MW01701120

The COBOL Programmer's Design Book

The COBOL Programmer's Design Book

Gary Robert Rogers
IBM Canada Limited Laboratory

A Wiley-Interscience Publication
JOHN WILEY & SONS
New York • Chichester • Brisbane • Toronto • Singapore

Copyright © 1986 by John Wiley & Sons, Inc.

All rights reserved. Published simultaneously in Canada.

Reproduction or translation of any part of this work beyond that permitted by Section 107 or 108 of the 1976 United States Copyright Act without the permission of the copyright owner is unlawful. Requests for permission or further information should be addressed to the Permissions Department, John Wiley & Sons, Inc.

Library of Congress Cataloging in Publication Data:

Rogers, Gary Robert.
The COBOL programmer's design book.

"A Wiley-Interscience publication."
Bibliography: p.
Includes index.
1. COBOL (Computer program language) I. Title.
QA76.73.C25R64 1986 005.13'3 86-1714
ISBN 0-471-82666-9

Printed in the United States of America.

10 9 8 7 6 5 4 3 2 1

For my Dearest Wife

Preface

In this age of software engineering, it seems as if novice computer programmers still assume that coding is the primary programming task. Design is haphazard with techniques attributable to social associations and residual coding school habits. Each new generation of programmers relearns or reinvents past programming history and propagates myths about the goodness or badness of various programming methods. No two programmers produce a similar solution to any programming problem, and few programmers understand modularity. This situation results in maintenance difficulty and expense.

This book treats programming as a design rather than a coding exercise. As such, it is really a book about problem solving. I have found that most COBOL texts usually discuss language semantics, such as how to code a SEARCH verb. Those that discuss design issues describe only general concepts or concepts that cannot be applied easily to frequently changing business application programs. Few books contain detailed examples of modern business programming problems taken completely into COBOL language solutions. This text is specifically directed at business computer programmers who work in COBOL. It describes methods that can be used to construct simple, maintainable, reliable programs for most common types of business applications. Both good and bad techniques are discussed.

Chapter 1 instructs the reader in structured programming concepts. Chapter 2 follows with a different, yet practical, perspective of modular programming. A COBOL-like high-level English design language is introduced in Chapter 3 and this design language is utilized in Chapters 7, 8, and 9 to document classical functions and in Chapters 13, 14, 15, and 16 to describe the designs of the example programs. The use of the design language ensures clear logic definition earlier in the programming cycle with follow-up coding a mere mechanical exercise. Many COBOL texts discuss design languages, but the design languages bear no relation to the structure and semantics of the COBOL programming language; this text offers a relevant, useful design language.

Chapters 4 and 5 analyse program flow and data considerations for program reliability and maintainability while Chapters 11 and 12 discuss briefly auditing and documentation considerations for programmers.

The key requirement for ease of design and ease of maintenance is a single structural design method or architecture that can easily be employed in business application program design. Chapter 6 describes a simple program decomposition strategy to achieve the necessary one-architecture design consistency.

Reusable code models (called classical functions) for many of the logic components found in business programming are described in detail in Chapters 7, 8, and 9. These functions improve the productivity of programmers by showing standardized solutions to programming problems. The use of such standardized approaches reduces maintenance costs for those organizations using these techniques. The models can be used in conjunction with a time-sharing editor to greatly speed the design and coding process.

Following the description of basic concepts and classical functions, Chapter 12 reviews the work that must be done by a programmer to initiate the design and implementation of a computer program. Then, four programs (two batch and two interactive) are described, designed in the design language, and coded in COBOL. A warehouse food item print program is designed and coded in Chapter 13. It is typical of many batch printing programs. The design and coding continues in Chapter 14 with a brokerage trades update program that duplicates complex match update logic often found in sequential batch update programs. In Chapter 15, the reader is introduced to interactive programs via an interactive credit authorization program. A more elaborate interactive program is solved in Chapter 16 where an employee information update program is taken through all steps to a COBOL solution. These sample programs are much larger than programs normally found in COBOL books. However, they realistically represent the types of programs found in business organizations and can be used as archetypes for the reader's production programs.

Programs are coded in American National Standard (ANS) 1985 COBOL that contains proper structured programming constructs, not available in previous COBOLs. In addition, the COBOL examples are independent of any particular machine or compiler environment. Different computer systems have different efficient data storage compression algorithms; therefore all example programs have the data in DISPLAY format so they are not biased toward any particular equipment. Readers will not have difficulty converting the examples into their particular COBOL.

Programmers who have COBOL coding training but require additional experience in design and associated problem-solving techniques will find this book most useful. The classical functions and COBOL program models also make it a handy reference for proficient COBOL programmers.

GARY R. ROGERS

West Hill, Ontario
April 1986

Acknowledgments

Several people assisted me in this work. Particular thanks go to IBMers: Bob Andrews, Paul Barrett, Susan Cholvat, Artur Reimann, and the management of IBM Canada's Laboratory. Bob looked after management approvals, which certainly saved me a lot of time. Paul "stick-handled" me through policies and procedures and arranged the transfer of relevant IBM copyrighted material to my publisher Wiley. Susan helped me interpret 85 ANS COBOL. Artur used his vast knowledge of COBOL and the new standard to perform a very beneficial technical review of my manuscript. IBM Canada Ltd. Laboratory management has always encouraged my publishing efforts

Wiley people have been superb. Carol Beasley, publisher, Jim Gaughan and Maria Taylor, editors; and Sheck Cho, editorial supervisor, and Lisa Van Horn, production supervisor, deserve my special thanks for their very professional production work.

COBOL is an industry language and is not the property of any company or group of companies, or of any organization or group of organizations. No warranty, expressed or implied, is made by any contributor or by the CODASYL Programming Language Committee as to the accuracy and functioning of the programming system and language.

Moreover, no responsibility is assumed by any contributor or by the committee in connection therewith.

The authors and copyright holders of the copyrighted material used herein:

FLOW-MATIC (trademark of Sperry Rand Corporation), Programming for the UNIVAC® I and II, Data Automation Systems copyrighted 1958, 1959, by Sperry Rand Corporation; IBM Commercial Translator Form No. F 28-8013, copyrighted 1959 by IBM; FACT, DSI 27A5260-2760, copyrighted 1960 by Minneapolis-Honeywell

have specifically authorized the use of this material in whole or in part, in the COBOL specifications. Such authorization extends to the reproduction and use of COBOL specifications in programming manuals or similar publications.

G.R.R.

Contents

1 Elemental Control Structures

In procedural language programming, the instruction sequence must be specified by the programmer. This flow of control operates through points in a program called nodes. Three types of nodes can exist in a program: process nodes, predicate or decision nodes, and collecting nodes. A predicate node always has an associated collecting node. These nodes can be represented graphically with flowcharting symbols as shown in Figure 1.1.

The process node represents an instruction in a program (such as ADD INPUT TO TOTAL) that is executed unconditionally. The predicate node and the associated collecting node provide the boundaries for conditional logic testing.

Data is associated with the nodes. It is either processed or tested at these program points. However, only program flow will be discussed in this chapter. The discussion of data will be deferred to later chapters.

Nodes are assembled to form program control structures. It can be shown (Bohm and Jacopini, 1966; Mills, 1972; Dahl, Dijkstra and Hoare, 1972) that any program can be constructed from five basic control structures: sequence structures, IF THEN ELSE structures, PERFORM WITH TEST BEFORE structures, PERFORM WITH TEST AFTER structures, and EVALUATE structures.

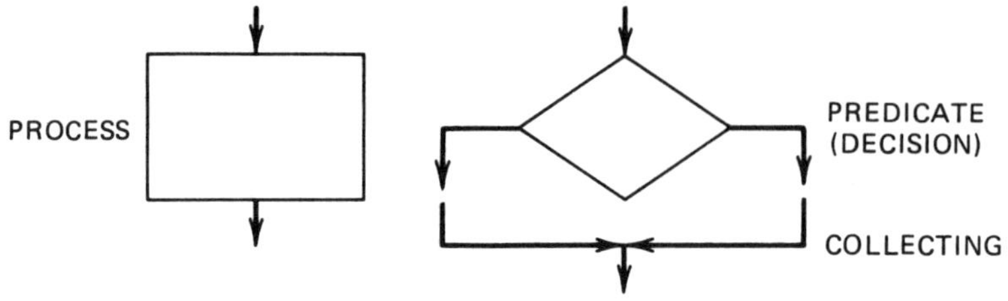

Figure 1.1. *Nodes.*

The sequence structure of Figure 1.2 is the simplest of the five structures. It occurs when one program instruction immediately follows a prior instruction.

Conditional branching is controlled with the IF THEN ELSE structure portrayed in Figure 1.3.

Each IF THEN ELSE structure will have a THEN action performed when the predicate condition test gives a true value. The ELSE action happens when the predicate condition test results in a false value. The ELSE process node is usually optional and, if not present, the ELSE branch takes the sequence control directly to the collecting node.

Iteration or looping is handled with two types of structures: the PERFORM WITH TEST BEFORE and the PERFORM WITH TEST AFTER. Both of these structures place the collecting node at the beginning and the predicate node at the end.

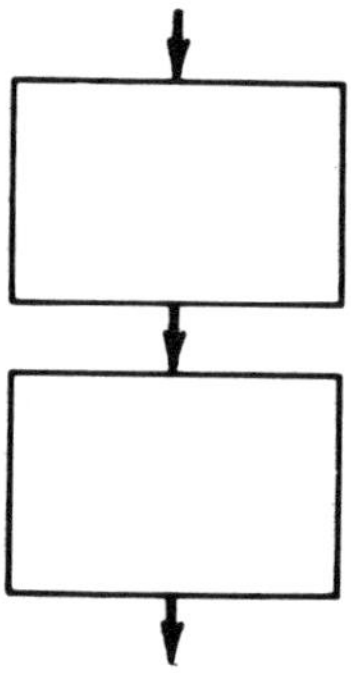

Figure 1.2. *Sequence structure.*

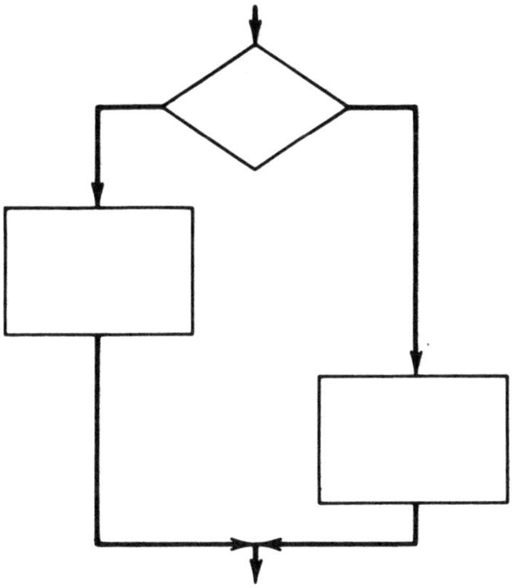

Figure 1.3. *IF THEN ELSE structure.*

The PERFORM WITH TEST BEFORE structure of Figure 1.4 tests the looping condition before processing commences. The iteration cycle will continue as long as the predicate condition gives a true value from its test. Another name for this structure, used in literature, is a DO WHILE structure.

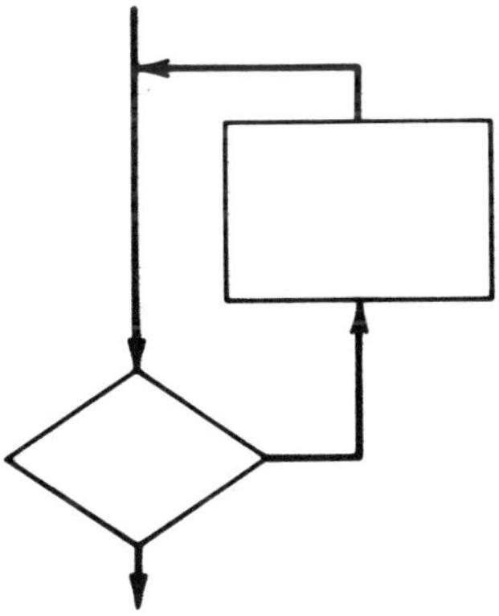

Figure 1.4. *PERFORM WITH TEST BEFORE structure.*

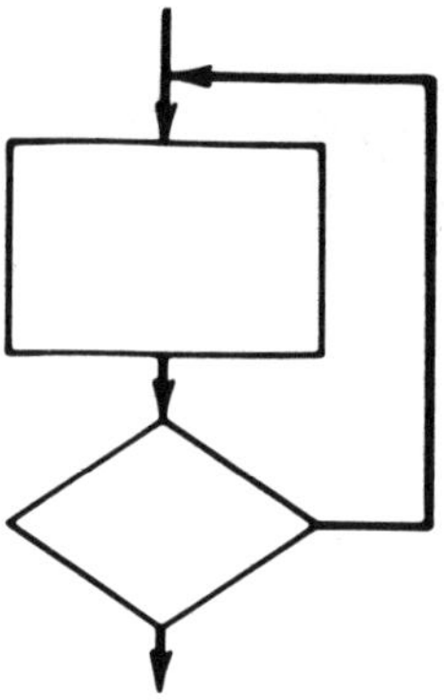

Figure 1.5. *PERFORM WITH TEST AFTER structure.*

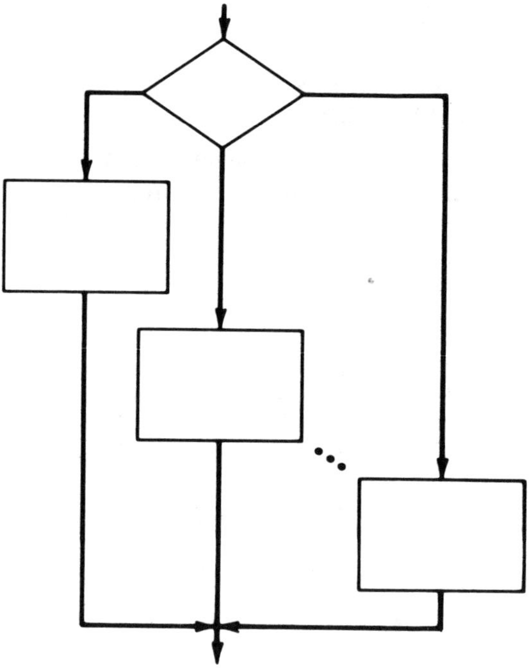

Figure 1.6. *EVALUATE structure.*

Figure 1.5 demonstrates that the PERFORM WITH TEST AFTER structure is similar to the previous PERFORM WITH TEST BEFORE structure. However, the process node is executed once before the looping condition is tested. Thereafter, the iteration logic is identical to the PERFORM WITH TEST BEFORE structure. DO UNTIL is another name for this structure.

In business application programming there are many examples where a test of more than two alternatives must be evaluated. In such circumstances the IF THEN ELSE structure becomes awkward and the EVALUATE structure of Figure 1.6 is more suitable.

An example of such a requirement would be a billing program that supports five different billing methods. The EVALUATE structure provides multiple paths from the predicate node to the collecting node. Process nodes occur along all paths from the predicate node to the collecting node. The last path (shown on the right side of Figure 1.6) is the default or WHEN OTHER path. If none of the other logical paths is taken, the flow will default to this path, thereby enabling the programmer to provide handling for all values that are not specifically tested in the predicate node. The EVALUATE structure is sometimes called a CASE structure.

All of the five program structures are proper program structures; that is, they have a single entry point and a single exit point. Proper structures are combined to form a proper program having a single entry point (from the operating system) and a single exit point (back to the operating system). These program structures can be combined in two ways to form the program.

In the first method, the structures are chained together. The exit point of the first is connected to the entry point of the second. Figure 1.7 shows an example is a PERFORM WITH TEST BEFORE followed by an IF THEN ELSE. This is called a bottom up design approach. The chaining method is repeated until the program is formed.

The second program building approach is to examine the process node of each structure and replace it with another structure. For example, in Figures 1.8 and 1.9, the process node of a PERFORM WITH TEST AFTER is replaced by a PERFORM WITH TEST BEFORE structure. This is called the top down design approach. The procedure is repeated until the process nodes can be decomposed no further.

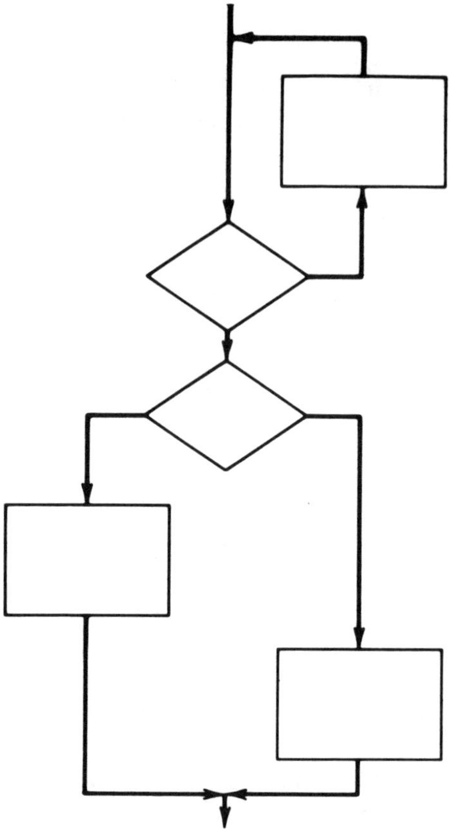

Figure 1.7. *Bottom up design.*

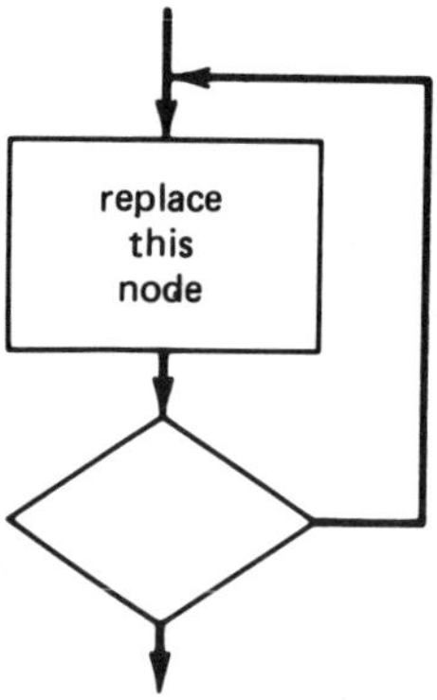

Figure 1.8. *Top down design—step 1.*

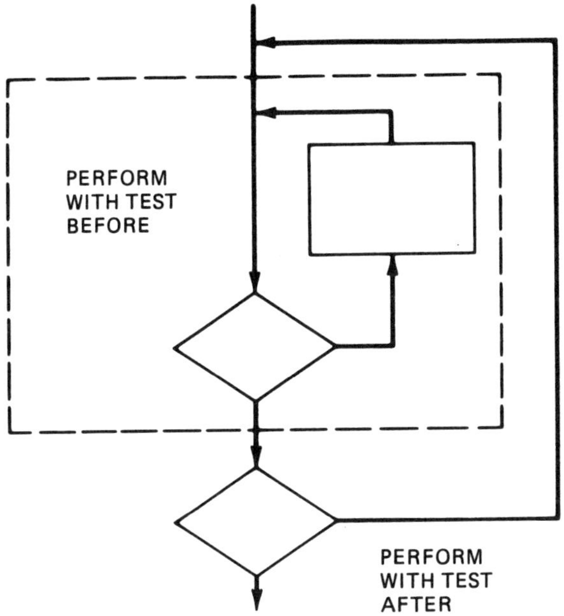

Figure 1.9. *Top down design—step 2.*

When building a program, a programmer uses a combination of top-down and bottom-up approaches to arrive at the overall product. The top-down method is used to translate general concepts into details and the bottom-up method is employed when the details are known and the programmer must connect them in a specific order to form the program.

2 Module Construction

Computer programming is a complex human activity. As the number of things a program has to do increases, the size and complexity of the program also increases. Once a certain size is attained, it becomes difficult for a programmer to comprehend the simultaneous interaction of all logic and data factors. Thereafter, the only way to reduce the complexity to comprehensible bounds is by partitioning the problem.

The units of partition are called modules. They enable us to narrow the focus of our attention and create well defined boundaries.

Yourdon (Yourdon, 1975) has correctly pointed out that most programmers do not understand modularity. The reason for this situation is the small amount of definitive work pertaining to the subject. The primary references are Parnas (Parnas, 1972) and Myers (Myers, 1978). These authors have defined general principles of modularity but leave identification of actual module units to the individual programmer.

A number of authors have suggested that modules be restricted to units having a fixed maximum number of lines of program instructions (code). However, this approach gives module definition problems, and the defined modules may be arbitrarily large or arbitrarily small. A better approach to module definition is described in the following pages.

The construction of a computer program is analagous to the building of a house . A general contractor manages the whole job. As the contractor progresses, he or she distributes parts of the work to subcontractors. Each subcontractor may, in turn, elect to have certain parts of the work distributed to other subcontractors. As each subcontractor completes his or her portion of the work, control returns to a higher level authority. The work structure is represented by the structure chart of Figure 2.1.

A computer program is decomposed in a similar fashion. The highest level of overall control remains at the highest level of the program, and functions are broken down into manageable tasks (modules) at subservient levels.

Once the unit, known as a module, has been identified, it is further subdivided into the elemental structures described in Chapter 1.

Each module in a program should be considered a functional black box similar to that of Figure 2.2. Control flows into the module; input data passes to it; certain data transformations are performed; output data is created; and control is returned to a higher authority (a calling module).

Control passes to the beginning of a module when it is called by another. Control returns from the last statement in a module (when pro-

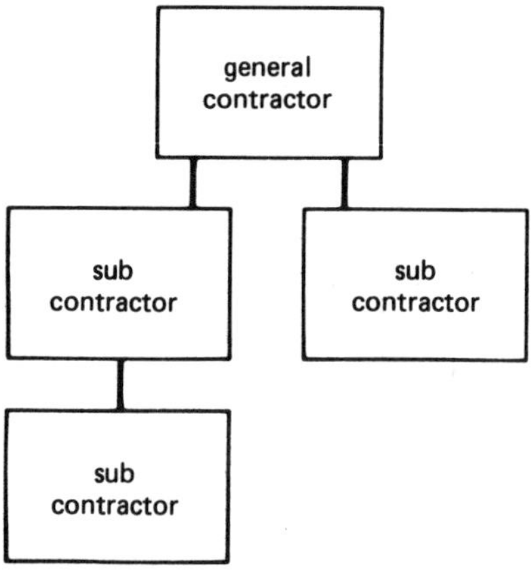

Figure 2.1. *Subdivision of construction work.*

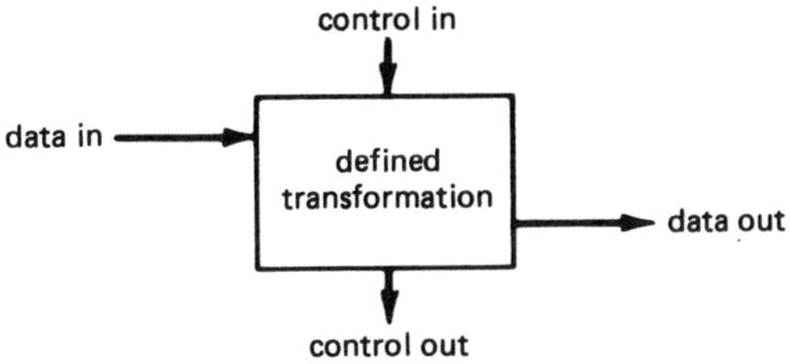

Figure 2.2. *Black box module.*

cessing is finished for that module) to the calling point in the calling module. This can be seen in Figure 2.3.

The called module can contain calling points for further modules. The hierarchy of calling and called modules is taken to as many levels as necessary to solve the programming problem. Once a program has been decomposed into modules, it is much easier to make changes since specific functions are isolated in the modules.

Parameters is the term used to describe the data that passes from module to module. These parameters are discussed in later chapters.

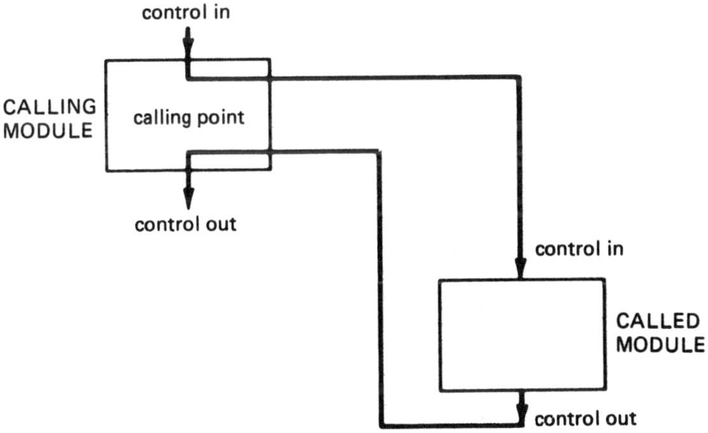

Figure 2.3. *Calling and called modules.*

The relationship of calling and called modules is known as coupling. Good programs have weak coupling; that is, one module is not closely tied to another. With the black box module concept, the calling module does not *see* the inside of the called module. Rather, it passes control and data and has other data returned after a specific function is performed.

Similarly, the called module knows nothing about the calling module. All it *sees* is control and data on its doorstep. It returns control and data after completing its required work.

The ideal module is one which can be replaced without disturbing any other parts in a program or requiring any other parts of the program to be recompiled.

In COBOL, each module should be a separately compiled subprogram. All such separately compiled subprograms are brought together in a separate step (often called link editing) to form the executable machine language program. Internal subroutines (out-of-line PERFORMed procedures) that are compiled as part of a module, should not be used. Such internal subroutines are common coupled with other parts of the module and share data field definitions (a data item is known by the same name in all areas). Similarly, some versions of COBOL support global data definitions, whereby the data is known by the same name in many modules and is referenced directly rather than being passed as parameters. This produces the same effect as internal subroutines: the functions are also common coupled. These types of data references should not be used as problems occur when changes are made in one area without realization of the impact or occurrnces in other areas. Such changes often produce disastrous results.

Ideally, the contents of a module should be a single specific function. In reality, only a few program modules exhibit these characteristics. However, all modules must have very distinct boundaries and be simple and easily comprehensible by the original programmer and subsequent generations of maintenance programmers.

A big problem facing programmers is the definition of the contents of modules. The most effective approach is to categorize modules by the type of business programming function contained therein and provide one module for each occurrence of the functions. The following paragraphs describe the types of modules found in business application programs.

MAINLINE

This is the key control module of programs. Its functions are described in Chapter 7.

DECISION LOGIC

This module characterizes the particular type of application program and contains the decision control logic. Its functions are described in Chapter 8.

DETAIL PROCESSING

The decision logic module (as described in Chapter 8) in a program defines the subservient detail processing modules. These detail processing modules perform the data processing functions in programs.

INITIALIZATION

In business computer programming, the grouping of initialization operations appears unavoidable. Totals have to be set to zero, security checks have to be done, control records have to be read and verified, and other starting values have to be established.

END OF JOB

As with initialization at the beginning of programs, there are functions which must be performed at the end of programs. Audit totals may be printed, records may be written to log files, and indicators may have to be set to cause certain program shutdown functions to happen. These requirements are best met via an end of job module.

INPUT/OUTPUT

There should be one module for each input, output, or update operation with each file or device connected to the program. Examples are read a file sequentially, read a file directly, read a data base sequentially, read a data base directly, update a file, update a data base, print report data, write to an output file, send a message to a terminal, receive a message from a terminal. When these operations are isolated in separate modules, device types or characteristics can be changed without causing a great impact to the logic of the program. In addition, status and error checks can be included with the input/output operation to provide a direct check on the operation.

The only exception to this is unformatted auditing report messages written to the system printer in an end of job module. They are generally too trivial to require a separate module. However, if the end of job module writes a log file, produces a formatted report, and so on, these functions must be contained in separate modules.

In some COBOL implementations there is no universal access to file definitions thereby preventing a file from being opened in one module, read in a second module, written to in a third module, and closed in a fourth module. If you are faced with this awkward situation, the functions for input/output module should be as described previously; but all of the physical operations (opening, closing, reading, writing) should be performed in a single module which operates below each of the described input/output modules. A parameter is passed to indicate which physical operation is to be utilized.

SECURITY

Each security checking operation should be contained in a separate module. This type of module is usually associated with interactive programs, but does not have to be, where the user data access status must be checked. This allows systems to be set up to provide restricted data access and restricted functional capability (e.g., inquiry only) to certain operational user groups.

TRANSACTION VALIDATION

One module should exist for each transaction that has to be validated. (*Editing* is a term frequently used to describe validation.) It is convenient to have all fields of a transaction checked together. A transaction is defined to be the data brought in to the program via a single input operation or written via a single output or update operation.

TRANSACTION PROCESSING

After a transaction has been validated, it may require other additional processing. There should be one module to perform processing operations for each transaction. A transaction processing module may call a transaction validation module before processing commences.

DATE FUNCTIONS

A single module should be provided for each date function in the program. Several examples of these functions are described in Chapter 9.

TABLE MANAGEMENT

There should be one module for each separate aspect of table management. Examples are enter elements into a table, sort a table, rearrange a table, search a table, and unload elements from a table.

COMPLEX CALCULATIONS

When programs require complex repeated arithmetic, each calculation should be isolated in a separate module.

GRAPHICS FUNCTIONS

A module should exist for each graphics icon that has to be drawn in a picture. The icon modules should be called by a higher level display placement module that positions all elements for each picture panel. Any input or output graphics operations should be handled by input or output modules according to the rules for input/output modules as specified earlier in this chapter.

Some of the previously described modules may require the services of the other modules described. In these instances, one module should call the other module. Under no circumstances should the separate modules be combined to form a single module. The sequence of events determines the order of subdecomposition (calling). For example, an initialization module in a program needs a table search to verify a control field. Because the sequence of events is a table search while in initialization, the table search will be called from the initialization module.

In this chapter the construction of the individual program units called modules is described. In later chapters the decomposition of programming solutions into modules will be examined.

3 A Design Language

In the discussion of structured programming in Chapter 1 and modular programming in Chapter 2, a graphical flowcharting notation was used to represent programming constructs. While this is a practical method of describing computer programs, it is not very compact and large components of programs cannot be pictured easily. A design language gives a more concise method of expressing program designs and is more easily retained by computerized text processing systems.

The origins of programming design languages are not readily evident. However, both Caine, Farber & Gordon, Inc. (Caine and Gordon, 1975) and McDonnell Douglas Automation Company (Leer, 1976) were developing practical implementations at about the same time.

A program design language retains the constructs of structured and modular programming and is similar to the COBOL procedural programming implementation language. It enables the programmer to express the design in natural English prose, and provides a means for documenting the intent of the design with functions referred to in summary or abstract. It is not a coding language, it does not have IDENTIFICA-

TION nor ENVIRONMENT nor DATA divisions, and it cannot be compiled. Designs produced in the design language are more easily understood by people other than the designer and, thus, can be used in inspection processes to find design flaws.

Design languages are sometimes called pseudo languages or pseudo code. A simple design language, suitable for describing solutions to COBOL business programming problems, is presented in the remainder of this chapter; it maps directly to American National Standard (ANS) 1985 COBOL.

BASIC DESIGN LANGUAGE CONCEPTS

All key structured and modular programming constructs are identified with uppercase letters. All data, conditions, actions, and imperative statements are shown in lowercase letters.

Each statement in the design language will expand to one or more COBOL program statements. Each design language statement summarizes related groups of COBOL statements. Examples such as *print summary lines, calculate mortgage interest, check field value range, update data base segments, display data on terminal; place arrow icon on third line in center* are common occurrences of the one-to-many design language/COBOL relationship.

Numeric literal data values are shown as numbers (e.g., 3) and character literal data values are shown in double quotation marks (e.g., "a?b").

Punctuation is identical to that of the COBOL language.

Spacing is used to enhance readability, and indentation and alignment are used to define the bounds of the programming constructs. Each modular or structured unit should be separated from others by a blank line. When constructs appear inside other constructs, the outer construct begins on the left, and each inner construct is indented to the right. Alignment of the constructs should appear as illustrated in this chapter and the example programs in Chapters 13 through 16.

Data is referenced, but attributes or PICTUREs of the data, nor-

mally are not described. If the attributes of the data are important to the understanding of the design solution, the design will be annotated with associated notes. Data attributes, sometimes requiring this form of annotation, might be tables and data data structures. The programmer should not be concerned with machine field characteristics, such as decimal, packed, binary, float, character, and so on in the design language. These can be left until the design is complete and coding in COBOL is underway.

When a data structure is passed as a parameter to a module, data fields referenced within the structure should be qualified to indicate the source. For example:

```
data element name in structure name
```

All data names should be in full English. Abbreviations should not be used.

SEQUENCE CONSTRUCT

The sequence structure of Chapter 1 is expressed in the design language as an imperative statement.

```
accumulate pay totals
```

This is a high level form of expression which may translate into multiple expressions when coded in COBOL. For example, the preceding sequence structure may appear as:

```
ADD CURRENT-PAY TO TOTAL-PAY
ADD CURRENT-DEDUCTIONS TO TOTAL-DEDUCTIONS
ADD NET-PAY TO TOTAL-NET-PAY
```

Although COBOL provides a mechanism for establishing initial values for data items, all indications of initial value settings are done via imperative statements in the design language or noted via comments.

IF THEN ELSE CONSTRUCT

The form of this construct used in the design language is:

```
IF condition
   THEN
      imperative statement(s) or continue
  [ELSE                             ]
  [   imperative statement(s)       ]
END-IF
```

Note how the keywords in this structure are aligned.

The imperative statement(s) under the THEN can be optional. However, if they are not present, the COBOL reserved word "continue'' must be present to indicate a null THEN. Somtimes the logic can be made simpler when a null THEN is used with an ELSE component.

The ELSE component of the structure appears within square brackets to indicate that it is optional. (Whenever these square brackets appear in the remainder of this book, they also denote optional items.) If there is a null THEN, an ELSE component must be present.

PERFORM WITH TEST BEFORE CONSTRUCT

This construct provides a mechanism for program looping (iteration). The PERFORM WITH TEST BEFORE structure invokes the iteration condition test each time the beginning of its structure is encountered. The format is:

```
PERFORM WITH TEST BEFORE UNTIL condition
   imperative statement(s)
END-PERFORM
```

As in the IF THEN ELSE construct, imperative statement(s) may be any valid combination of structured and modular programming constructs.

PERFORM WITH TEST AFTER CONSTRUCT

The PERFORM WITH TEST AFTER is similar to the PERFORM WITH TEST BEFORE construct. However, the condition for execution is not tested until one full iteration of the logic has been completed.

```
PERFORM WITH TEST AFTER UNTIL condition
   imperative statement(s)
END-PERFORM
```

A variation of this construct can be used when the loop must be performed a specific number of times.

```
PERFORM integer or data name TIMES
   imperative statement(s)
END-PERFORM
```

If integer is used, then data name is not used and vice versa. *Data name* must contain an integer value.

EVALUATE CONSTRUCT

The EVALUATE construct provides multipath logic branching. It is often useful when more than two values of a data variable must be specifically tested. In such circumstances, complex IF THEN ELSE structures can be avoided.

```
EVALUATE [data variable or conditional statement]
   WHEN condition-1
      imperative statement(s)
   WHEN condition-2
      imperative statement(s)
            .
            .
            .
```

```
    WHEN condition-N
       imperative statement(s)
          .
          .
          .
   [WHEN OTHER                  ]
   [   imperative statement(s)  ]
  END-EVALUATE
```

There must be a WHEN statement for each case that is to be tested. WHEN OTHER provides the alternative actions for all cases that aren't specifically tested. As with the previously described constructs, imperative statement(s) may be any valid combination of structured and modular programming constructs (including an EVALUATE).

PROGRAM-ID CONSTRUCT

This construct enables a programmer to define the beginning and end of a module (separately compiled subprogram). It shows the physical beginning of a module and the physical ending of a module.

```
  PROGRAM-ID. module name [<MAIN>]
                              [USING parameters].
                      .
                      .
                      .
                      .
  END PROGRAM module name.
```

The PROGRAM-ID statement combines the information for both the PROGRAM-ID and PROCEDURE DIVISION statements of COBOL. These COBOL statements would be created after the design is complete and coding is underway.

<MAIN> is strictly a design language notation and appears when the module is the root module of the program. A root module is the one

that first receives control from the operating system when program execution commences.

Here, also, the square brackets are used to denote optional items: MAIN and the parameters in this construct. There can be multiple parameters separated by commas. For example:

```
total 1, total 2, total 3
```

are three input parameters.

END PROGRAM indicates the physical end of the module. Note that it is not a COBOL statement, but is merely a separator between separately compiled subprograms.

CALL CONSTRUCT

The CALL construct provides the means for a calling module to pass control to another module (termed the *called* module).

```
CALL "module name" [USING parameters]
```

The parameters of both the CALL statement in the calling module and the PROGRAM-ID statement in the called module must have identical positions and definitions. Control passes from the CALL statement of the calling module to the first statement of the called module and returns from the last statement of the called module to the next statement after the CALL statement in the calling module.

By default, the parameters are assumed to be BY REFERENCE unless BY CONTENT is specifically stated. In a number of design language examples, literals are utilized for parameters. This is done for convenience in the design language. ANS 85 COBOL does not support literals in CALL statements. When literals appear in the design language, they must be converted to WORKING-STORAGE variables in COBOL programs, given literal VALUES and referenced via their data names in CALL statements.

EXIT PROGRAM CONSTRUCT

Normally, control passes from a called module back to a calling module when the last of the executable statements in the called module is encountered. This situation really means that an implicit EXIT PROGRAM statement has been executed. In some circumstances, it is convenient to leave a module immediately rather than trying to structure the logic to provide a path through the physical end of the program. The mechanism for achieving this is execution of an explicit EXIT PROGRAM construct.

EXIT PROGRAM

This statement must appear on a line by itself.

Without the EXIT PROGRAM statement, a piece of logic could be expressed:

```
PROGRAM-ID. test USING field 1, field 2, message.

   IF field 1 = "a"
      THEN
         move "message 1" to message
      ELSE

         IF field 2 = "x"
            THEN
               move "message 2" to message
            ELSE
               move "message 3" to message
         END-IF
   END-IF.

END PROGRAM test.
```

With the EXIT PROGRAM statement, the same logic appears as:

```
PROGRAM-ID. test USING field 1, field 2, message.

   IF field 1 = "a"
      THEN
         move "message 1" to message
```

```
      EXIT PROGRAM
  END-IF.
  IF field 2 = "x"
    THEN
      move "message 2" to message
      EXIT PROGRAM
  END-IF.

  move "message 3" to message.

END PROGRAM test.
```

The use of the EXIT PROGRAM construct makes the logic simpler, more straightforward, and, thus, easier to comprehend and modify. It can sometimes be used as a substitute if the particular COBOL implementation does not have an EVALUATE construct.

COMMENTS

Designs expressed in the design language should be self-explanatory However, from time to time, the designer may need to annotate the design to clarify understanding. In COBOL, comments must appear on a separate line and be marked with an asterisk in an identification column (often column 7). This form is not compact and is somewhat awkward for annotating designs; therefore, in this design language, a different comment form will be used. The form is:

```
≪ comment ≫
```

The basis for this method of annotation is the CODASYL 1984 Journal of Development. (CODASYL is for *Conference On DAta SYstem Languages*, an organization composed of volunteer representatives of computer manufacturers, computer users, the United States federal government, and the Canadian government.) In the *Journal of Development*, annotated comments are identified by ≪ to the right of the COBOL code. Be aware that this notation is not part of the COBOL language standard, but is used only for design language comments.

Comments should be unobtrusive and to the right of the item requiring explanation.

At the beginning of each module, there should be a comment line stating the function of the module. This comment also helps to separate that module from any others that may be documented nearby.

A reference summary of design language constructs, in tabular form, can be found in the appendix.

The reader is advised to spend a few minutes briefly browsing the classical functions noted in Chapters 7 through 9 and the example programs in Chapters 13 through 16. These show how structured programming constructs, modular programming constructs, and comments are used in program designs.

ALTERNATE STRUCTURES

The structured and modular programming constructs described in preceding sections can be directly coded in ANS 1985 COBOL. This may be seen in the example programs in Chapters 13, 14, 15, and 16. However, many of the constructs do not exist in ANS 1974 and other prior versions of COBOL. Equivalent COBOL structures are described in the following pages.

Pre-1985 COBOLs do not have construct terminators (END PROGRAM, END-IF, END-PERFORM, END-EVALUATE). Such terminators make it easier for program readers to see the scope of the structures. These terminators can be simulated with appropriate comment lines. For example:

```
      IF RECORD-COUNT = 50
         THEN
            ADD 1 TO NUMBER-OF-SETS.
*     END-IF.
```

Note how the prior statement is ended with a period and the asterisk marks the END-IF as a comment.

The reader will observe that the PERFORM constructs of the design language are in-line PERFORMs; that is, there is no referenced procedure name. Pre-1985 COBOLs do not provide this feature; the PER-

FORM must be out-of-line and reference a procedure name. To make an equivalent structure, one may *hide* these out-of-line procedures after comments at the end of the module, and use a straight PERFORM rather than a PERFORM THROUGH option.

```
                .                                             )
                .                                             |
      PERFORM CALL-DATE UNTIL                                 |  body
            DATA-STREAM-STATUS = "AT END".                    >   of
*     END-PERFORM                                             |  module
                .                                             |
                .                                             |
                .                                             )
********************************** ← logical end of module
 CALL-DATE.
      CALL "DATE" USING DATE-VALUES.
```

COBOLs with a PERFORM UNTIL statement have the equivalent of a PERFORM WITH TEST BEFORE. In such circumstances, the effect of a PERFORM WITH TEST AFTER can sometimes be achieved by altering the exit condition to force the loop to be executed at least once for a PERFORM UNTIL. If this cannot be done, two PERFORMS, with indentation to show the structure, may be used to simulate a PERFORM WITH TEST AFTER.

```
      PERFORM CALCULATE-TAX.
         PERFORM CALCULATE-TAX UNTIL DEDUCTION-COUNT = 0.
*     END-PERFORM.
```

The END PROGRAM header is unique to ANS 1985 COBOL. It can be simulated in prior COBOLs as a comment.

```
* END PROGRAM EXAMPLE.
```

Pre-1985 COBOLs do not have an EVALUATE construct. Therefore, multiway branching is best handled with nested IF THEN ELSE structures. For example, a test for three specific values can be coded:

```
       IF RECORD-TYPE = "A"
          THEN
             ADD 1 TO TYPE-A-COUNT
          ELSE
             IF RECORD-TYPE ="B"
                THEN
                   ADD 1 TO TYPE-B-COUNT
                ELSE
                   IF RECORD-TYPE = "C"
                      THEN
                         ADD 1 TO TYPE-C-COUNT
                      ELSE
                         ADD 1 TO OTHER-TYPE-COUNT.
*                  END-IF
*            END-IF
*      END-IF.
```

Sometimes, the EXIT PROGRAM can simulate an EVALUATE situation (provided no subsequent processing is done in the module). The previous example would be coded:

```
       IF RECORD-TYPE = "A"
          THEN
             ADD 1 TO TYPE-A-COUNT
             PERFORM EXIT-PROGRAM.
*      END-IF.
       IF RECORD-TYPE = "B"
          THEN
             ADD 1 TO TYPE-B-COUNT
             PERFORM EXIT-PROGRAM.
*      END-IF.
       IF RECORD-TYPE = "C"
          THEN
             ADD 1 TO TYPE-C-COUNT
             PERFORM EXIT-PROGRAM.
*      END-IF.
       ADD 1 TO OTHER-TYPE-COUNT.
*      END PROGRAM EXAMPLE.
*****************************************************
   EXIT-PROGRAM.
       EXIT PROGRAM.
```

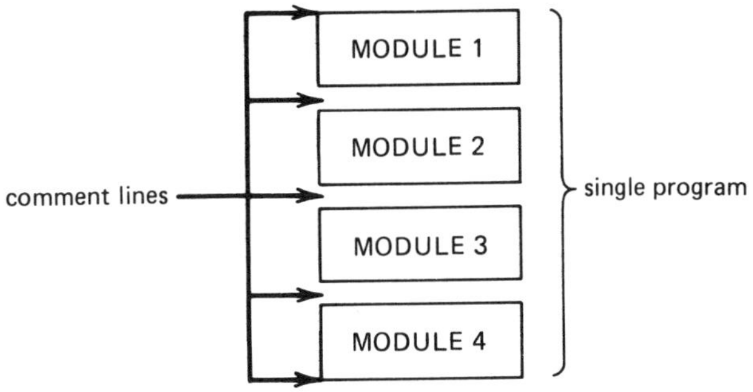

Figure 3.1. *Simulated modularity.*

Most COBOL compilers provide a mechanism for separate module compilation and object program linkage. However, some can only have a single program module and do not support parameters in subroutine calls. When using these versions, a crude form of modularity can be obtained by partitioning the logical pieces of the program with comment statements. This is shown in Figure 3.1.

In the remainder of this book only the recommended constructs will be used in both design language and COBOL code examples. The alternates do not appear.

4 Program Flow

In procedural programming languages such as COBOL, the programmer controls program flow. Flow is the sequence of instruction execution. In contrast, nonprocedural languages such as RPG, provide the means for a programmer to specify what has to be done, rather than how to do it. (The sequence of doing it may be a minor concern or no concern.)

A procedural language computer program is a complicated manifestation of the human thought process. At best, it may be incomprehensible, and, at worst, it can be a terrible nightmare. To overcome this enigma, programs should be designed with simplicity as a primary consideration. Avoid complications when simple solutions suffice. The simplest solutions are the most durable and the first to work correctly.

Program designers must plan for future maintenance of their products. Programs last a very long time and must survive many visits by repairpersons. Maintenance programming is a very difficult task. It requires one human being to understand the thought mechanisms of another. Simplicity and consistency of design can significantly reduce maintenance expense.

Simple programs occur when the control flow is kept simple. Unidirectional top-to-bottom flow is the simplest and should be a design goal; it gives more reliable programs. The method of achieving it is to chain elemental structures rather than nesting them. The sequence structure is preferable to the other conditional and iterative structures.

Each conditional program test resulting from IF, PERFORM, or EVALUATE structures causes a horizontal flow digression, disturbing the top-to-bottom order; increasing the flow complexity and, thus, increasing the potential for reliability problems. While these structures cannot be completely eliminated from programs, their scope should be kept simple. Nesting levels (one structure within another) greater than two deep may indicate that design simplification is needed. Deeper nesting levels become progressively more difficult to comprehend and lead to maintenance programmer confusion.

When a programmer has established a design, he or she should review it to see if flow simplification can be achieved.

First, nested IF conditionals should be examined to determine if EVALUATE constructs would simplify the logic. For example, the nested test:

```
IF transaction code = "a"
   THEN
      move "x" to output code
   ELSE

      IF transaction code = "b"
         THEN
            move "y" to output code
         ELSE
            move "z" to output code
      END-IF

END-IF.
```

can be replaced with:

```
EVALUATE transaction code
   WHEN "a"
      move "x" to output code
   WHEN "b"
      move "y" to output code
   WHEN OTHER
      move "z" to output code
END-EVALUATE.
```

Next, the programmer should examine nested IF statements to see if EXIT PROGRAM statements can be profitably used to give shorter path lengths through the end of the module. Consider:

```
PROGRAM-ID. test USING transaction code, message.

   IF transaction code = 1
      THEN
         move message q to message
      ELSE

         IF transaction code = 2
            THEN
               move message r to message
            ELSE
               move message s to message
         END-IF

   END-IF.

END PROGRAM test.
```

which can be expressed more simply as:

```
PROGRAM-ID. test USING transaction code, message.

   IF transaction code = 1
      THEN
         move message q to message
         EXIT PROGRAM
   END-IF.

   IF transaction code = 2
      THEN
         move message r to message
         EXIT PROGRAM
   END-IF.

   move message s to message.

END PROGRAM test.
```

In the next simplification analysis, the programmer should look carefully at conditional tests to determine those that can be replaced by logical expressions. Never use conditional branches as a substitute for logical expressions (Kernighan and Plauger, 1974). The following nested conditional expressions:

```
IF amount greater than or equal to lower value
   THEN

      IF amount less than or equal to upper value
         THEN
            move 0 to total
      END-IF

END-IF.
```

can be restated more simply as:

```
IF amount less than lower value or
     greater than upper value
   THEN
      continue
   ELSE
      move 0 to total
END-IF.
```

Next, review the program logic to determine if it can be reordered or restated to eliminate redundancies. If not, a review of modularity may be in order. Too much logic may be contained in one module producing deeply nested PERFORM and IF constructs. Small modules do not cause inefficient program execution. There is evidence (Brooks, 1981) that the opposite is true.

Express conditional statements in positive terms to be easily understood by others. Negative compound conditionals are vague and should not be used. They cause perceptual meanings for humans, but literal ordered computer interpretations often produce errors. For example, the conditional statement:

```
IF data item 1 not = data item 2 or
     not = data item 2
```

seems to make sense, but when interpreted by a computer always tests true (a yes value). Bracketing related conditional operators helps, but restating in postiive terms produces clearer understanding.

```
IF field 1 or field 2
   THEN
      continue
```

```
    ELSE
        handle exception
END-IF.
```

When your COBOL version allows, use full English operatives for conditional tests as these increase reader comprehension. A GREATER THAN is preferable to a GT.

In any program, events affect flow. Events may be error conditions, data conditions, terminal replies, and so forth. Such events demand immediate action and should be treated where they happen. Potential for error increases in proportion to the number of modules traversed before the event is dealt with. In the module where the event occurs, the programming logic has access to all conditions and settings associated with the event. The further the logic is away from the event, the weaker the information.

In Figure 4.1, module 1 calls module 2 which calls module 3. An event occurs in module 3. If treated in module 3, action can be immediate (say, stop the program) and all relevant data and conditions are present. If the problem is not treated until control passes either back to module 2 or, subsequently, back to module 1, some of the causitory data and conditions may be lost. Diagnosis then becomes more difficult.

No consideration of program flow is complete without a discussion of the GO TO statement. Dijkstra (Dijkstra, 1968) was the first to condemn publicly its use. One major problem with it occurs because the GO TO enables a programmer to build an unstructured and, thus, less reliable program. Consider Figure 4.2.

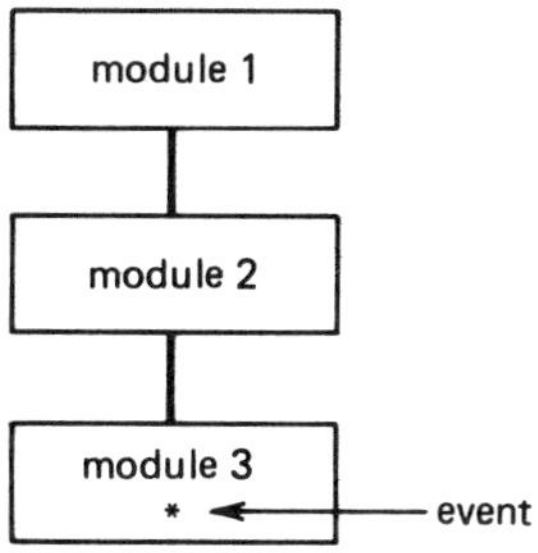

Figure 4.1. *Event dispersion.*

```
procedure name.
    IF condition 1
       THEN
          imperative statement(s)
          GO TO procedure name
    END-IF.

    IF condition 2
       THEN
          imperative statement(s)
          GO TO procedure name
    END-IF.
```

Figure 4.2. *GO TO branching.*

Examining *procedure name* in the code, we cannot tell where control came from. Did it come from the statement immediately prior to procedure name? Did control come from the first GO TO? Did it come from the second GO TO? Did it come from somewhere else? This phenomenon, identified by Clark (Clark, 1973), is the other major problem associated with the GO TO statement.

Do not use GO TO statements in your program. Without them, structured programs are easy to produce and control flow reliability concerns are greatly reduced. Fortunately, GO TO usage is easy to police. If there are no GO TOs, there will be no labels (procedure names) other than module names found at the beginning of modules.

5 Data

Computer programming is more commonly known as data processing. With no data to be processed, there would be no need for computer programs.

Data is the machine representation of alphabet letters, numbers, characters, conditions, signals, and events. It exists as data elements, parameters, files, segments, data bases, transactions, and messages. Data can be stored permanently outside the program (on devices such disks or tapes), temporarily outside the program, or temporarily within the program.

There are many reference books available for programmers who want to study data in its external form. In this chapter, data kept internally within the program is discussed.

In business computer programs the basic data element is called a data item or data element. A data element may be one or more characters long and can be alphabetic, numeric (decimal, binary, fixed, floating point), or character in nature.

Data elements may be referenced individually or may be assembled to form data structures and arrays (also known as tables).

NET-AMOUNT is a data element

NET-AMOUNT and GROSS-AMOUNT within PAY-STUB form a structure

DEDUCTIONS (INDEX) is a subscripted array

When data elements, structures, and arrays are written to external media (tape, disk, terminal, etc.), the access unit is called a record, segment, transaction, or message.

Data is referenced in a program via its name. The name given to data should be fully spelled out in the language of the programmer (e.g., English for this author). If the given name is more than 30 characters in length, a proper dictionary abbreviation is the best alternative.

The name given to a data item should clearly represent its usage. For example,

TOTAL-INPUT-TRANSACTION-COUNT

is clearly more comprehensible than

T1

In the long name, hyphens are utilized as word separator characters to clarify understanding. Such separators should be used. (TOTALINPUTTRANSACTIONCOUNT takes much longer to mentally decode.) COBOL prohibits the use of blank characters (SPACES) as separators. However, in our design language, described in Chapter 3, blanks are acceptable.

People who are not the authors of programs, and who are called upon to make changes or urgently correct mistakes (commonly called bugs), must be able to find things in a hurry. If the data name clearly defines usage (without reference to other sources or other documentation), then that person has eliminated a significant comprehension problem and can immediately analyze program logic. If the programmer has to look in reference documents or data dictionaries to understand the data usage, it will take much longer to find logical problems. Time will be spent looking up meanings and keeping mental track of cryptic values.

(This is not meant as a condemnation of data dictionaries. Data dictionaries can be more profitably used to show editing rules, formats, sources, dispositions, and locations (where used) of data elements, structures, and arrays.)

Sometimes, programmers express concern about coding effort when full data names are used. With available technology this becomes a very minor concern. The wide availability of shorthand preprocessors and powerful full screen display editors provide rapid data creation and entry to sidestep this concern.

Data having the same meaning should always have the same name throughout the program. The various occurrences are distinguished via high-level structure name qualifiers. In COBOL, a data element named GROSS-PAY may appear in the following structures:

```
01 INPUT-RECORD.
   02 GROSS-PAY          PICTURE 9(8).
   02 FILLER             PICTURE X(28).

01 OUTPUT-RECORD.
   02 GROSS-PAY          PICTURE 9(8).
   02 FILLER             PICTURE X(50).

01 TERMINAL-RECORD.
   02 GROSS-PAY          PICTURE 9(8).
   02 FILLER             PICTURE X(30).
```

The three different GROSS-PAY item locations are referenced via qualifiers.

GROSS-PAY IN INPUT-RECORD.

or

GROSS-PAY IN OUTPUT-RECORD.

or

GROSS-PAY IN TERMINAL-RECORD.

Without the qualifying names, the COBOL compiler would not know which data element to use.

In application programs, data structures often must pass through many modules as input/output layouts and as parameters. If a data description is coded separately for each occurrence of a structure, changes become major headaches. The results are data mismatches and subsequent program failures. COBOL has the COPY statement to overcome this problem. It is a mechanism for copying a piece of code from a system library into numerous locations in any module. The programmer defines the data item, array, or structure and stores each definition in a separate library member (e.g., an input transaction layout). For each reference in a program, the programmer codes the appropriate COPY statement and the compiler automatically inserts the defined code at the specified location.

The use of such copy facilities greatly simplifies program maintenance. If a data field changes, the definition only has to be changed in one place (the copy library member), thus minimizing the number of program areas to be changed. If one or more components in a common copy library changes, all program modules in all programs using the item must be recompiled to ensure all references are correctly reestablished.

If a data field, array, or structure is used in more than one location in a program, it should be stored in a copy library. File record definitions and data base segment definitions should always be stored in copy libraries as these usually appear in more than one module and more than one program.

When data must be transferred from one storage area in a module to another storage area in the module, the move should be done on an element-by-element basis to make certain all needed data fields are moved. When the from and to data structures are identical, with each containing many individual fields, a group move may be considered:

```
MOVE INPUT-RECORD TO OUTPUT-RECORD.
```

You should not use MOVE CORRESPONDING. Simple spelling mistakes can cause data to suddenly disappear with the problem undetected for long periods of time. At some point in future time, the data loss may be unrecoverable.

In business applications, associated data items usually have a natural data structure. When such data structures are encountered, data handling is greatly simplified when the structure is retained throughout the program. Error prone techniques, such as data element concatenation and substringing, should not be used.

COBOL provides a substringing mechanism via the UNSTRING statement and reference modification technique. These features enable the programmer to address a portion of a data element by specifying the starting character location and length. Figure 5.1 shows an example of a substring operation. The upper portion of the diagram contains a structure handled via UNSTRING manipulation and reference modification. Examination of the lower portion of the figure, where the data items are structured, reveals an error in the upper operations

```
77 INPUT-PERSONNEL-DATA          PICTURE X(65).

77 WORK-MONTH                    PICTURE X(9).

77 START-CHARACTER               PICTURE 999 VALUE 30.

   UNSTRING INPUT-PERSONNEL-DATA INTO WORK-MONTH
              WITH POINTER START-CHARACTER.

                        or more simply

   MOVE INPUT-PERSONNEL-DATA (30:9) TO WORK-MONTH.
----------------------------------------------------------------
01 INPUT-PERSONNEL-DATA.
   02 NAME                       PICTURE X(30).
   02 DATE-OF-BIRTH.
      03 MONTH                   PICTURE X(9).
      03 DAY                     PICTURE X(2).
      03 YEAR                    PICTURE X(4).
   02 EMPLOYER                   PICTURE X(20).

77 WORK-MONTH                    PICTURE X(9).

   MOVE MONTH TO WORK-MONTH.
```

Figure 5.1. *Substringing versus a structure.*

(MONTH will be offset by one character). However, if you only have either of the upper code forms, the the error is very difficult to detect.

Always deal with data directly. Avoid switches as they are a form of indirect data reference.

The switch is a very popular form of indirect data reference. Unfortunately, a common malady among programmers is *switchitus*. A switch contains the results of a condition set as a result of another conditional test. It is always better to test the original condition, if possible, rather than resort to switches. When switches are used, a data element is tested and the switch is given a value.

```
IF RECORD-TYPE = "A"
   THEN
      MOVE 1 TO SWITCH
   ELSE
      MOVE 0 TO SWITCH
END-IF.
```

Sometime later the switch is tested.

```
IF SWITCH = 1
   THEN
      ADD AMOUNT TO GROSS-TOTAL
END-IF.
```

Difficulties arise when subsequent maintenance is being performed. If the record type field assumes a value other than *A* or *not A*, the test has to be modified in multiple locations (everywhere the switch is set and everywhere it is tested).

A better method is to save the actual data value for later testing.

```
MOVE RECORD-TYPE TO SAVED-RECORD-TYPE.
```

The later test then becomes:

```
IF SAVED-RECORD-TYPE = "A"
   THEN
      ADD AMOUNT TO GROSS-TOTAL
END-IF.
```

Here, when record type requires additional values to be tested, only the relevant tests need be adjusted.

Programmers cannot completely avoid switches because procedural programming languages do not have constructs to test conditions that are transient in time (first time in a module and end of file/data base are very common conditions). If switches cannot be eliminated, the values given to them should reflect the actual conditions being tested instead of on/off binary values. *YES* and *NO* are preferable to *1* and *0* for a first time indicator.

Each data variable should be used for only one purpose (Kernighan and Plauger, 1974). Trying to economize on storage by using one data area for multiple purposes causes headaches for maintenance programmers. An apparently irrelevant value may be overridden without the realization that it has another purpose.

All required initial values should be specifically set by the programmer. Do not use compiler default values because compiler developers, for valid system reasons, may eliminate or change the defaults. A production program that relies on storage being initialized to binary zeros may go haywire if a new compiler release uses blanks for all its default values.

A programmer should never assume that input data coming from an uncontrolled source, such as a terminal operator, will be valid or in the correct sequence. If you have no control over the source of data, you have no control over its quality. Always validate input data and check file and data base sequence if the logic of the program is dependent on correct values or correct sequence.

You can count on program volume growth; therefore, to accommodate growth, always design data element sizes to contain values much larger than the current known maximum sizes. With such provision, growth is easier to accommodate.

Sometimes it is convenient to store data in tables or arrays and process it via indices. However, errant subscript values are difficult to trace and can cause damage in distant portions of the program. When using subscripts, upper and lower bound value checks should be performed to ensure the subscripts stay within valid ranges. (Many compilers now include this check. If yours is one of those, the following code is redundant.) For example, consider the following method.

```
calculate subscript value.

IF subscript value greater than table range or
        subscript value less than 1
   THEN
      handle error condition
   ELSE
      move data to table (subscript value)
END-IF.
```

Many organizations issue a dictum that literals should not be used in the PROCEDURE DIVISION. Instead, the character or numeric values should be defined in the WORKING-STORAGE SECTION. In general, this is a good policy, but it should be tempered with logic understanding and maintenance considerations. For example, suppose the literal 1 is defined and used in the following manner:

```
77  ONE                      PICTURE 9 VALUE 1.

        IF COUNT = ONE
           THEN
              MOVE SPACES TO OUTPUT-LINE
        END-IF.
```

If someone tries to make fast changes to check for a different value of count, the following quick adjustment will lead to disaster:

```
77  ONE                      PICTURE 9 VALUE 2.
```

A better rule is to use literals in the PROCEDURE DIVISION for things that have an unchangeable meaning and value. Use the WORKING-STORAGE SECTION for values that will likely change as program maintenance is undertaken: subscript values, range values, page sizes, editing values, and so on.

Rounding precision can produce strange calculation results. The order of calculation may have a dramatic effect on the rounding of the result. Whenever multiplication and division of numerical data take place, the answer should be carefully reviewed to verify absence of rounding errors. Many financial systems cannot tolerate rounding errors (someone's money is involved).

6 Program Decomposition

A major problem facing programmers is how to subdivide a particular program into modular components after the overall program functions have been defined and documented. In this chapter, a simple design approach for general business application programs is described. This approach has been published in the *IBM Systems Journal* (Rogers, 1983) and is suitable for most programs written in COBOL. It utilizes a single simple architecture that views computer application programs as four-level hierarchies of logical modules. Benefits of this technique include improved maintenance productivity through design consistency, faster learning curves for novice programmers, and some simplification of the system design process (described in Chapter 12).

Procedural language application programs have four key parts: iteration, decision control, data detail processing, and support operations. These functions are organized into a modular structural hierarchy of four logical levels to form the program structural architecture. This architecture is shown in Figure 6.1.

LEVEL 1—MAINLINE

The mainline module is the root of the program at the top of the structural hierarchy. It controls overall program iteration and main event

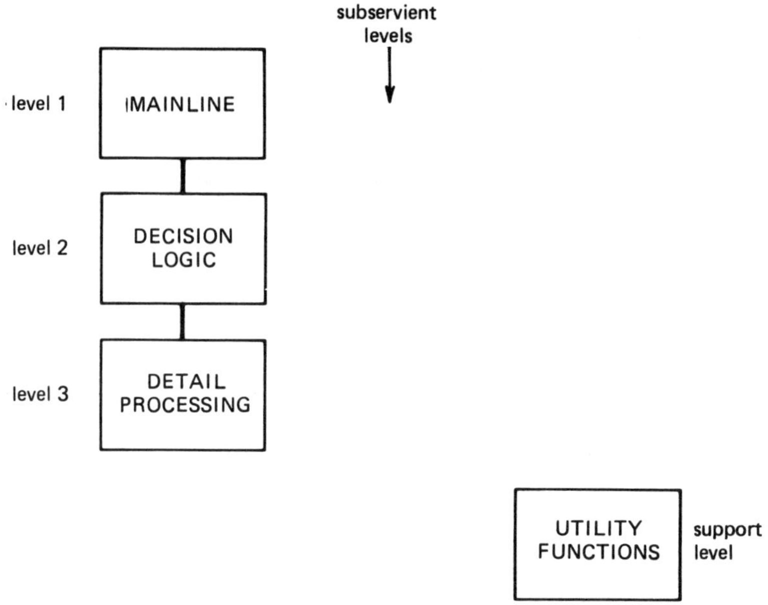

Figure 6.1. *Program structural architecture.*

processing for the program. This module is usually prepared by the programmer. Sometimes it is supplied as part of a software control system, as with the special processing option of IBM's Application Development Facility (ADF).

The program begins executing when control passes from the operating system to the mainline module. Program execution ends when processing reaches the end of the mainline module and control returns to the operating system.

The primary purpose of the mainline logic is to make the key program operative conditions clearly visible. With consistent documentation standards, programmers should be able to comprehend readily the reason for program execution.

One of the biggest problems facing maintenance programmers is determining the exact conditions under which a program executes. Often, maintenance programmers examine several levels in the hierarchy of a program and are perplexed as to why the program runs, given certain input conditions. When the logic for primary control is widely dispersed, the initial programmer and subsequent maintenance programmers may have difficulty fully understanding all the interactions of the program. It is extremely important for maintenance programmers to know under what circumstances the program functions, and this knowledge should be easily obtainable. When the run conditions of the program are buried in the hierarchy, programmers can easily make changes in the wrong places, causing unpredictable results.

There is limited data processing and data handling at this top level in the hierarchy. A condition or conditions controlling execution of the program, data to be initialized, data passed to the end of job processing module, and data base and data communication work areas (which may be parameters when control is given to the mainline module) are the likely data to be handled.

Mainline logic is discussed in further detail in Chapter 7.

LEVEL 2—DECISION LOGIC

Decision logic is the second level in the program structural hierarchy. Here the characteristic logic of the processing solution appears. Most general business application programs can be classified in one of four groups: control break, balance line, single panel interactive, or multi-panel interactive. Decision logic for these four groups is discussed further in Chapter 8.

Again, practically no data is processed at this level. However, the amount of data handling increases significantly. The decision logic provides, in a sense, a message switching/control function and ensures that the appropriate data is correctly passed among the subservient program levels.

LEVEL 3—DETAIL PROCESSING

Detail processing is the next level down from decision logic in the program hierarchy. The modules that appear are defined by the decision logic that invokes them. (The examples of Chapters 13, 14, 15, and 16 provide further insight into this phenomenon.)

At this level in the hierarchy, the modules primarily process the data. Control logic should be simplified and data processing should be maximized. For these reasons, the modules at this level in the structure in the program will be larger than those found at the mainline and decision logic levels.

Since the detail processing level of a program deals with specific data manipulation, the code at this level is generally unique for each program.

LEVEL 4 (SUPPORT)—UTILITY FUNCTIONS

Acting for all levels in the hierarchy are the utility function modules. These operate at the support level and provide common functions usable by all levels in the application program hierarchy.

Utility functions occur in most business application programs. They perform tasks that are called from various locations throughout the program. Utility modules can be supported by other utility modules. Therefore, although the program structure has four logical levels, it may have more than four physical levels. (This will be demonstrated in examples in later chapters.)

Utility functions tend to be relatively simple modules that process data rather than affect control logic. Some common utility functions are described in Chapter 9.

CLASSICAL FUNCTIONS

In business application programs many functions occur repeatedly. In the following chapters, a number of these are documented. They are called *classical* functions and can be reused in many programs.

In application programs, great amounts of data, often in complex structures, must traverse most of the key modules. To accommodate this situation, the classical functions must be able to handle different elements and data structures that occur in various programs. Ideally, a programmer should have these in ready-to-run object code form. However, this requires a code generator. A practical alternative, used in this book, is to specify the functions in the design language (rules described in Chapter 3). The programmer takes the classical functions, adds his or her data references to complete those module designs, and adds program-specific functions and company-wide reusable functions to complete the program design.

In addition to classical functions, businesses have additional sets of utility functions characteristic of the enterprise. These functions will be identified by the organization itself. A common security authorization module is an example of a company-specific reusable function.

Chapters 7, 8, and 9 define classical function modules for three program structural levels: mainline, decision logic, and utility functions. As yet, classical functions have not been identified at the detail processing level, since the logic at this level appears to be unique for each program.

You should strive to use the classical modules as is. Program variations can be handled by program-unique modules. If the classical function logic is changed, a programmer must re-debug it. *Reinventing the wheel* is a senseless waste of time.

This author has found that classical functions used with a time sharing text editor is a very useful productivity tool. The classical functions are stored in editor-accessible computer libraries and are used as the *shell* for each program design. The shell is enhanced with programmer-provided program-unique logic and program data fields to complete the design. This author has also found it convenient and productive to retain a copy of a COBOL module of each classical function used. Once the design in the design language is finalized, it can be quickly implemented by modifying copies of existing COBOL code using the time-sharing text editor. (This technique is explained further in the discussion of the example programs of Chapters 13, 14, 15, and 16.)

7 Classical Mainline Module

The mainline module is the root module at the top of the program hierarchy. When a COBOL program commences its operation, control passes from the computer operating system to the beginning of this module. When the program completes its processing, control normally returns to the operating system from the last executed statement in this module. Control reverts to the operating system from other than the mainline module only when an abnormal situation occurs and immediate program termination is specifically requested. An example of such an abnormal situation would be a module that reads a sequential input file and discovers a sequence error in it—processing should then be ended immediately (with an appropriate error message).

The mainline module can be written by the programmer or may be supplied as part of a software manager. When a programmer designs his or her own mainline function, he or she should use the classical function, shown in Figure 7.1, as a basis for it. To utilize this logic, the programmer takes the classical function and adds his or her data references to it.

One of the biggest problems facing maintenance programmers is determining the exact conditions under which a program executes. Often people examine several levels in a program's hierarchy and cannot determine why the program runs, given some or all of the input condi-

```
*                     MAINLINE MODULE

 PROGRAM-ID. mainline ⟨MAIN⟩ [USING system parameters].

    CALL "initial" USING initialization variables.

    PERFORM WITH TEST BEFORE UNTIL condition for program to end
       CALL "decide" USING decision logic variables
    END-PERFORM.

    CALL "endjob" USING end of job variables.
    [end of program command.]

 END PROGRAM mainline.
```

Figure 7.1. *Classical mainline module.*

tions. When the logic for primary control is widely dispersed, the initial developer and subsequent maintenance programmers may have difficulty understanding all the interactions of the program. It is extremely important for maintenance programmers to know under what circumstances the program functions, and this knowledge should be easily obtainable. When the run conditions of the program are buried in the hierarchy, programmers can easily make changes at the wrong places, causing unpredictable results.

The mainline logic of Figure 7.1 is very simple, and its prime purpose is to show overall program iteration for the major condition or conditions affecting continued program execution. It is suitable for both batch and interactive types of programs.

The code of Figure 7.1 shows the PROGRAM-ID statement with optional system parameters. These are data fields that may be passed between the operating system and the application program. When present, they are often work areas for interactive reentrant programs or parameters passed from the system command or job control language.

The next statement issues a call to the initialization module (named *initial*). Initialization is handled by a utility level module. It can give starting values to data fields and performs any processing that must occur when the program starts operating.

Following the initialization call is a PERFORM statement that controls the main processing of the program. This statement checks the validity of program execution conditions and iteratively invokes the decision logic module (named *decide*) at the next lower level in the program hierarchy. An input data stream that is not yet at the end, or a terminal user who has not told the program he or she is finished, are examples of conditions resulting in continued program operation.

After the PERFORM construct, there is a statement containing a call to the end of job module (named *endjob*). The end of job module is a utility level module for processing that occurs at the end of the program. The end of job module may print grand totals, produce summary reports, write audit totals onto a log file, save program work areas, and process program shutdown functions.

Finally, an optional end of program command may appear. This is usually a STOP RUN statement. However, in some environments an end of program command may, instead, set specific system fields or return codes before control is returned to the operating system or software manager.

8 Classical Decision Logic Modules

Decision logic appears at the second level in a program's structural hierarchy and contains the characteristic logic of the programming solution. For business applications, the decision logic for a program generally falls into one of four categories: control break, balance line, single panel interactive, or multipanel interactive. This chapter describes the classical functions for each of these categories.

The four decision logic functions are each contained in separate modules. There can be one decision logic module in each program and all four modules are designed to work with the classical mainline module described in Chapter 7.

Decision logic is invoked from the mainline module. For consistency, all classical modules in this chapter have been given the same name (*decide*) to reinforce this relationship.

CONTROL BREAK MODULE

Control break logic is a very common programmer-written logic. It appears in batch report programs, batch validation programs, batch random update programs, copy programs, and data reduction programs (where data is condensed and written to a file for processing by subsequent programs), and is based on the concept of change-of-sequence keys of a sequenced input data stream. The sequenced input data stream can be a sequential file, a sequentially read indexed file, a sequentially read data base, or a sequentially read table. A control break occurs when a key field changes value. At this time, related processing, such as totaling takes place.

The classical logic for the control break module is shown in Figure 8.1.

In order to understand the logic, one must view the key field of the sequenced input subdived into N sub keys.

| sub key N | ......| sub key 3 | sub key 2 | sub key 1 |
high level sub keys ←→ low level sub keys

When the lowest level sub key changes value break 1 occurs. When the next higher level changes, break 2 occurs. These breaks are defined up to the highest level (break N). At each break level, the control break processing for that level and all lower levels must be operated in lowest-to-highest level order. For example, if a report is prepared for employees in a company with the employees printed by department within city, the report has two levels of control breaks. Break 1 (lowest level) occurs when either department or city changes value. Break 2 (highest level) occurs when city changes value. It is important to note that the program will only work correctly when the input data exists, or is sorted into, the key sequence of department within city.

If there are no data key fields or no control breaks taken, the program is a zero level control break program. A simple copy program is an example of a zero level control break program.

The logic of Figure 8.1 allows for any number of control breaks, and these are shown as noted options in square brackets.

The first operation, after control enters the module, is the invocation of a utility level module (seqread) to read the sequential input. (This input could be a sequential file, a sequentially read data base, or a sequentially read table.) Usually, one of the classical sequential read modules of Chapter 9 can be called at this point.

The check for first time in the module is necessary because no break processing should occur for first invocation of the decision logic. A

```
*                        CONTROL BREAK MODULE

PROGRAM-ID. decide USING decision logic variables.

    CALL "seqread" USING data stream status,
                         current sequential key,
                         previous sequential key, data fields.

    IF data stream status = "at end"
       THEN
         [CALL "break1" USING break1 variables]     《 note 1 》
         [CALL "break2" USING break2 variables]     《 note 2 》
         [CALL "break3" USING break3 variables]     《 note 3 》
                        .
                        .
                        .
         [CALL "breakN" USING breakN variables]     《 note 4 》
          EXIT PROGRAM
    END-IF.

    IF first time in module
       THEN
          CALL "detail" USING detail processing variables
          reset first time indicator
          EXIT PROGRAM
    END-IF.

   ┌IF current keys for breaks 1 through N not equal to ┐
   │     previous keys for breaks 1 through N           │
   │   THEN                                             │    《 note 1 》
   │      CALL "break1" USING break1 variables          │
   └END-IF.                                             ┘

   ┌IF current keys for breaks 2 through N not equal to ┐
   │     previous keys for breaks 2 through N           │
   │   THEN                                             │    《 note 2 》
   │      CALL "break2" USING break2 variables          │
   └END-IF.                                             ┘

   ┌IF current keys for breaks 3 through N not equal to ┐
   │     previous keys for breaks 3 through N           │
   │   THEN                                             │    《 note 3 》
   │      CALL "break3" USING break3 variables          │
   └END-IF.                                             ┘
                        .
                        .
                        .
   ┌IF current key for break N not equal to         ┐
   │     previous key for break N                   │
   │   THEN                                         │ 《 note 4 》
   │      CALL "breakN" USING breakN variables      │
   └END-IF.                                         ┘

    CALL "detail" USING detail processing variables.

END PROGRAM decide.
```

Notes: 1. Required if there are one or more control breaks.
2. Required if there are two or more control breaks.
3. Required if there are three or more control breaks.
4. Required if there are N control breaks.

Figure 8.1. *Classical control break module.*

break cannot occur unless there are at least two input records present in the data before end of data is encountered. If this precautionary check is not taken, erroneous totaling for the first data record will be the result.

The subsequent logic to the end of the module checks, in order, for lowest to highest level breaks. For each change in the appropriate key field, associate processing is invoked via a called module. In the previously described example of the employee report, the low level break (break 1) occurs when department value changes and a module for break 1 processing is called. A city value change causes the lower level (break 1) processing to be invoked for the last department in the prior city followed by the invocation of the processing for the prior city (break 2) to ensure the previous city is fully accounted for.

The modules handling the break processing are detail processing functions found at level 3 in the program's structural hierarchy.

BALANCE LINE MODULE

Programmers are often faced with the problem of combining two sequential streams of items. The data streams may be sequential tables, sequential files, sequentially read indexed files, or sequentially read data bases, or a combination of these. The combination process can be called a merge, a selection program, or an update program, and one of the data streams is matched to another similarly sequenced data stream.

Consider two data streams with the following key field values.

stream 1	stream 2
1	2
3	4
5	5

In balance line processing, input consists of two streams of data in acsending, similarly sequenced order. The output will be a single stream of sequential data resulting from the combination. In the preceding example, the order of processing of items is:

Stream 1 key value 1
Stream 2 key value 2
Stream 1 key value 3
Stream 2 key value 4
Stream 1 and stream 2 key value 5

The items in the data stream with lowest key value are always taken first. This is reflected in the balance line logic module documented in Figure 8.2. The logic assumes that there is only one logical record for each unique key value in each of the input streams. If the possibility exists for more than one record with a particular key to be present in either input data stream, the simplest method of handling this situation is to have the reading module load related sets into a table. The balance line match key is then the key of the items in the table. However, some problems have record sets with an indeterminate large number of records in each set. The balance line logic can also handle this situation as shown in the example program of Chapter 14.

The module name in the classical code is again *decide* to show compatibility with the classical mainline module of Figure 7.1.

Upon entry to this module, the logic tests to see if it is the first time for invocation of this module in the program. During first time invocation, the first time indicator is reset and both input data streams must be read (via utility read modules) to have the logic positioned to the initial data records. Here, also, both data streams are tested for joint end of data condition, as such a condition obviates the need for further processing. With no data in both input streams, control exits to the main line module.

Next, the key of stream 1 is evaluated to determine if it has the lowest value. It can be lowest when stream 2 is at end (no more records), or if it is found lowest when its key is compared to the key of the other data stream. If stream 1 has the lowest key, the key 1 low module at the detail processing level is called with a subsequent call to the read module to get the next record in data stream 1.

If the key of stream 1 is not the lowest, a similar check is made to see if the key of stream 2 is lowest. If it is, the key 2 low module at the detail processing level is called followed by a call to the utility level module to read the next record in stream 2.

```
*                          BALANCE LINE MODULE

   PROGRAM-ID. decide USING decision logic variables.

      IF first time in module
         THEN
            reset first time indicator
            CALL "seqread1" USING data stream 1 status,
                                  current sequential key 1,
                                  previous sequential key 1,
                                  stream 1 data fields
            CALL "seqread2" USING data stream 2 status,
                                  current sequential key 2,
                                  previous sequential key 2,
                                  stream 2 data fields

            IF data stream 1 status = "at end"
                       and
               data stream 2 status = "at end"
                THEN
                   EXIT PROGRAM
            END-IF

      END-IF.

      IF data stream 2 status = "at end"
                  or
         current sequential key 1 less than
            current sequential key 2
          THEN
            CALL "key1low" USING key1low module variables
            CALL "seqread1" USING data stream 1 status,
                                  current sequential key 1,
                                  previous sequential key 1,
                                  stream 1 data fields
            EXIT PROGRAM
      END-IF.

      IF data stream 1 status = "at end"
                  or
         current sequential key 2 less than
            current sequential key 1
          THEN
            CALL "key2low" USING key2low module variables
            CALL "seqread2" USING data stream 2 status,
                                  current sequential key 2,
                                  previous sequential key 2,
                                  stream 2 data fields
            EXIT PROGRAM
      END-IF.

      CALL "keyseq" USING keyseq module variables.
      CALL "seqread1" USING data stream 1 status,
                            current sequential key 1,
                            previous sequential key 1,
                            stream 1 data fields.
    [ CALL "seqread2" USING data stream 2 status,       ]
    [                       current sequential key 2,   ]  « note 1 »
    [                       previous sequential key 2,  ]
    [                       stream 2 data fields.       ]

   END PROGRAM decide.
```

Notes: 1. Not required for selection programs.

Figure 8.2. *Classical balance line module.*

If stream 1 hasn't the lowest key and stream 2 hasn't the lowest key, the keys must, therefore, be equal. In this circumstance, the detail processing logic of the *keyseq* module is called with subsequent invocation of both utility read modules to get the next input record of both input data streams. The reader will note that the second read module call is shown to be optional. This read is left out for selection programs when one record of stream 2 is matched against many records in stream 1.

The identified detail processing modules *key1low, key2low, keyseq*, perform the necessary data processing for each of the three key match situations.

SINGLE PANEL INTERACTIVE MODULE

For interactive processing, a programmer may create a program that is called by the classical mainline module to process a single type of transaction or create a program that operates under a menu management system. Menu management systems (such as the special processing option of IBM's Application Development Facility) provide an umbrella mechanism of selection menus and control features to enable users to transfer from transaction to transaction in an interactive environment to facilitate simpler programming. The single panel interactive classical module is compatible with both the classical mainline and menu management systems.

There are two major types of single panel interactive programs: those which *see* a complete session for each connected terminal device and those which process only one interaction for a terminal device at a time. IBM products, such as TSO, VM/CMS, and the Personal Computer, provide the first type of environment, while IMS provides the second type of environment. (Depending on the options chosen, CICS can be made to support either type.) The classical single panel interactive decision logic works for both types of environments.

The design logic for this module is shown in Figure 8.3. It can be applied to both interactive update and interactive inquiry processing as indicated by the square option brackets ([ ]). The module is again named *decide* to indicate compatability with the classical mainline module.

```
*                    SINGLE PANEL INTERACTIVE MODULE

PROGRAM-ID. decide USING decision logic variables.

 [CALL "profile" USING user profile variables).]  « note 1 »

  IF first time in module for user
       THEN
          reset first time indicator
          CALL "prompt" USING prompt display variables
         [make current and previous data]
         [   display keys different     ]        « note 2 »
          CALL "send" USING send module variables
          EXIT PROGRAM
    END-IF.

    CALL "receive" USING receive module variables.

  [IF user not allowed to access data              ]
  [    THEN                                        ]
  [       set up error message                     ]  « note 1 »
  [       CALL "send" USING send module variables  ]
  [       EXIT PROGRAM                             ]
  [END-IF.                                         ]

  [IF current data display key not equal to]
  [   previous data display key            ]        « note 2 »
      THEN
         CALL "getdata" USING data base variables
        [move current data display key to]         « note 2 »
        [   previous data display key    ]
         CALL "send" USING send module variables
  [      EXIT PROGRAM]                             « note 2 »
  [END-IF.           ]

 [[IF user not allowed to update data            ]  « n »  ]
 [[    THEN                                      ]  « o »  ]  « n »
 [[       set up error message                   ]  « t »  ]  « o »
 [[       CALL "send" USING send module variables]  « e »  ]  « t »
 [[       EXIT PROGRAM                           ]  «   »  ]  « e »
 [[END-IF.                                       ]  « 1 »  ]  «   »
 [                                                         ]  « 2 »
 [ CALL "dataup" USING data base update variables.         ]
 [ move current data display key to                        ]
 [      previous data display key.                         ]
 [ CALL "send" USING send module variables.                ]

END PROGRAM decide.
```

Notes: 1. Required if security checking not provided by software control system.
2. Required for data update.

Figure 8.3. *Classical single panel interactive module.*

After control enters the module, the first (optional) operation is a call to the user profile module to get the user profile parameters. Many software environments supply a security control scheme that is adequate. However, if this is not present in your system, or if more thorough security checks are required, such as users who are restricted to certain sections of files, a utility profile module should be used. When used, the security profile module is called for each invocation of the decision logic and, thus, allows security status changes in long running applications.

Next, the logic checks to see if this is the first invocation of decision logic for the particular user. (Because the logic is usually applied in multiuser interactive environments, the first time indicator is normally a data variable stored in the user's terminal work area.) For first time, a utility module is called to build an output prompt transaction asking the user to enter input. The user can be a person or a machine, and the prompt can vary from a sophisticated, formatted display to a simple data request indicator. After the prompt is constructed, the first time indicator is reset and, if the program is to perform data updating functions, the current and previous field data keys are made different to force a *get* data situation during the next subsequent module invocation for that user. The prompt is then dispatched to the user via a utility send module and control leaves the decision logic module.

If it is not the first time in this module, a call is issued to get the user's input reply data.

An optional test follows to determine if the user is allowed to access the data. If the system parameters or the prior call the the profile module show data access is not allowed, an appropriate error message is sent to the user and control leaves the module.

For data updates, a check is made to verify that no data key changes have occurred between interactions with this user. This means the user has viewed and, perhaps, updated the data, but has not changed its key fields. If the key fields were changed by the user, the logic will get the new data (via the get data detail processing module), set up the data display keys, send the data to the user and exit from the module.

For inquiry usage, the logic gets the data each time. This is done under the assumption that an additional request for the same data by the user is a mistake. Logic simplicity is of greater value than optimizing code for once-in-a-while errors. Thus, it is a waste of coding effort to code a check to avoid input/output requests when the same data key is reentered.

Before data updating actually occurs, an optional test may be used to ensure that the user is actually allowed to change the selected data. If not, an error message is sent via the utility send module and control exits from this module.

For valid updates, the detail processing update module is invoked. The current display key is moved to the previous display key and the update is then acknowledged via the send utility module, and control leaves this module at the end of the code marked by the END PROGRAM header.

MULTIPANEL INTERACTIVE MODULE

In sophisticated interactive computer applications, the programmer often needs, or wants, to control the processing flow from transaction to transaction. Some transactions process data updates, some process data inquiries, some are used to select other transactions (menus), while others are combinations of these types. The multipanel interactive decision logic module is suitable for all these kinds of programs.

As with the single panel interactive programs, there are also two major types of multipanel interactive programs: those which "see" a complete session for each connected terminal and those which process only one interaction for a terminal device at a time. The classical multipanel interactive decision logic also works in both types of environments.

The logic is shown in Figure 8.4. Note that the module name is also *decide* to indicate compatibility with the classical mainline module.

After entry into the module, the logic has an optional call to a utility user profile module. The profile module would be included when the software control system, under which the application operates, does provide security checking or if elaborate security precautions must be taken (e.g., restricted access to certain portions of files or data bases). The profile module is invoked each time the decision module is entered to give continuous security checking for long running interactive applications where user profiles can be varied dynamically by system administrators.

If this is the first run of the decision logic for a terminal user, the prior panel identifier is set to a value to enable subservient modules to

```
*                    MULTIPANEL INTERACTIVE MODULE

 PROGRAM-ID. decide USING decision logic variables.

   [CALL "profile" USING user profile variables.]   « note 1 »

   IF first time in module for user
      THEN
         reset first time indicator
         make previous panel identifier show no prior panel
      ELSE
         CALL "receive" USING receive module variables
   END-IF.

   PERFORM WITH TEST AFTER UNTIL processing control = "send"

      EVALUATE panel code
         WHEN first panel
            CALL "panel1" USING panel1 variables,
                                previous panel code,
                                panel code,
                                processing control
            move "first panel identifier" to previous panel code
         WHEN second panel
            CALL "panel2" USING panel2 variables,
                                previous panel code,
                                panel code,
                                processing control
            move "second panel identifier" to previous panel code
                                .
                                .
                                .
         WHEN Nth panel
            CALL "panelN" USING panelN variables,
                                previous panel code,
                                panel code,
                                processing control
            move "Nth panel identifier" to previous panel code
         WHEN OTHER
            move previous panel code to panel code
            set up message for bad panel id
            move "send" to processing control
      END-EVALUATE

   END-PERFORM.

   CALL "send" USING send module variables.

 END PROGRAM decide.
```

Notes: 1. Required if security checking not provided by software control system.

Figure 8.4. *Classical multipanel interactive module.*

know there have been no prior panels (transactions) processed for that user. Detail processing modules, called by the decision logic, often need to establish if they, or another transaction, last dealt with the user.

If this module is not being run a first time for the user, a utility receive module is called to get input data from the user.

The PERFORM logic uses a processing control data field to switch control from one transaction to another or return control to the terminal user. The loop logic ends when the value of the processing control data field becomes *send*.

Within the PERFORM loop there is an EVALUATE construct for each transaction that can be processed. Each transaction is handled via a subservient detail processing module (panel1, panel2, . . ., panelN) and a previous panel identifier value is established. The WHEN OTHER option provides for handling of invalid panel code situations.

Finally, before control leaves the decision logic, a send utility module is called to send a response to the user. Control then exits from the module.

9 Classical Utility Modules

Utility modules appear at the fourth (support) level in a program's structural hierarchy. They perform tasks that are invoked from all levels in the hierarchy, including other support level modules. A large program may have many utility modules.

This chapter describes classical utility functions that can be used in various types of business application programs. They are grouped into four categories: input/output modules, field manipulation modules, table processing modules, and calendar modules.

INPUT/OUTPUT MODULES

Print Report Detail

This logic appears in a majority of batch processing applications. It controls the layout and page numbering of report pages. There should be one of these modules for each different report that is to be produced.

The logic appears in Figure 9.1. The input parameters are the report variables that are to be printed. Note that this logic depends on a high

```
*                       PRINT REPORT DETAIL MODULE

 PROGRAM-ID. print USING report variables.

          « page number should have an initial value of zero »
          « line number should have an initial value of 999  »
          « page size is the maximum number of lines to be   »
          «  on a page                                       »

   IF line number greater than page size
      THEN
         add 1 to page number
         move zero to line number
         print page headings
   END-IF.

   print detail line(s).
   add 1 to line number for each line printed.

 END PROGRAM print.
```

Figure 9.1. *Classical print report detail module.*

initial value for the line number, and the initial value must always be greater than the value of page size to ensure that headings are printed on the first page of the report.

Because this function is normally associated with batch programs, the starting values can be initialized by the compiler. However, when the report function must operate in a multiuser interactive environment, all initial values are established by executable statements in the initialization module and will be passed as parameters through the program's hierarchy to the print report detail module.

The logic of this module first checks to see if there is page overflow (line number greater than page size). For a page overflow condition, the title lines are printed on the top of the next physical page.

After the page heading condition is checked, detail lines for the report are printed and the line number is incremented by one for each line printed.

Simple Sequential Read

This module is applicable where input records must be read from a sequenced file or data base. The logic for it is portrayed in Figure 9.2.

Data stream status and audit data fields are parameters that are updated by this module. Data stream status is set externally to *not at end* in the program's initialization module and is changed to *at end* by this module when the end of the input data stream is reached (i.e., end of file). The data stream status must be given its starting value by the initialization module because the mainline logic often relies on a test for end of input data.

Audit data items contain record counts and summary elements to verify the program is operating correctly. Audit parameters may also include parameters passed from the software control system (such as status values).

The module logic first checks to see if end of file has been previously attained. If it has, it signifies that the program contains a logic error and the error must be handled. The most appropriate action is to stop the program immediately with a suitable error message display.

The current key value is moved to the data item containing the previous key value, and the next record in the data stream is read. If there are no more records, data stream status is set to *at end.*

For the not at end condition, the auditing data values are accumulated, and the current key value element is set up.

For first invocation of this logic in a program, *low values* are established in the previous key element. Control then returns to the higher level calling module.

When it is not the first time in this module, an optional sequence check of input data occurs. The sequence check helps ensure correct program logic functions. If the program has a dependency on the sequence of input data, the sequence check is a must. Control break logic (Chapter 8) is an example of logic that depends on a certain input sequence.

Sequential Read and Table Load

Sometimes sequential input data is presented to a program in sets and it is convenient to load each set of records into a table for subsequent pro-

```
*               SIMPLE SEQUENTIAL READ MODULE

  PROGRAM-ID. seqread USING data stream status,
                            current sequential key,
                            previous sequential key,
                            audit data fields, data fields.

     IF data stream status = "at end"
        THEN
           indicate error - program attempting to read past end
                            data
          handle error condition
         [EXIT PROGRAM]
     END-IF.

     move current sequential key to previous sequential key.
     read file or data base sequentially to get data.

     IF end of data reached
        THEN
           move "at end" to data stream status
           EXIT PROGRAM
     END-IF.

     set up linkage data.
     accumulate audit data fields.
     set up current sequential key.

     IF first time in module
        THEN
           reset first time indicator
           move low values to previous sequential key
           EXIT PROGRAM
     END-IF.

    [If current sequential key not greater than  ]
    [  previous sequential key                   ]
    [   THEN                                     ]
    [      indicate error-data out of sequence   ]   《 note 1 》
    [      handle error condition                ]
    [END-IF.                                     ]

  END PROGRAM seqread.
```

Notes: 1. Required if program logic has dependency on input sequence.

Figure 9.2. *Classical simple sequential read module.*

cessing. The logic of Figure 9.3 provides a sequential read and table load function.

The parameters are identical to those of the simple sequential read module with the exception that the data read is in table form rather than record form. This makes it easy to exchange modules, minimizing program logic changes when problems change and groups of records replace single record entities.

The module produces sets of records, in sequential chronological order, for its calling modules. However, the logic, internally, is always one record ahead in order to detect set completion criteria. To facilitate this process, two sets of keys are maintained: current and previous sequential keys for external reference, and local current and previous sequential keys for internal reference.

Again, in this logic, the existence of an end of data condition is tested to check for program logic errors whereby the module is entered with an end of data condition in existence. When such an error occurs, the logic shows the condition and takes appropriate action (most likely terminating the program with a message).

The first time the module logic is executed, the processing parameters and key values are set up and the first record is read. If end of data occurs on the first record, the appropriate indicators are set. Otherwise, the table key values are established.

If the local end of data indicator shows at *end*, the external end of data indicator is set and control returns to the higher level calling module.

After the above end of data check, the logic loops, thereby loading the table until an end of set is detected. The end of the set is marked either with a key value change or an end of data condition.

Once a set is loaded into the table, sequence is checked. This test is mandatory because the logic will fall apart, giving disastrous results, if the input data is not in the correct sequence.

Direct Read

The direct read module is used when a program must directly access files or data bases via key values (either indexed or by relative record numbers). The logic is presented in Figure 9.4. The parameters are the key values used to locate the desired data records, an optional locking

```
*          SEQUENTIAL READ AND TABLE LOAD MODULE

     PROGRAM-ID. seqread USING data stream status,
                               current sequential key,
                               previous sequential key,
                               audit data fields,
                               table of data fields, table index.

        IF data stream status = "at end"
           THEN
              indicate error - program attempting to read past end of
                               data
              handle error condition
             [EXIT PROGRAM]
        END-IF.

        IF first time in module
           THEN
              move low values to current sequential key
              reset first time indicator
              move "not at end" to local data stream status
              read file or data base sequentially to get first record

              IF end of data reached
                 THEN
                    move "at end" to local data stream status
                 ELSE
                    set up current table key
              END-IF

        END-IF.

        IF local data stream status = "at end"
           THEN
              move "at end" to data stream status
              EXIT PROGRAM
        END-IF.

        move current sequential key to previous sequential key
        move current table key to previous table key
        move zero to table index

        PERFORM WITH TEST BEFORE UNTIL
              current table key not = previous table key
                                  or
              local data stream status = "at end"
           add 1 to table index
```

Figure 9.3. *Classical sequential read and table load module.*

```
        IF table index greater than table size
            THEN
                indicate error - table overflow condition
                handle error condition
              [EXIT PROGRAM]
        END-IF

        load table (table index) from input data
        accumulate audit data
        move previous table key to current table key
        read file or data base sequentially to get data

        IF end of data reached
            THEN
                move "at end" to local data stream status
            ELSE
                set up current table key
        END-IF

    END-PERFORM.

    set up current sequential key.

    IF current sequential key not greater than
            previous sequential key
        THEN
            indicate error - data out of sequence
            handle error condition
    END-IF.

END PROGRAM seqread.
```

```
*                       DIRECT READ MODULE

 PROGRAM-ID. diread USING key fields,
                          audit data fields,
                          data fields, message
                         [,locking indicator].        « note 1 »

   set up file or data base access parameters and key.

  [IF locking indicator = "yes"                       ]
  |   THEN                                            |
  |      read record with specified key and lock it   |        « note 1 »
  |   ELSE                                            |
  [           read record with specified key          ]
  [END-IF.]                                                    « note 1 »

   IF record found
      THEN
         move spaces to message
         set up data fields from record
         accumulate audit data fields
      ELSE
         move "data not found" to message
   END-IF.

 END PROGRAM diread.
```

Notes: 1. Locking required if simultaneous update situation can occur and lock not controlled by operating system.

Figure 9.4. *Classical direct read module.*

indicator, audit data items, the data retrieved from the files and data bases, and messages.

In many application situations, numerous users must simultaneously update files and/or data bases; therefore, to accommodate such situations a locking mechanism must be provided by the software control system. The reason for this is to correctly sequence updates. Chaos will occur if the first user reads a record with the intention to update it, and, while he or she changes the data, a second user also accesses the record. The second user's changes will not be built on the modifications of the first user, but will likely override them. Locking ensures the first user's changes are applied before subsequent users *see* the data.

Often the locking mechanism is external and transparent to the COBOL program. For performance reasons, some systems allow user programs to control the locking mechanism. (Records that are read but not to be updated can avoid the locking overhead.) To handle programs running in locking control environments, the optional locking parameter is provided in the direct read logic.

The audit data items are those parameters containing system control parameters and auditing totals. An example of system control parameters would be data base attributes. Auditing totals assist with program data control and balancing (see Chapter 10).

Output parameters that are created by the logic are the data elements or records retrieved from the file or data base and messages to show results of the read operation. The messages can be either in the language of the user (e.g., English for this author) or, alternatively, codes that are acted on by the calling modules.

In the logic of Figure 9.4, the file or data base access parameters, identifying the type of access and the key(s) of the record(s) are set up. A read to retrieve the data follows. If the record is found the data is moved to the output parameter area and auditing data is accumulated. For unsuccessful reads, an appropriate error message is established instead.

Control then leaves the module for the return to the calling module.

Sequential Write

Sequential write logic is contained in a very simple module (Figure 9.5). It appears in many different kinds of programs.

The data items that come in to this module as parameters are written to the output sequential file or data base after the output record has been set up. Auditing totals are accumulated, and control returns to the calling module.

Direct Insert

The direct insert module is applicable when records must be added (as opposed to being changed) to a directly updated file or to add directly

```
*                    SEQUENTIAL WRITE MODULE

 PROGRAM-ID. seqwrite USING data fields, audit data fields.

     set up output record.
     write file or data base sequentially.
     accumulate audit data.

 END PROGRAM seqwrite.
```

Figure 9.5. *Classical sequential write module.*

accessed segments to a data base. Its logic, documented in Figure 9.6, requires the record to be added to have unique keys, and for there not to be exiting records with the same keys in the file or data base.

Input parameters for this module are the key values (used to locate the records) and the data to be inserted into the file or data base. In some systems, the key data items may be contained within the data to

```
*                    DIRECT INSERT MODULE

 PROGRAM-ID. insert USING key fields, data fields,
                          audit data fields,
                          message.

     set up file or data base access parameters and key.
     set up output record.
     insert record into file or data base.

     IF record already exists
        THEN
           move "data already exists" to message
        ELSE
           move "data inserted" to message
           accumulate audit data fields
     END-IF.

 END PROGRAM insert.
```

Figure 9.6. *Classical direct insert module.*

be inserted. Audit data elements encompass the audit data to be updated plus any applicable system control parameters. *Message* is an output parameter containing an indicator (either an English message or a coded value) reflecting the status of the insertion.

The logic first sets up the information to access the records and then attempts to add the record to the file or data base. If the write is successful, a *data updated* (or equivalent value) is established, auditing counts are accumulated, and control returns out of this module to the calling module.

However, if the data record is found to exist already, the update fails, the message is set to *data already exists*, and control leaves this module without further processing or audit data accumulation.

Direct Update

The direct update logic of Figure 9.7 is suitable for those applications which require data updates to existing records in files or data bases. The logic requires the records being updated to be directly accessable via key fields (that are input parameters to the module).

In the preceding discussion of the direct read logic in this chapter, record locking was discussed. If program controlled locking is employed, the optional locking indicator must be used as an input parameter to this module.

Again, as in previously described input/output modules, the updated parameters are the audit data fields, and the output parameter is the message field.

After entry into this logic, the file or data base access parameters and key field values are set up. If the record hasn't been previously locked, it is read and locked. Locking ensures that no other users can access the record while it undergoes changes. If the record that is to be locked cannot be found, that is there is no match with the access key fields, the message field is set to *data not found*, and control exits this module to return to the calling module.

For found records, the appropriate data is updated and the record is replaced in the file or data base. When the update is successful, the message field is given a value to show the data has been updated, and control returns to the calling module. After the update the affected re-

```
*                         DIRECT UPDATE MODULE

 PROGRAM-ID. update USING key fields, data fields,
                          audit data fields,
                          message
                         [,locking indicator].        « note 1 »

    set up file or data base access parameters and key.

   [IF locking indicator not = "yes"                          ]
   |   THEN                                                   |
   |      read record with specified key and lock it          |  « n »
   |                                                          |  « o »
   |      IF record not found or already locked               |  « t »
   |         THEN                                             |  « e »
   |            move "data not available for update" to message|  «   »
   |            EXIT PROGRAM                                  |  « 1 »
   |      END-IF                                              |
   |                                                          |
   [END-IF.                                                   ]

    update the data in record.
    replace record [and unlock it].                    « note 1 »

    IF replace is successful
       THEN
          move "data updated" to message
          accumulate audit data fields
       ELSE
          move "update failure–call administrator" to message
          handle error condition
    END-IF.

 END PROGRAM update.
```

Notes: 1. Locking used if simultaneous update situation can occur and lock mechanism not controlled by system software.

Figure 9.7. *Classical direct update module.*

cord is unlocked so that other users may now access the information contained in that record. (Most software systems automatically unlock the record as part of the update process. If the update did not take place, the affected record will normally be unlocked when that user accesses a different record.)

Unsuccessful updates are usually due to system, file, or data base integrity problems. In such circumstances, there is little the program can do other than provide a notification message and then give up control. The programmer should plan to have higher level modules (or the operating system) inform the user and the system operator and shut down the program.

FIELD MANIPULATION MODULES

Left Justify

Many computer applications allow users to enter the data in a free format anywhere in the input fields. It is usually mandatory for subsequent processing that alphanumeric data be left justified in its respective fields.

The logic module of Figure 9.8 performs a left justification operation. It scans input data from left-to-right looking for the first nonblank character. It then commences the scanning and justifying. Imbedded blanks (spaces) remain imbedded in the justified field.

The input parameters consist of a one-dimensional array of single characters that are to be left justified, along with a count of the number of actual characters in the array (the input field size) and the size of the output array. The output array is a one-dimensional array of single characters that will contain the left-justified data at the completion of the execution of the logic.

Normally, programs deal with unitary data elements rather than arrays. Therefore, the input and output arrays will likely be *REDEFINED* as elemental data items in the modules that call the left justify module. The output array can be larger or smaller than the input array—processing stops when the smallest array's data area is exhausted.

```
*                    LEFT JUSTIFY MODULE

PROGRAM-ID. leftjust USING input array,
                           output array,
                           number of input characters,
                           number of output characters.

  move spaces to output array.
  move "no" to non blank character indicator.
  move 1 to input array index.
  move 1 to output array index.

  IF number of input characters greater than
     number of output characters
     THEN
        move number of output characters to justify limit
     ELSE
        move number of input characters to justify limit
  END-IF.

  PERFORM WITH TEST BEFORE UNTIL input array index
        greater than justify limit

     IF input array (input array index) = spaces and
        nonblank character indicator = "no"
        THEN
           continue
        ELSE
           move input array (input array index) to
              output array (output array index)
           add 1 to output array index
           move "yes" to nonblank character indicator
     END-IF

     add 1 to input array index
  END-PERFORM.

END PROGRAM leftjust.
```

Figure 9.8. *Classical left justify module.*

The logic of the left justify module begins by initializing its work data. It then sets a justification limit, in number of characters, equal to the smaller of the input or output array.

The logic next loops through the input array looking for the first nonblank character. After locating the left-most nonblank character, it continues the scan moving characters (blank and nonblank) to the output array. Processing ends when the end of the smallest of the input or output arrays is reached.

Right Justify

To enhance usability, numerous applications dictate a requirement for free-form numeric input. This is very common in interactive data entry systems employed by casual users. Such free-form data must be right justified, and imbedded decimal points must be removed with an associated data item showing the number of decimal places. (COBOL cannot perform arithmetic functions on fields containing decimal point editing symbols.)

The logic of the module in Figure 9.9 executes right justification. Input data is scanned from right to left (opposite to the left justification logic) to locate the digits and the decimal point.

Parameters that are input to this module are a one-dimensional array of single characters that are to be right justified, a count of the number of characters in this array, and a count of the number of characters in the output array. The output array is also a one-dimensional array of single characters created by this module with an associated data element indicating the nimber of decimal places. In addition, there is a message data element showing the status of the processing—blank (spaces) for successful completion.

The output array can be larger than the input array but cannot be smaller.

Again, as with the left justify module, right justification is usually required for unitary or elemental data items. For such processing, the input and/or output arrays must be *REDEFINED* by the higher level modules that call the right justify module.

The logic begins with a check on input and output array sizes. If the output array is smaller than the input array, *output array too small* indication is entered into the message area and control leaves this module.

```
*                         RIGHT JUSTIFY MODULE

 PROGRAM-ID. rtjust USING input array,
                          output array,
                          number of decimal places, message,
                          number of input characters,
                          number of output characters.

   IF number of output characters less than
      number of input characters
      THEN
         move "output array too small" to message
         EXIT PROGRAM
   END-IF.

   move 0 to location of first nonblank character.
   set output array to all zeros.
   move 0 to location of decimal point.
   move 0 to location of last blank after a character.
   move number of input characters to input array index.
   move number of output characters to output array index.

   PERFORM WITH TEST BEFORE UNTIL input array index less than 1

      EVALUATE input array (input array index)
         WHEN spaces

            IF location of first nonblank character not = 0
               THEN
                  move input array index to
                        location of last blank after a character
            END-IF

         WHEN "."

            IF location of decimal point not = 0
               THEN
                  move "multiple decimal points" to message
                  EXIT PROGRAM
            END-IF
```

Figure 9.9. *Classical right justify module.*

```
            move output array index to location of decimal point

        WHEN OTHER

            IF location of last blank after a character not = 0
                THEN
                    move "imbedded blanks" to message
                    set output array to all spaces
                    EXIT PROGRAM
            END-IF

            IF location of first nonblank character = 0
                THEN
                    move input array index to
                         location of first nonblank character
            END-IF.

            move input array (input array index) to
                 output array (output array index)
            subtract 1 from output array index

    END-EVALUATE

    subtract 1 from input array index

END-PERFORM.

IF location of decimal point = 0
    THEN
        move 0 to number of decimal places
    ELSE
        compute number of decimal places =
            number of output characters - location of decimal place
END-IF.

move spaces to message.

END PROGRAM rtjust.
```

Working data elements are given initial values and the output array is initialized to all zeros. Zeroing the output array to start simplifies the subsequent logic since the data created must have left-most leading zeros.

A PERFORM loop scans the input array looking for nonblank characters and decimal points. Multiple decimal points can be detected, and this condition causes control to leave the module with an appropriate value in the message area.

At the completion of the scanning loop, the number of decimal places is calculated, the message data element is set to blanks, and control returns to the calling module.

Field Centering

Information displayed on video terminals and paper reports sometimes needs titles and other information centered in their respective data field areas. The field centering logic will handle the centering application.

The logic in the field centering module of Figure 9.10 scans the input data looking for the first (left-most) and last (right-most) nonblank characters. It then calculates the actual data area size and centers the data in an output parameter.

Parameters that are input to this module are a one-dimensional array of single characters that are to be centered, a count of the total characters in the input array (field size), and a count of the total number of characters in the output array (field size). The output array is a one-dimensional array created in this module and contains the centered data. The message data is also created by this module and shows the correct or incorrect result of the operation.

Since the modules calling the field centering logic probably use the input, uncentered data and the output, centered data as elemental items, they should have the appropriate *REDEFINES* for the input and output arrays.

The field centering logic begins by setting initial values for the work data. Then the input array is scanned via a PERFORM loop to locate the first and last nonblank characters. After the scan, a check is made to see if there were any nonblank characters. If not, the message data ele-

```
*                      FIELD CENTERING MODULE

PROGRAM-ID. center USING input array,
                         output array, message,
                         number of input characters,
                         number of output characters.

    move 1 to input array index.
    move 0 to location of first character.
    move 0 to location of last character.

    PERFORM WITH TEST BEFORE UNTIL input array index
        greater than number of input characters

       IF input array (input array index) not = spaces
          THEN
             move input array index to location of last character

             IF location of first character = 0
                THEN
                   move input array index to
                        location of first character
             END-IF

       END-IF

        add 1 to input array index
    END-PERFORM.

    IF location of last character = 0
       THEN
          move "all blank input field" to message
          EXIT PROGRAM
    END-IF.

    compute number of characters = location of last character -
        location of first character + 1.

    IF number of characters greater than
      number of output characters
       THEN
          move "output array too small" to message
          EXIT PROGRAM
    END-IF.

    compute offset = (number of output characters -
        number of characters)/2 with decimal truncated.
    set output array = all spaces.
    move spaces to message.
    move location of first character to input array index.
    compute output array index = offset + 1.

    PERFORM WITH TEST BEFORE UNTIL input array index
        greater than location of last character

       move input array (array index) to
            output array (output array index)
       add 1 to input array index
       add 1 to output array index
    END-PERFORM.

END PROGRAM center.
```

Figure 9.10. *Classical field centering module.*

ment is set to indicate that the input is all blank and control returns to the calling module.

The output data size is calculated and, if too big for the output array, control is returned to the calling module with a signifying error message.

The next calculation figures the centering offset. The output array is filled beginning at the offset, and control leaves the module.

TABLE PROCESSING MODULES

Table Inversion

If a programmer needs to reverse the order of all entries in a table he or she can use the table inversion module. Parameters that are input to this module are the table, specified in the form of an array, and the number of table elements which represents the table size. The output parameter created by this logic is the inverted table (also an array). The output table must be identical to the input table in both element size and number of elements.

Figure 9.11 illustrates how data is transferred from the table to the inverted table. Since the inverted data is not the same as the original data it is stored in a separate table in order not to destroy the original data. (See data discussion in Chapter 5.)

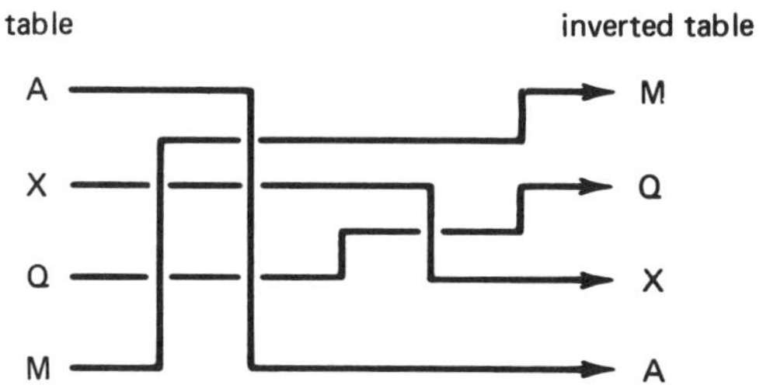

Figure 9.11. *Table inversion.*

In the logic of Figure 9.12, indexes for both the table and its inverted counterpart are set up. A PERFORM loop follows to complete the data transfer. The table is processed from beginning to end as the inverted table is simultaneously processed from end to beginning.

Sequential Search

Many COBOL compilers have implemented the sequential form of the SEARCH verb for sequential table searching. However, if your compiler does not have the sequential SEARCH or your searching is more complex and, therefore, cannot be handled by the compiler, the sequential search logic of Figure 9.13 can be employed.

Sequential searching is best suited for small-sized, in-memory tables. Searches involving large in-memory tables are normally better served by a binary search (see next section).

The sequential search logic does not require the table to be in any particular sequence. For situations where duplicates are to be avoided,

```
*                    TABLE INVERSION MODULE

   PROGRAM-ID. invert USING table, number of table elements,
                                   inverted table.

      move 1 to table index.
      move number of table elements to inverted table index.

      PERFORM WITH TEST BEFORE UNTIL table index greater than
            number of table elements
         compute inverted table (inverted table index) =
               table (table index)
         add 1 to table index
         subtract 1 from inverted table index
      END-PERFORM.

   END PROGRAM invert.
```

Notes: 1. Table and inverted table must be identical in element size and number of elements.

Figure 9.12. *Classical table inversion module.*

```
*                       SEQUENTIAL SEARCH MODULE

 PROGRAM-ID. search USING search key,
                          [ table,                        ]  « note 1 »
                          [ number of table elements,     ]
                            found indicator
                          [,table index]                     « note 1 »
                          [,output data].                    « note 2 »

    move 1 to table index.

    PERFORM WITH TEST BEFORE UNTIL table index greater than
          number of table elements

       IF key field (table index) = search key
          THEN
            move "yes" to found indicator
           [set up output data from table (table index)]     « note 2 »
            EXIT PROGRAM
       END-IF

       add 1 to table index
    END-PERFORM.

    move "no" to found indicator.

 END PRCGRAM search.
```

Notes: 1. Required if table supplied by calling module.
2. This logic used if data that is found on match is to be returned to calling module.
3. Each element in the table must have a unique key.

Figure 9.13. *Classical sequential search module.*

ascending sequence is the best order. Where performance is a concern, the most actively found items should be located at the beginning of the table.

Input parameters to the module are a data item that is the search key and, optionally, the table to be searched along with a value showing the number of elements (rows) in the table. With the optional table, the programmer may elect to store the table in this module or have varying sizes of tables passed from a number of calling modules. If the table has fixed values, such as a table of error messages, it it better to store it in this module.

The output parameters, established by this logic, are a found indicator and, for tables that are input parameters, a table index and output data. The found indicator contains a *yes* or *no* value to let the calling module know if there was, or was not, a match to key values in the table. Table index contains the index for the input table where a match is made. Output data is the information returned to the calling module from the matched element in the table. Output data would not be required when the search is done to test the validity of the input search data, since the calling module does not require any resultant data.

Upon entry to the module the logic sets up the initial values to start the search. It then proceeds in an iterative loop from the beginning, matching the search key to the key data in each table element. When a match is found, the search is discontinued, the found indicator is set to *yes*, output data is set up, and control leaves the module.

The search continues until the end of the table is reached; if no match is found, found indicator is set to *no*, and control leaves the module.

Binary Search

Some COBOL compilers have a binary search option of the SEARCH verb. Many compilers do not. A binary search is an effective method for searching very large sequenced, in-memory tables.

The search works by successively dividing the table in two in the following manner:

1. split the table into two halves and determine if the search key is above or below the split line in the table;
2. divide the portion selected into two halves and again determine if the search key is above or below the split line;
3. repeat step 2 until a match is found or the table cannot be subdivided further.

The logic for the binary search appears in Figure 9.14. The table being searched must be in ascending key sequence. In general, if there are N elements in the table, a binary search requires approximately

```
*                         BINARY SEARCH MODULE

  PROGRAM-ID. binary USING search key,
                           [table,                          ]  << note 2 >>
                           [number of table elements,       ]
                            found indicator
                           [,table index]                      << note 2 >>
                           [,output data].                     << note 3 >>

     move spaces to found indicator.
     compute search base = number of table elements + 1.
     move 0 to table index.

     PERFORM WITH TEST BEFORE UNTIL found indicator not = spaces
        compute search half = search base/2 with decimal truncated

        IF search half = 0
           THEN
              move "no" to found indicator
              EXIT PROGRAM
        END-IF

        add search half to table index
        subtract search half from search base

        IF key field (table index) greater than search key
           THEN
              subtract search half from table index
           ELSE

              IF key field (table index) = search key
                 THEN
                    move "yes" to found indicator
                   [set up output data from table (table index)]
                                                               << note 3 >>
              END-IF

        END-IF

     END-PERFORM.

  END PROGRAM binary.
```

Notes:
1. Table must be in ascending sequence.
2. Required if table supplied by calling module instead of resident in this module.
3. Required if found data is to be returned.
4. Each element in table must have a unique key.

Figure 9.14. *Classical binary search module.*

$\log_2 N$ comparisons. A search of a one million element table requires 20 comparisons while a sequential search requires, on average, one-half million comparisons. The advantage of the sequential search is that it is simple and relatively easy to make work, while the binary search is more complex and difficult to debug if the logic is not followed exactly.

The parameters of the binary search module are identical to those of the sequential search module (Figure 9.13). Thus, if a sequential search is found to be inefficient, a binary search can be substituted without changing any other modules in the program.

The logic begins by setting up the initial values for the search. An iteration loop follows encompassing the division strategy. Note that all division arithmetic truncates decimal places (i.e., 7.5 would be truncated to 7).

The found indicator has the same meaning and values as that of the sequential search (see the previous section) and output data can be optionally returned to the calling module.

Bubble Sort

For most sorting problems the computer system stand-alone sorting utility is a practical and effective solution. In other circumstances the COBOL SORT verb may be employed for sorting. However, the use of system sorting functions involves a substantial overhead of file opening, closing, and accessing, and can sometimes give unacceptable program performance (especially interactive response times) for small tables. The bubble sort of Figure 9.15 provides a simple solution for sorting small in-memory tables.

Input parameters are the input table that is to be sorted along with a data item showing the number of elements in it. The key value defining the sorting order must be part of each record (element) in the table. The output parameter is the sorted table. Although the logic will work on an input table directly to sort it in place, an output table is used to avoid destroying the input data—once the input data is rearranged, the input data ceases to exist in its original form.

The logic proceeds forward in the table comparing key fields of adjacent elements. When an out-of-sequence condition is detected, the logic descends the table, interchanging elements. When an in-sequence con-

```
*                    "BUBBLE" SORT MODULE

 PROGRAM-ID. bubble USING input table, number of elements,
                          output table.

    move input table to output table.
    move 1 to forward index.

    PERFORM WITH TEST BEFORE UNTIL forward index not less than
        number of elements

      IF output table key field (forward index + 1) less than
         output table key field (forward index)
         THEN
           interchange output table (forward index) and
              output table (forward index + 1)
           move forward index to backward index

           PERFORM WITH TEST BEFORE UNTIL
                backward index not greater than 1 or
                output table key field (backward index) not less
                than output table key field (backward index - 1)
              interchange output table (backward index) and
                 output table (backward index - 1)
              subtract 1 from backward index
           END-PERFORM

      END-IF

      add 1 to forward index
    END-PERFORM.

 END PROGRAM bubble.
```

Notes: 1. Output table is assumed to be the same size as input table.

Figure 9.15. *Classical "bubble" sort module.*

dition is again detected, all elements up to the point at which the first interchange took place are then in sequence.

Consider a table with the following keys:

1
3
4
2
5

The sorting steps are:

1. Compare 1 and 3. They are in sequence
2. Compare 3 and 4. They are in sequence
3. Compare 4 and 2. They are out of sequence
4. Interchange 4 and 2; the table appears as:

   1
   3
   2
   4
   5
5. Start processing backward. Compare 3 and 2. They are out of sequence
6. Interchange 3 and 2; the table appears as:

   1
   2
   3
   4
   5
7. Compare 1 and 2; they are in sequence—stop backward processing
8. All elements up to the point of the first interchange are now in sequence; continue forward processing at 4
9. Compare 4 and 5; they are in sequence
10. 5 is the last item in the table; stop the sort

When the end of the table is reached, all elements are then in ascending key sequence.

CALENDAR MODULES

Date Validation

Dates appear in many kinds of programs. If they are entered by people, they should be given a validity test as humans can be prone to err. This module verifies that the date given to it is numeric and falls within a valid calendar. For example, one might want to know if February 29, 1984 is a valid date.

The validation logic, exhibited in Figure 9.16, uses an internal two-dimensional array as part of the validation process. The indexes to the array are type of year (leap year or not) and month. The intersection data in the array contains the number of days in the month for nonleap year and leap year respectively.

Input parameters to this module are day, month, and year. Day and month are two-character numeric fields, while year is a four-character numeric field. The output parameter is a message field containing the results of the validation—an error value or blanks. Alternatively, programmers may choose to use a status indicator value instead of an English message. For example, the indicator could be an key to locate a message record set on a disk file and, thus, provide the ability to issue messages in any language.

At first, day is tested for numerics. If not numeric, control leaves this module with error message set to *invalid day*.

Next, month is tested for numerics within the range of 01 through 12. If this test fails, message is given the value of *invalid month* and control returns to the calling module.

Then, year is tested to verify its validity. A numeric test precedes the valid range check. Then the logic must determine if the year is, or is not, a leap year in order to establish the first index dimension value.

Every fourth year except a century year is a leap year. Only every fourth century year is a leap year. The logic uses division by four and

```
*                    DATE VALIDATION MODULE

  PROGRAM-ID. validate USING day, month, year, message.

     IF day not numeric
        THEN
           move "invalid day" to message
           EXIT PROGRAM
     END-IF.

     IF month numeric and greater than 00 and less than 13
        THEN
           continue
        ELSE
           move "invalid month" to message
           EXIT PROGRAM
     END-IF.

     IF year not positive numeric
        THEN
           move "invalid year" to message
           EXIT PROGRAM
     END-IF.

     IF last 2 digits of year = 00
        THEN

           IF first digits of year evenly divisable by 4
              THEN
                 move 2 to type of year
              ELSE
                 move 1 to type of year
           END-IF

        ELSE

           IF last 2 digits of year evenly divisable by 4
              THEN
                 move 2 to type of year
              ELSE
                 move 1 to type of year
           END-IF

     END-IF.

     IF day less than 01 or greater than
           table (type of year, month)
        THEN
           move "invalid day" to message
        ELSE
           move spaces to message
     END-IF.

  END PROGRAM validate.
```

Notes:
1. Day and month each are two characters.
2. Year is four characters.
3. This module uses a two-dimensional array with indexes: (type of year, month). The intersection data contains the number of days in the month for a nonleap year of leap year (type of year 1 or 2 respectively).

Figure 9.16. *Classical date validation module.*

the presence or absence of a remainder to identify the leap year. Type of year is 1 for leap years and 2 for non-leap years. If year fails its validity checks, control leaves this module with message set to *invalid year*.

Day is now checked to see that it falls within an acceptable range. Type of year and month are used to locate the range of days in the table of number of days. If day does not fall between 01 and the number of days specified in the table, it is in error and control returns to the calling module with message set to *invalid day*.

When the date passes all checks, message is blanked and control leaves the date validation module to return to the higher level calling module.

Julian Date Calculation

When one needs to do arithmetic to determine the number of days between dates, or to arrive at a new date, one needs the date in an absolute numeric form before proceeding. The Julian date conversion module provides the Julian day value. The calculation formula (Tantzen, 1963) was published many years ago. Note that the date is a large number, is the offset from a base date, and is not in the form YYDDD often found in computer systems. YYDDD dates do not facilitate simple calculations when dates cross year boundaries.

The input parameters are day, month, and year. The output parameters are the Julian day number and a message to show the status of the conversion

Upon entry to the module, the validation module (described in a preceding section) is invoked to check the validity of the input parameters. If the date is in error, control immediately returns to the calling module. (The validation module completes the message value.)

The logic (Figure 9.17) then calculates the Julian day according to the algorithm (Tantzen, 1963). As you can see from the logic, most divisions rely on truncation arithmetic, and the Julian day can be seven or more digits long.

Gregorian Date Calculation

The Gregorian date calculation module reverses the operation of the Julian date calculation. It changes a Julian date into a Gregorian calendar date (day, month, year).

```
*                JULIAN DATE CALCULATION MODULE

  PROGRAM-ID. julian USING day, month, year, julian day, message.

     CALL "validate" USING day, month, year, message.

     IF message not = spaces
        THEN
           EXIT PROGRAM
     END-IF.

     move year to work year.
     move month to work month.

     IF work month greater than 2
        THEN
           subtract 3 from work month
        ELSE
           add 9 to work month
           subtract 1 from work year
     END-IF.

     compute century = work year/100 with decimal truncated.
     compute year in century = work year - (100 * century).
     compute work field 1 = 146097 * century/4
                             with decimal truncated.
     compute work field 2 = 1461 * year in century/4
                             with decimal truncated.
     compute work field 3 = ((153 * work month) + 2)/5
                             with decimal truncated.
     compute julian day = work field 1 + work field 2 +
                           work field 3 + day + 1721119.

  END PROGRAM julian.
```

Notes: 1. Day and month each are two characters.
2. Year is four characters.
3. Julian day can be seven or more digits long.

Figure 9.17. *Classical Julian date calculation module.*

```
*              GREGORIAN DATE CALCULATION MODULE

   PROGRAM-ID. gregorian USING julian day, day, month, year,
                                         message.

      IF julian day numeric and greater than 1721119
         THEN
            continue
         ELSE
            move "invalid julian date" to message
            EXIT PROGRAM
      END-IF.

      compute work field 1 = julian day - 1721119.
      compute work field 2 = ((4 * work field 1) - 1)/146097
                              with decimal truncated.
      compute work field 3 = (4 * work field 1) - 1 -
                              (146097 * work field 2).
      compute work field 4 = work field 3/4 with decimal truncated.
      compute work field 5 = ((4 * work field 4) + 3)/1461
                              with decimal truncated.
      compute work field 6 = (4 * work field 4) + 3 -
                              (1461 * work field 5).
      compute work field 7 = (work field 6 + 4)/4
                              with decimal truncated.
      compute work field 8 = ((5 * work field 7) - 3)/153
                              with decimal truncated.
      compute work field 9 = (5 * work field 7) - 3 -
                              (153 * work field 8).
      compute work field 10 = (100 * work field 2) + work field 5.
      compute day = (work field 9 + 5)/5 with decimal truncated.

      IF work field 8 less than 10
         THEN
            compute month = work field 8 + 3
            compute year = work field 10
         ELSE
            compute month = work field 8 - 9
            compute year = work field 10 + 1
      END-IF.

   END PROGRAM gregorian.
```

Notes: 1. Julian day is seven or more digits long.

Figure 9.18. *Classical Gregorian date calculation module*

Julian day is the input parameter and the Gregorian day, month, and year are the output parameters created by the logic. An output message parameter is also created to show the result of the conversion.

The logic, as presented in Figure 9.18, first checks the Julian day number to verify that it is numeric and large enough for the conversion. If the test fails, the message data item is given a value of *invalid julian date*, and control returns to the calling module immediately.

The calculations (Tantzen, 1963) are subsequently performed to compute the Gregorian date. Again, truncation arithmetic is employed. The final operations are the setting of the message to blanks and the return of control to the calling module.

New Date Calculation

The new date calculation logic uses the Julian and Gregorian date calculation modules to derive a new date.

The logic appears in Figure 9.19. Input parameters are input day, input month, and input year, plus a data item containing the number of days to be added to or subtracted from (the offset) the input date. Input day and input month are two characters long, while input year is four characters long. Offset days can be positive or negative (representing addition or subtraction respectively). Output parameters consist of the resultant output day, output month, and output year, along with a message field.

At first, the Julian date calculation module is called to convert the calendar date to a Julian number. If the conversion module detects any problems, it will return a nonblank message, and control exits to the calling module.

Then, the offset days value is added to the Julian day to give a new Julian day number. The Gregorian date calculation module is called to convert the new Julian day to an output calendar date. Control leaves this module with the message value set by the Gregorian date module.

Date Difference

The date difference module utilizes the Julian date module as a basis to calculate the number of days between two dates. The logic appears in Figure 9.20.

```
*                    NEW DATE CALCULATION MODULE

PROGRAM-ID. newdate USING input day, input month, input year,
                          offset days, output day,
                          output month, output year, message.

   CALL "julian" USING input day, input month, input year,
                       julian day, message.
   IF message not = spaces
      THEN
         EXIT PROGRAM
   END-IF.

   add offset days to julian day.

   CALL "gregorian" USING julian day, output day, output month,
                          output year, message.

END PROGRAM newdate.
```

Notes:
1. Offset days can be positive or negative.
2. Input day, output day, input month, output month, are two characters.
3. Input year, output year are four characters.

Figure 9.19. *Classical new date calculation module.*

DATE DIFFERENCE MODULE

```
PROGRAM-ID. datediff USING day 1, month 1, year 1, day 2,
                           month 2, year 2, number of days,
                           message.

   CALL "julian" USING day 1, month 1, year 1, julian day 1,
                       message.

   IF message not = spaces
      THEN
         EXIT PROGRAM
   END-IF.

   CALL "julian" USING day 2, month 2, year 2, julian day 2,
                       message.

   IF message not = spaces
      THEN
         EXIT PROGRAM
   END-IF.

   compute number of days = julian day 2 - julian day 1.

END PROGRAM datediff.
```

Notes:
1. Day 1, day 2, month 1, month 2 are two characters.
2. Year 1, year 2 are four characters.
3. Number of days can be positive or negative.

Figure 9.20. *Classical date difference module.*

The input parameters are two calendar dates, each consisting of day, month, and year. The days and months data items are two characters in size, and the years fields are four characters. The output parameters are the calculated number of days and a message showing the status of the calculation.

The Julian date calculation is invoked with the first date as input parameters to translate this first date into a Julian day number. If there are problems with this conversion, the message data item will not be blank when control returns from the Julian date module. This causes control to leave the date difference module.

The Julian date module is called again with the second date as input parameters to establish a second Julian day value. Again, if there are conversion problems with this date, the message will be nonblank causing control to leave the date difference module.

The difference in days between the two dates is obtained by subtracting one Julian date from the other. The result can be either positive or negative depending on which date is later.

Control then returns to the module that called for the date difference calculation.

Zeller's Congruence

In data processing, one sometimes needs to know the day of the week on which a particular event takes place. Certain functions may have to be executed every Wednesday, or a programmer may have to account for employees not working on Saturday or Sunday.

The formula for the conversion (Uspenski and Heaslit, 1939) was published before the advent of computers. It is known as Zeller's congruence. The formula is stated:

$$f = \{[2.6m - 0.2] + k + D + [D/4] + [C/4] - 2C\} \bmod 7$$

where:

m is month

k is day of the month

C is century

D is year in century

f is the day of the week (between 0 and 6).

```
                      ZELLER'S CONGRUENCE MODULE

PROGRAM-ID. zellers USING day, month, year,
                          numeric day of the week,
                          alphabetic day of the week, message.

   CALL "validate" USING day, month, year, message.

   IF message not = spaces
      THEN
         move 0 to numeric day of the week
         EXIT PROGRAM
   END-IF.

   move day to work day.
   move year to work year.
   compute work month = month - 2.

   IF work month less than 1
      THEN
         subtract 1 from work year
         add 12 to work month
   END-IF.

   compute century = work year/100 with decimal truncated.
   compute year in century = work year - (century * 100).
   compute work field 1 = 2.6 * work month - 0.2 with results
                           truncated to 1 decimal place.
   compute work field 2 = work field 1 with decimal truncated.
   compute work field 3 = year in century/4 with decimal
                           truncated.
   compute work field 4 = century/4 with decimal truncated.
   compute work field 5 = work field 2 + work day +
                           year in century + work field 3 +
                           work field 4 - (2 * century).
   compute work field 6 = work field 5/7 with decimal truncated.
   compute work field 7 = work field 5 - (work field 6 * 7).

   IF work field 7 less than 0
      THEN
         add 7 to work field 7
   END-IF.

   compute numeric day of the week = work field 7 + 1.
   compute alphabetic day of the week =
                  table of days (numeric day of the week).

END PROGRAM zellers.
```

Notes:
1. Day and month each are two characters.
2. Year is four characters.
3. Numeric day of the week goes from 1 (Sunday) to 7 (Saturday).
4. Alphabetic day of the week is stored in a table. The index is numeric day of the week.

Figure 9.21. *Classical Zeller's congruence module.*

The arithmetic is mod 7 based, and the logic of Figure 9.21 is laid out so that it does not require an intrinsic mod 7 function as a prerequisite in the COBOL compiler.

Input parameters are day, month, and year. Day and month fields are two characters long and year field is four characters long.

Output parameters are a numeric day of the week, an alphabetic day of the week, and a message regarding the status of the conversion. The relationship of days is:

Numeric Day of the Week	Alphabetic Day of the Week
1	Sunday
2	Monday
3	Tuesday
4	Wednesday
5	Thursday
6	Friday
7	Saturday

The aphabetic days of the week are stored in a table in the module. They are indexed with the numeric day of the week value.

The first step of the logic is to validate the input date. The validation module (see the section entitled ''Date Validation'') is invoked to perform this utility service. If the date is invalid, the message data item will not contain blanks, and causes control to leave Zeller's congruence for its calling module.

Following validation, the arithmetic of the conversion formula is completed. Truncation is used extensively in the calculations. The result of the calculation is a value for numeric day of the week (running from 1 to 7 for proper indexation). This value is used as an index to the table that establishes a value for alphabetic day of the week. Control then exits from Zeller's congruence.

10 Program Audit Trails

When your program has been designed, built, tested, and put into production, how will the operations staff know the program runs correctly? What precautions can be taken to ensure correct files and data bases are used? How will the staff know that the program doesn't lose data? How will they know the program doesn't destroy data? How will they ascertain that someone isn't stealing from the system?

To address these questions, we build audit trails into each program. Audit trails are counted data values used as a cross-check to verify that processing is progressing as it is supposed to.

As a minimum, all input, output, and update transactions, segments, and records for all files and data bases should be counted. If the program handles financial data, hash totals should also be taken. A hash total is simply a total of the absolute values of the control fields. The absolute values discount the effect of negative values on the balance.

The auditing totals should be balanced against external values maintained by machine or manual processes. For master files or data bases, a good check is the count of the number of records on the prior version (old master if you like). For transactions, the counts must match values produced by previous programs that generate the transactions or manual control totals prepared by the clerks who manually prepare the data.

Batch programs should have the auditing totals printed on the system printer at the end of the program run. Interactive programs should have their auditing data written to a log file to be printed later in a separate run.

If the programming system is using a backup/recovery mechanism for transaction, file, and data base recovery, the auditing log should also be operated under the same backup/recovery mechanism. If this is not done, the record counts can never be balanced because the log will have lost appropriate data that cannot be matched with missing log records.

When you have completed your system design, have it reviewed by your company's auditors before programs are designed and coded. This will ensure that the control mechanisms are suitable for the intended purposes and are consistent with company auditing practices.

The example programs in later chapters show simple samples of auditing and control totals.

11 Program Documentation

Programmers have a vested interest in good documentation. Without it, they may put themselves in a position of *living* with their programs forever. Or, at least, until their employers decide they need neither the programs nor the programmers.

Which kind of programming documentation is best? This topic provides fodder for many arguments among programmers, themselves, and management. Are specifications more important? Code? Design language? Logic diagrams? To discover the answer, we must ask ourselves: Where does a programmer first look to find the source of errors in the program? The code, of course.

The program source code listing, either printed on paper or displayed on a terminal, is a programmer's most important piece of documentation. It describes exactly what the logic accomplishes in its most current state.

The source code should *speak for itself*; that is, it should be simple, straightforward, and clear. The rules described in previous chapters of this book should be followed, and the code should be laid out consistently for all programs. Notes can be used to clarify particular aspects of the logic but they should never dominate. This author finds that he can't locate things in others' programs when they are overloaded with comments.

Each program module needs a prolog giving the author's name, the original creation date, an overview of the contained logic functions, and a history of program changes. All changes, including deletions, made to the code itself, should be annotated with a short comment and a number cross-referencing the change to the change history summary in the prolog.

COBOL code must be aligned and indented, as shown in the various examples in this book, to ensure that code structures are readily evident. To aid clarity, full use of scope terminators (END-IF, END-PERFORM, etc.) is necessary.

The design can be greatly clarified by putting the module linkage chart as comments in the mainline module of the program. This shows all modules necessary to make the program and the relationship of one to another. (In the example programs of Chapters 13, 14, 15, and 16, this has not been done because of space constraints and because the module linkage design is specified in prior paragraphs.)

The next most important type of documentation is the program functional specification. This documentation sets forth the external aspects of program function. It must be prepared before coding commences or not done at all. It describes the functions of the program in language clear enough to give a nonprogrammer *buyer* a lucid impression of what the proposed program will do.

The functional specification describes input files, displays, and data bases, and output files, reports, data bases, and displays. It must detail all calculations and data flow throughout the program. Included must be a full description of all error conditions to be detected along with the associated error messages.

The programmer ought to be aware that the reader of the specifications may not fully understand the implications of what is being said. This could be due to technical, perceptual, cultural, or organizational barriers. By discussing the writing with the potential *buyers* and users in a walk-through discussion format, the programmer can minimize these barriers and ensure better comprehension.

Programmers often debate the necessity for retaining the designs that have been written in the design language. The answer to this question depends on whether the programmer's business organization is prepared to maintain design language libraries. If they are not committed to maintenance of the design language, the designs should be destroyed after the program is coded in COBOL and is running in the production environment. Otherwise, there will be confusion as to which is the correct version of the logic.

However, the benefits of keeping the designs that have been specified in the design language are substantial. When programs are very complex, the design language specification is usually much smaller than the COBOL code. This makes it much faster for a programmer, who is not familiar with the program, to make program changes quickly. Similarly, one often finds that, in large organizations, programs change hands quickly because the organizations want people cross-trained on many programs, and people may be promoted frequently. The advantage of the design language is that it facilitates training of the programmer who must take responsibility for the code.

Retention of designs, specified in the design language, is beneficial to those organizations that use Fagan's (Fagan, 1976) design and code inspection techniques. When program logic must change as a result of changing business requirements, it is simpler to inspect the design language version of the program rather than the COBOL version.

If the design language interpretation of the program is kept, it must always be up-to-date. An effective method of retaining it is to set up the design language version of each module as a comment copy library member (asterisks in column 7 on all lines). This member is copied into the beginning of the COBOL code for the same module via the COPY statement.

User operating documentation is usually required before a program begins to run in its production mode. This documentation may be considered part of system documentation, but if the run documentation is required for each program, it needs to be straightforward and simple. In fact, the best programs have no, or next to no, run documentation. The programs prompt for information as they run without resort to written material. Sometimes, additional help text is provided as part of the system environment and is requested via *help* keys. Wherever possible, the programmer should strive to eliminate *paper-type* documentation.

A log of design rationale can be a great time saver for programmers. Every time you make an important decision, note the reasons for it in a log book. When programs are revisited after long periods of time, the reasons that particular pieces of logic were set up in certain ways may not be clear. A lot of time can be wasted rediscovering conclusions that determined design parameters. A log eliminates this time-wasting headache.

After-the-fact documentation is a waste of time and useless. This includes logic documentation, flowcharts, narrative descriptions, and any other documentation produced after the program is running. Maintenance programmers view such material with a great deal of skepticism because they know there will not be an exact match to the COBOL code. There may be misleading information, simply because the documentation was rushed to finish the programming job. A wise maintenance programmer avoids after-the-fact documentation.

12 Getting Started With The Design

Chapters 13, 14, 15, and 16 contain example programs for each of the characteristic decision logic types found in business programs. These designs begin with a statement of the functions the proposed programs are to perform. However, there are a number of things that must happen before that stage of program development can be reached.

In the beginning, the most important thing for the programmer to accomplish is to ascertain that the users' problems really will be solved by the proposed program. This means that the programmer must truly understand the users' problems. This author has seen some fantastic programming solutions to problems no one cares about.

The best starting point is a discussion with the user (or users) about the problem, in question, that might be solved with a computer program. The programmer must always remember that although the user may not understand computers and programming, the user is an expert in his or her own work endeavor. Therefore, the discussion of the problem must proceed in nondata processing language. As the discussion continues, the programmer should document key requirements, concerns, sequences, calculations, assumptions, dependencies, and volumes in a notebook. This notebook will form the basis for the functional specification which is, in a sense, a contract between the user or buyer and the programmer.

The programmer next determines the data required for the program and its relationship to sources and subsequent processes. All files and data bases that are input, output, or updated by the program are documented along with the relationship to the preceding requirements, dependencies, calculations, and so on. Transaction files, with formats, should also be noted.

As this text is concerned with the programming aspects of data processing, it will be assumed that the structural organization and layout of the relevant files and data bases exists prior to the program design phase.

From the users' statement of requirements and the analysis of the data, the programmer can document the functional specifications for the program design. The document should be written in simple English, understandable by programmers and users. It should provide an overall description of the problem, a detailed description of all files and data bases (along with field validation rules for input data), documented calculations, error message descriptions, and display and report layouts. The programmer should concentrate on the core functions of the programming problem. Often, prospective users of the program may not fully understand what the program may do for them (even though they agree to the written specification) and may not understand how the program will alter the way they do business. It is better to get the core functions correct and implement peripheral *nice to have* functions later.

When the specifications for the program are documented, the programmer should have the user agree that the functions and data that are described are what is needed to solve the problem. The programmer should always keep in mind that these specifications are just a guideline. They document the result of human communications—a communication form that is very imprecise. Both the specification and the resulting program should be easily changeable to reflect the dynamic nature of the human environment the program will operate in.

Next, the programmer decides which of the four characteristic types the program will be. Chapter 8 describes the detailed characteristics and rationale for each. The detailed design can now be done.

First, the module hierarchy chart is drawn. This chart shows all of the functional modules in the hierarchical relationship of one to another. Each module appears as a box with its function named inside.

The chart is drawn in a top-to-bottom fashion as in the example shown in Figure 12.1.

Following completion of the module hierarchy chart, the design proceeds from top to bottom in the design language. "Top to bottom" means from the mainline level to the utility module levels. At each level, all logical functions are specified and all related data is identified. At this stage, all logical details should be worked out—no logic should be left to the COBOL coding phase.

Once the detailed design has been specified in the design language, all data items occurring more than once can be defined and stored in COBOL COPY libraries. The benefit of COPY libraries is that if a data definition changes, either by size or data type, only the copy library definition is changed and all program modules are recompiled. The programmer does not have to go searching throughout the program for occurrences of changed data items. COPY libraries significantly reduce the potential for error due to missed data item changes.

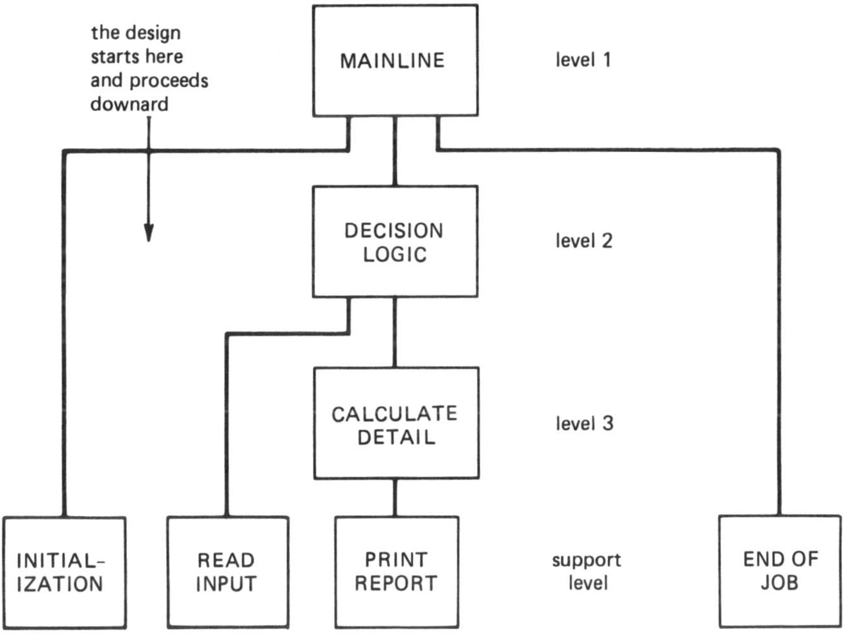

Figure 12.1. *Sample module hierarchy chart.*

The COBOL program can now be coded. With the logic design and the COPY libraries in existence, this becomes a simple mechanical task that can be completed quickly. This author uses computer libraries along with a text editor to speed the coding process, and keep representative samples of all types of program modules and copies, and modifies them to create the programs as specified by the design language.

Following coding, the program can be tested and put into production. If it has been designed properly, a minimum amount of effort will be expended in the debugging process. Most problems will be related to data type inconsistencies. Because COBOL is a programming language supporting strong data typing, these problems will be readily apparent and simple to fix.

In Chapters 13, 14, 15, and 16, four typical programs are designed and coded: a warehouse print program representing control break logic, a brokerage trades update program representing balance line logic, a credit authorization program representing single panel interactive logic, and an employee data update program representing multi-panel interactive logic. These programs realistically duplicate programs found in business applications. The major difference between these programs and those you, the programmer, will encounter in a programming job, is the data. The examples have less data than typically found in real life applications. However, the design architecture is the important consideration; programmers can easily accommodate the data differences.

13 Example Control Break Program

PROBLEM DEFINITION

This control break program is similar to a sample program that has been used (Bergland, 1981) to illustrate different program decomposition techniques. It is fairly straightforward, but is characteristic of many printing problems.

The warehouse for a restaurant chain receives and distributes food items. A program is to be designed to produce a weekly management report showing the net change in inventory for each item. The input consists of records, stored on a disk file, containing the following data layout:

Item code	Type	Quantity

Item code is four characters long. Type is one character long and can be either *R* for received or *D* for distributed. Quantity is a six-digit numeric field. These input transactions are sorted into ascending sequence of item code.

The management report is laid out according to the following format: it shows the net change (receipts minus distributed) for each item;

	MANAGEMENT REPORT	PAGE 1
ITEM	NET CHANGE	
BMAC	+25	
FRFR	-200	
HAMB	+300	
OPND	-65	
NUMBER CHANGED =	4	

Figure 13.1. *Report Layout.*

at the end of the report, one line is printed showing the number of items having a net change value not equal to zero. A sample report appears in Figure 13.1.

You, as the programmer, are to design and build a COBOL program to satisfy the requirements.

First, you should follow the guidelines laid out in Chapter 12. When you have satisfied yourself that the problem definition is correct and preliminary data definitions are established, you can proceed with the design. The initial design phase covers the identification of module functions and the construction of the module hierarchy chart which shows the hierarchical relationship of the functional program units.

MODULE HIERARCHY

The module identification process begins at the top of the program. As this program will operate under the regular operating system, without the use of a software control system to provide mainline functions, a mainline module must be constructed. It is obtained by taking the standard mainline of Figure 7.1 and modifying it with the data needed by this program. The mainline calls decision logic at the second level in the module hierarchy and utility initialization and end of job modules at the fourth or support level in the hierarchy. Figure 13.2 portrays the first step in the module hierarchy design.

We must now determine the type of decision logic that is to be used for this program. The choice is one of four: control break, balance line, single panel interactive, or multipanel interactive. Because there is no direct interaction with a user, but with a file, instead, the program is a batch program. This means that we can discard the single panel interactive and multipanel interactive decision logics. This leaves a choice between control break and balance line logic.

There are two clues that help us choose. Only one file is present and break totaling must be done. Therefore, control break logic is the obvious candidate. Because only one level of totals are to be accumulated (total by item), the logic must be a one-level type of control break. When we look at the total for the end of the report, we notice that it is not a regularly printed value, but, rather, a one time value and can be considered an end of job value.

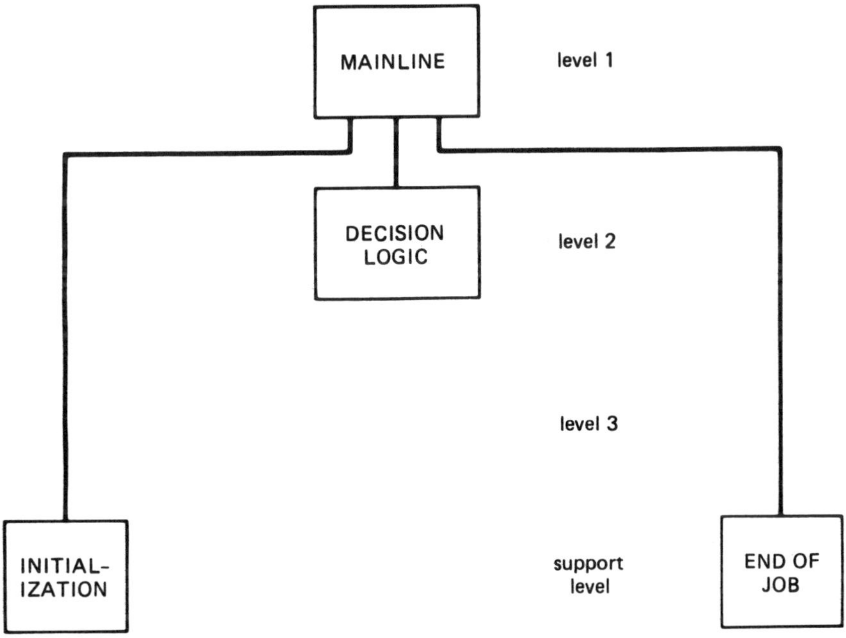

Figure 13.2. *First design step.*

One level control break logic automatically identifies the modules below the decision logic in the hierarchy: process group to print the totals for each item (at the detail processing level), process detail for each input record to be accumulated (at the detail processing level), and a sequential read module to read the input records (at the support level). This second design step in the design process is shown in Figure 13.3.

Next, we examine the process group module to decide if it will call any lower level modules. Because the report contents are printed for item totals, a print report utility module will be called by the process group module.

The process detail module simply accumulates totals without any other functions. Therefore, it does not call any lower level modules. The third step in the module hierarchy design is illustrated in Figure 13.4.

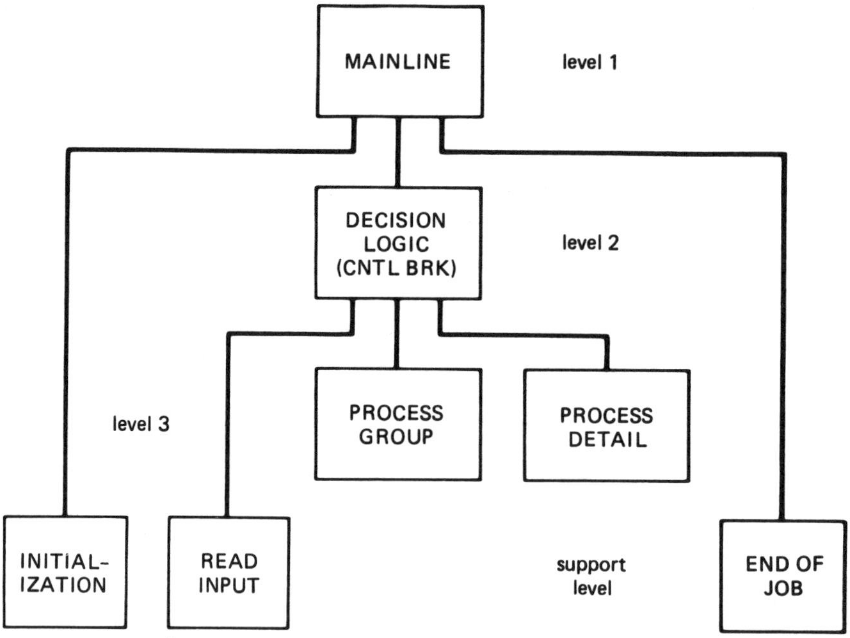

Figure 13.3. *Second design step.*

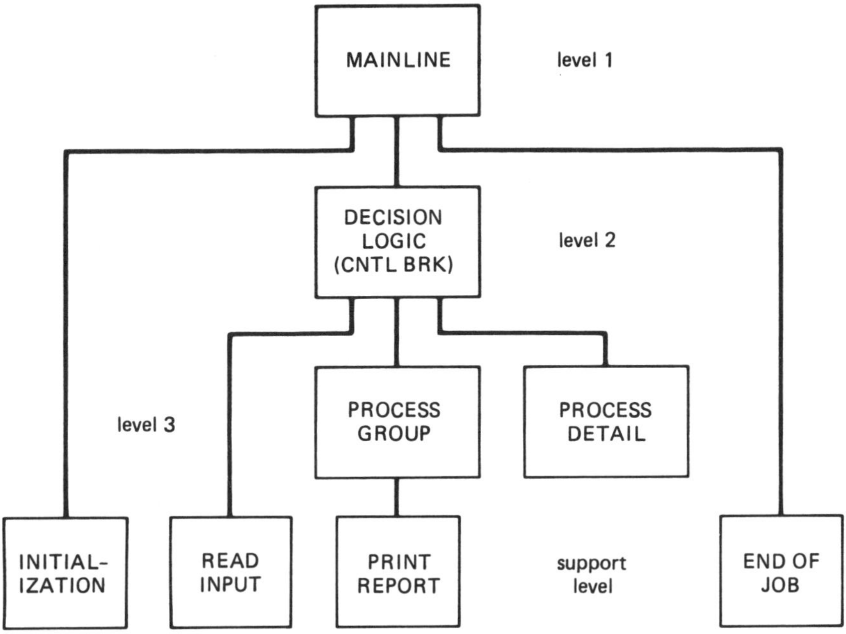

Figure 13.4. *Third design step.*

The overall design has been established. We must now try to refine it to ensure that the design has been decomposed as far as possible. Chapter 2 provides guidance. The modules of the preceding design fit the categories of Chapter 2 and cannot be subdivided further.

We now have one remaining problem: the net change total at the end of the report. Because it is printed at the end of the run, and because it must appear on the same report (instead of on a separate audit sheet), the print report detail module must be called by the end of job module. The result of our efforts is the final module hierarchy chart of Figure 13.5. Note that although this design has four logical levels, it has five physical levels due to a utility module that is called both by a detail processing module and another utility module.

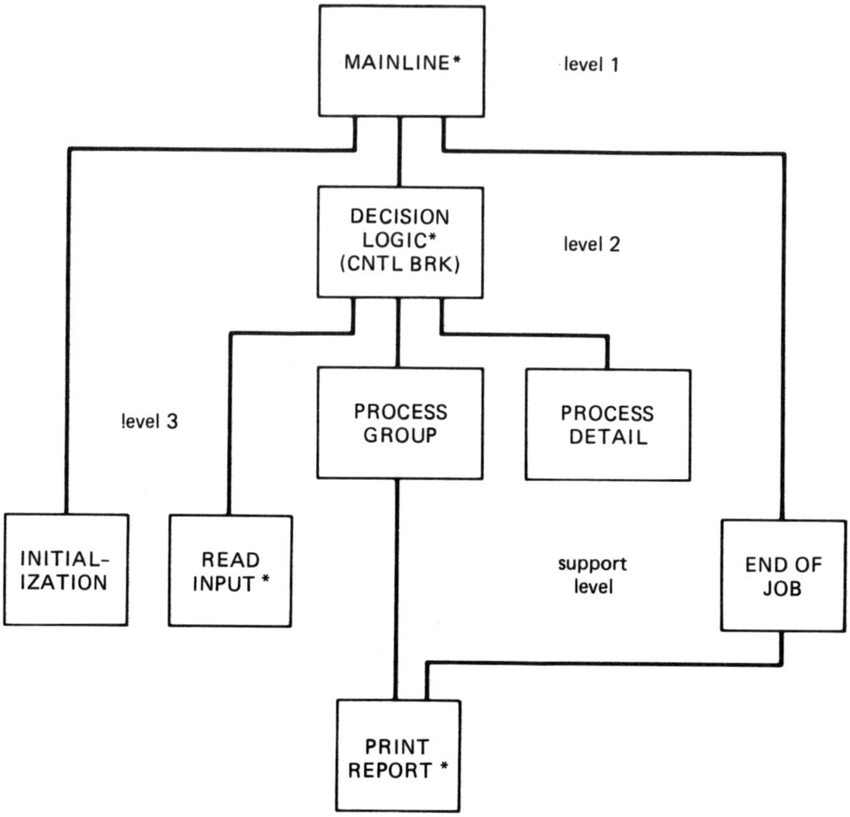

Figure 13.5. *Fourth design step.*

DETAIL DESIGN

The detail design, specified in the design language, can now be done. However, we first need to examine the module chart to identify those modules that are classical functions in order to avoid having to redesign that logic. Classical modules are the mainline, decision logic, read input, and print report (identified with an asterisk in Figure 13.5). Modules that have to be designed are process group, process detail, initialization, and end of job. Note that these are simpler than the previous four classical functions.

Again, begin at the top of the program hierarchy with the mainline module. We take the classical function and add the data fields needed for this program. The result is the logic of Figure 13.6.

The iteration logic is controlled by the data stream status data item. When the file of input records reaches the end, the value of data stream status changes from *not at end* to *at end* and the program finishes.

The other data items that appear in this module are total fields that must be initialized and subsequently accumulated. Net change and

```
*                  WAREHOUSE PRINT—MAINLINE MODULE

  PROGRAM-ID. prmain ⟨MAIN⟩.

    CALL "prinit" USING data stream status, net change,
                        number changed,
                        number of input records.

    PERFORM WITH TEST BEFORE UNTIL data stream status = "at end"
      CALL "prdec" USING data stream status, net change,
                         number changed,
                         number of input records
    END-PERFORM.

    CALL "preoj" USING number changed, number of input records.

  END PROGRAM prmain.
```

Figure 13.6. *Mainline module.*

number changed are used for the report, while number of input records is an audit trail value that is to be printed at the end of job.

The decision logic is next in the module hierarchy and is called by the mainline module. To arrive at a final design for this module, take the classical logic of Figure 8.1 and apply it to the problem at hand. The module names are changed to conform to the naming for this program (e.g., *decide* becomes *prdec*), and the data to be used is included.

Because only one level of control breaks is required, the logic options are chosen to match. Thus break 1 logic is handled by module *prgrp* and detail logic by *prcard*. The decision logic is now that of Figure 13.7.

We now descend to another level in the program hierarchy. The decision logic invokes detail processing modules for groups of records and for the input records themselves. Neither of these modules can be obtained from classical functions and, therefore, must be designed without reference to models.

In the group processing module, a check is first made to ensure that some input records were present in the prior group. This condition will occur when an end of file status happens on the first file read (a null data file).

Next, the print report module is called to print the group details. After printing, a check is taken to determine if the net change is zero. If not, a value of one is added to the number changed field and the net change value is zeroed. The logic for this module appears in Figure 13.8.

The logic for the processing of detail records (prcard) module is very straightforward. The net change field is accumulated depending on whether the shipment is received (*R* type) or delivered (*D* type). No other modules are called by this module. The resultant logic is pictured in Figure 13.9.

We have now worked our way down to the utility modules at the support level in the program. The initialization module is the first one we will design at this level.

Here again, a suitable classical function is not available to provide the logic needed. The design is not complex; initial values are established and the input and report files are opened. This can be seen in Figure 13.10.

The next module to be designed is the read input module. This module reads the input file and the sequential read classical function should be utilized.

```
*       WAREHOUSE PRINT—DECISION LOGIC MODULE

 PROGRAM-ID.  prdec USING data stream status, net change,
                          number changed,
                          number of input records.

    CALL "prread" USING data stream status,
                        current item number,
                        previous item number,
                        number of input records,
                        input record.

    IF data stream status = "at end"
       THEN
          CALL "prgrp" USING previous item number,
                             net change,
                             number of input records,
                             number changed
          EXIT PROGRAM       reciept count
    END-IF.                  distrib count

    IF first time in module
       THEN
          CALL "prcard" USING input record, net change , reciept-count
          reset first time indicator                       distrib.-count
          EXIT PROGRAM
    END-IF.

    IF current item number not equal previous item number
       THEN
          CALL "prgrp" USING previous item number,
                             net change,
                             number of input records,
                             number changed
    END-IF.                  reciept count
                             distrib count
    CALL "prcard" USING input record net change. reciept-count
                                                 distrib-count
 END PROGRAM prdec.
```

Figure 13.7. *Decision logic module.*

```
*              WAREHOUSE PRINT—PROCESS GROUP MODULE

 PROGRAM-ID. prgrp USING previous item number,
                         net change, number of input records,
                         number changed.

    IF number of input records = 0        « no input data »
       THEN
          EXIT PROGRAM
    END-IF.

    CALL "prprt" USING  previous item number, net change,
                        "group".           reciept- count
                                           distrib -count
    IF net change not = 0
       THEN
          add 1 to number changed
          move 0 to net change
    END-IF.                          reciept -count
                                     distrib-count
 END PROGRAM prgrp.
```

Figure 13.8. *Process group module.*

```
*              WAREHOUSE PRINT—PROCESS DETAIL MODULE

 PROGRAM-ID. prcard USING input record, net change.

    IF type of shipment = "r"
       THEN                              add 1 to reciept-count
          add quantity to net change
          EXIT PROGRAM
    END-IF.

    IF type of shipment = "d"
       THEN                              add 1 to distribution-count
          subtract quantity from net change
    END-IF.

 END PROGRAM prcard.
```

Figure 13.9. *Process detail module.*

```
*            WAREHOUSE PRINT—INITIALIZATION MODULE

 PROGRAM-ID. prinit USING data stream status, net change,
                          number changed,
                          number of input records.

     move "not at end" to data stream status.
     set net change, number changed, number of input records to 0.
     open the files.

 END PROGRAM prinit.
```

Figure 13.10. *Initialization module.*

The logic of Figure 13.11 is identical to that of Figure 9.2 with the module name and data utilized reflecting this warehouse print problem. Where the classical design logic specifies that the error conditions are to be handled, we have chosen to display an appropriate message and stop the program.

The sequence check of the classical logic is retained. If it is not present, and the input data file is out of sequence, a completely meaningless report would be produced.

Continuing on the support level of the program's module hierarchy, we design the print report module next. The magic word *print* causes us to look at the classical logic for this function. The logic of Figure 9.1 is suitable for most report printing applications.

Again, the logic is adapted by using a module name compatable with the program naming convention and having the relevant program data processed by the module. Note that there are two types of report detail lines: the group total line created by the process group module (prgrp), and the end of program total line set up by the end of job module (preoj). The resultant design is displayed in Figure 13.12.

The final module to be designed is the end of job module. A classical function cannot be used for this, so we must also design it ourselves.

The logic first calls the print module to display the number changed total. It then displays the program auditing totals on the system printer.

```
*          WAREHOUSE PRINT—READ INPUT MODULE

PROGRAM-ID. prread USING data stream status,
                         current item number,
                         previous item number,
                         number of input records,
                         input record.

  IF data stream status = "at end"
    THEN
      display message "program reading past data end"
      stop the program
  END-IF.

  move current item number to previous item number.
  read file to get item number, type of shipment, quantity.

  IF end of data reached
    THEN
      move "at end" to data stream status
      EXIT PROGRAM
  END-IF.

  set up linkage record.
  add 1 to number of input records.
  move item number to current item number.

  IF first time in module
    THEN
      reset first time indicator
      move binary zeros to previous item number
      EXIT PROGRAM
  END-IF.

  IF current item number less than previous item number.
    THEN
      display "print program ended abnormally" and audit
        information on system printer
      stop the program
  END-IF.

END PROGRAM prread.
```

Figure 13.11. *Read input module.*

```
*            WAREHOUSE PRINT—REPORT MODULE

 PROGRAM-ID. prprt USING print item number, print quantity,
                         report line type.

         « page number has an initial value of zero  »
         « line number has an initial value of 999   »
         « page size is set to 25                    »

   IF line number greater than page size
      THEN
         add 1 to page number
         move 0 to line number
         print page and column headings
   END-IF.

   IF report line type = "group"
      THEN
         set up item print lines
         print double spaced item lines
   END-IF.

   IF report line type = "eoj"
      THEN
         set up number changed print line
         print double spaced number changed line
   END-IF.

   add 1 to line number.

 END PROGRAM prprt.
```

Figure 13.12. *Print report detail module.*

```
*           WAREHOUSE PRINT—END OF JOB MODULE

    PROGRAM-ID. preoj USING number changed,
                            number of input records.

        CALL "prprt" USING  dummy field, number changes, "eoj".
        display end audit information on system printer.
        close the files.

    END PROGRAM preoj.
```

Figure 13.13. *End of job module.*

The logic finishes by closing the input file and the output report file as shown in Figure 13.13.

THE COBOL CODE

The COBOL program can now be coded. Because the program logic has been worked out in the design language, coding is a mechanical exercise. You should have set up all COPY library members before commencing design in the design language. This data and the design logic are the starting basis for the code. The COBOL code appears in Figures 13.14 through 13.21.

There are a number of items of interest in this code. First, note that the version number and associated date are set up as WORKING STORAGE values. A major concern for programmers, examining program failures, is ascertaining that the correct version of the program was operating before the failure. Often compilers will store the date when the program was compiled. However, this doesn't prevent the wrong version of the program from being compiled. The version number and date in the WORKING STORAGE SECTION allows a programmer to check a storage dump and know the version that was run.

ANS COBOL 85 provides a set of language semantics that allows sequence and IF THEN ELSE structures to be combined in one statement. An example of this can be found in module *prread* where the

```
/***************************************************************
 IDENTIFICATION DIVISION.

 PROGRAM-ID.        PRMAIN.

 AUTHOR.            G.R. ROGERS.

**************************************************************
*                                                            *
* WAREHOUSE PRINT PROGRAM                                    *
* MODULE - MAINLINE                                          *
*                                                            *
*------------------------------------------------------------*
* CHANGE HISTORY                                             *
*   090785 NEW PROGRAM                                   GRR *
**************************************************************

 DATA DIVISION.

 WORKING-STORAGE SECTION.

 77  VERSION-NUMBER                    PICTURE X(27) VALUE
     "VERSION 1      SEPT. 7, 1985".

 COPY DCL05.
 77  DATA-STREAM-STATUS                PICTURE X(10).           COPY

 COPY DCL06.
 77  NET-CHANGE                        PICTURE S9(7).           COPY

 COPY DCL07.
 77  NUMBER-CHANGED                    PICTURE S9(7).           COPY

 COPY DCL08.
 77  NUMBER-OF-INPUT-RECORDS           PICTURE S9(7).           COPY
***************************************************************

/***************************************************************

 PROCEDURE DIVISION.

     CALL "PRINIT" USING DATA-STREAM-STATUS, NET-CHANGE,
                         NUMBER-CHANGED, NUMBER-OF-INPUT-RECORDS.

     PERFORM WITH TEST BEFORE UNTIL
        DATA-STREAM-STATUS = "AT END"
       CALL "PRDEC" USING DATA-STREAM-STATUS, NET-CHANGE,
                          NUMBER-CHANGED,
                          NUMBER-OF-INPUT-RECORDS
     END-PERFORM.

     CALL "PREOJ" USING NUMBER-CHANGED, NUMBER-OF-INPUT-RECORDS.
     STOP RUN.

 END PROGRAM PRMAIN.

***************************************************************
```

Figure 13.14. *Mainline module in COBOL.*

```
/*****************************************************************
 IDENTIFICATION DIVISION.

 PROGRAM-ID.        PRDEC.

 AUTHOR.            G.R. ROGERS.

*****************************************************************
*                                                               *
* WAREHOUSE PRINT PROGRAM                                       *
* MODULE - DECISION LOGIC                                       *
*                                                               *
*---------------------------------------------------------------*
* CHANGE HISTORY                                                *
*   090785 NEW PROGRAM                                      GRR *
*****************************************************************

 DATA DIVISION.

 WORKING-STORAGE SECTION.

 77  VERSION-NUMBER                     PICTURE X(27) VALUE
     "VERSION 1      SEPT. 7, 1985".

 COPY DCL01.
 01  INPUT-RECORD.                                          COPY
     02  ITEM-NUMBER                    PICTURE X(4).       COPY
     02  FILLER                         PICTURE XX.         COPY
     02  TYPE-OF-SHIPMENT               PICTURE X.          COPY
     02  FILLER                         PICTURE XX.         COPY
     02  QUANTITY                       PICTURE 9(6).       COPY
     02  FILLER                         PICTURE X.          COPY

 COPY DCL10.
 77  CURRENT-ITEM-NUMBER                PICTURE X(4).       COPY

 COPY DCL09.
 77  PREVIOUS-ITEM-NUMBER               PICTURE X(4).       COPY

 COPY DCL11.
 77  FIRST-TIME-IN-MODULE               PICTURE XXX VALUE "YES".   COPY

 LINKAGE SECTION.

 COPY DCL05.
 77  DATA-STREAM-STATUS                 PICTURE X(10).      COPY

 COPY DCL06.
 77  NET-CHANGE                         PICTURE S9(7).      COPY

 COPY DCL07.
 77  NUMBER-CHANGED                     PICTURE S9(7).      COPY

 COPY DCL08.
 77  NUMBER-OF-INPUT-RECORDS            PICTURE S9(7).      COPY
*****************************************************************

/*****************************************************************
 PROCEDURE DIVISION USING DATA-STREAM-STATUS, NET-CHANGE,
                          NUMBER-CHANGED,
                          NUMBER-OF-INPUT-RECORDS.

     CALL "PRREAD" USING DATA-STREAM-STATUS,
                         CURRENT-ITEM-NUMBER,
                         PREVIOUS-ITEM-NUMBER,
                         NUMBER-OF-INPUT-RECORDS,
                         INPUT-RECORD.

     IF DATA-STREAM-STATUS = "AT END"
       THEN
         CALL "PRGRP" USING PREVIOUS-ITEM-NUMBER,
                            NET-CHANGE,
                            NUMBER-OF-INPUT-RECORDS,
                            NUMBER-CHANGED
         EXIT PROGRAM
     END-IF.

     IF FIRST-TIME-IN-MODULE = "YES"
       THEN
         CALL "PRCARD" USING INPUT-RECORD, NET-CHANGE
         MOVE "NO " TO FIRST-TIME-IN-MODULE
         EXIT PROGRAM
     END-IF.

     IF CURRENT-ITEM-NUMBER NOT EQUAL PREVIOUS-ITEM-NUMBER
       THEN
         CALL "PRGRP" USING PREVIOUS-ITEM-NUMBER,
                            NET-CHANGE,
                            NUMBER-OF-INPUT-RECORDS,
                            NUMBER-CHANGED
     END-IF.

     CALL "PRCARD" USING INPUT-RECORD, NET-CHANGE.

 END PROGRAM PRDEC.
*****************************************************************
```

Figure 13.15. *Decision logic module in COBOL.*

```
/*************************************************************
 IDENTIFICATION DIVISION.

 PROGRAM-ID.        PRGRP.

 AUTHOR.            G.R. ROGERS.

*************************************************************
*                                                           *
* WAREHOUSE PRINT PROGRAM                                   *
* MODULE - PROCESS GROUP OF RECORDS                         *
*                                                           *
*-----------------------------------------------------------*
* CHANGE HISTORY                                            *
*   090785 NEW PROGRAM                                  GRR *
*************************************************************

 DATA DIVISION.

 WORKING-STORAGE SECTION.

 77  VERSION-NUMBER                   PICTURE X(27) VALUE
     "VERSION 1     SEPT. 7, 1985".

 77  GROUP                            PICTURE X(5) VALUE "GROUP".

 LINKAGE SECTION.

 COPY DCL09.
 77  PREVIOUS-ITEM-NUMBER             PICTURE X(4).            COPY

 COPY DCL06.
 77  NET-CHANGE                       PICTURE S9(7).           COPY

 COPY DCL08.
 77  NUMBER-OF-INPUT-RECORDS          PICTURE S9(7).           COPY

 COPY DCL07.
 77  NUMBER-CHANGED                   PICTURE S9(7).           COPY
**************************************************************

/*************************************************************

 PROCEDURE DIVISION USING PREVIOUS-ITEM-NUMBER,
                          NET-CHANGE, NUMBER-OF-INPUT-RECORDS,
                          NUMBER-CHANGED.

     IF NUMBER-OF-INPUT-RECORDS = 0
       THEN
         EXIT PROGRAM
     END-IF.

     CALL "PRPRT" USING PREVIOUS-ITEM-NUMBER, NET-CHANGE,
                        GROUP.

     IF NET-CHANGE NOT = 0
       THEN
         ADD 1 TO NUMBER-CHANGED
         MOVE 0 TO NET-CHANGE
     END-IF.

 END PROGRAM PRGRP.

**************************************************************
```

Figure 13.16. *Process group module in COBOL.*

```
/*************************************************************
 IDENTIFICATION DIVISION.

 PROGRAM-ID.        PRCARD.

 AUTHOR.            G.R. ROGERS.

************************************************************
*                                                          *
* WAREHOUSE PRINT PROGRAM                                  *
* MODULE - PROCESS DETAIL RECORDS                          *
*                                                          *
*----------------------------------------------------------*
* CHANGE HISTORY                                           *
*   090785 NEW PROGRAM                                 GRR *
************************************************************

 DATA DIVISION.

 WORKING-STORAGE SECTION.

 77  VERSION-NUMBER                    PICTURE X(27) VALUE
     "VERSION 1     SEPT. 7, 1985".

 LINKAGE SECTION.

 COPY DCL01.
 01  INPUT-RECORD.                                          COPY
     02  ITEM-NUMBER                   PICTURE X(4).        COPY
     02  FILLER                        PICTURE XX.          COPY
     02  TYPE-OF-SHIPMENT              PICTURE X.           COPY
     02  FILLER                        PICTURE XX.          COPY
     02  QUANTITY                      PICTURE 9(6).        COPY
     02  FILLER                        PICTURE X.           COPY

 COPY DCL06.
 77  NET-CHANGE                        PICTURE S9(7).       COPY
*************************************************************

/*************************************************************

 PROCEDURE DIVISION USING INPUT-RECORD, NET-CHANGE.

     IF TYPE-OF-SHIPMENT = "R"
       THEN
         ADD QUANTITY TO NET-CHANGE
         EXIT PROGRAM
     END-IF.

     IF TYPE-OF-SHIPMENT = "D"
       THEN
         SUBTRACT QUANTITY FROM NET-CHANGE
     END-IF.

 END PROGRAM PRCARD.

*************************************************************
```

Figure 13.17. *Process detail module in COBOL.*

```
/*****************************************************************

 IDENTIFICATION DIVISION.

 PROGRAM-ID.        PRINIT.

 AUTHOR.            G.R. ROGERS.

*****************************************************************
*                                                               *
* WAREHOUSE PRINT PROGRAM                                       *
* MODULE - INITIALIZATION                                       *
*                                                               *
*---------------------------------------------------------------*
* CHANGE HISTORY                                                *
*   090785 NEW PROGRAM                                      GRR *
*****************************************************************

 ENVIRONMENT DIVISION.

 INPUT-OUTPUT SECTION.

 FILE-CONTROL.

 COPY DCL12.
     SELECT INPUT-FILE ASSIGN TO DISK-INFILE.                        COPY
 COPY DCL13.
     SELECT PRINT-FILE ASSIGN TO PRINTER-PRFILE.                     COPY

 DATA DIVISION.

 FILE SECTION.

 COPY DCL03.
 FD  INPUT-FILE EXTERNAL                                             COPY
     BLOCK CONTAINS 10 RECORDS                                       COPY
     LABEL RECORDS ARE STANDARD.                                     COPY

 COPY DCL01.
 01  INPUT-RECORD.                                                   COPY
     02  ITEM-NUMBER                    PICTURE X(4).                COPY
     02  FILLER                         PICTURE XX.                  COPY
     02  TYPE-OF-SHIPMENT               PICTURE X.                   COPY
     02  FILLER                         PICTURE XX.                  COPY
     02  QUANTITY                       PICTURE 9(6).                COPY
     02  FILLER                         PICTURE X.                   COPY

 COPY DCL04.
 FD  PRINT-FILE EXTERNAL                                             COPY
     LABEL RECORDS ARE OMITTED.                                      COPY

 COPY DCL02.
 01  PRINT-RECORD                       PICTURE X(132).              COPY

 WORKING-STORAGE SECTION.

 77  VERSION-NUMBER                     PICTURE X(27) VALUE
     "VERSION 1     SEPT. 7, 1985".

 LINKAGE SECTION.

 COPY DCL05.
 77  DATA-STREAM-STATUS                 PICTURE X(10).               COPY

 COPY DCL06.
 77  NET-CHANGE                         PICTURE S9(7).               COPY

 COPY DCL07.
 77  NUMBER-CHANGED                     PICTURE S9(7).               COPY

 COPY DCL08.
 77  NUMBER-OF-INPUT-RECORDS            PICTURE S9(7).               COPY
*****************************************************************

/*****************************************************************

 PROCEDURE DIVISION USING DATA-STREAM-STATUS, NET-CHANGE,
                          NUMBER-CHANGED,
                          NUMBER-OF-INPUT-RECORDS.

     MOVE "NOT AT END" TO DATA-STREAM-STATUS.
     MOVE 0 TO NET-CHANGE.
     MOVE 0 TO NUMBER-CHANGED.
     MOVE 0 TO NUMBER-OF-INPUT-RECORDS.
     OPEN INPUT INPUT-FILE
          OUTPUT PRINT-FILE.

 END PROGRAM PRINIT.

*****************************************************************
```

Figure 13.18. *Initialization module in COBOL.*

```
/****************************************************************
 IDENTIFICATION DIVISION.
 PROGRAM-ID.        PRREAD.
 AUTHOR.            G.R. ROGERS.
****************************************************************
*                                                              *
* WAREHOUSE PRINT PROGRAM                                      *
* MODULE - READ INPUT RECORDS                                  *
*                                                              *
*--------------------------------------------------------------*
* CHANGE HISTORY                                               *
*   090785 NEW PROGRAM                                     GRR *
****************************************************************
 ENVIRONMENT DIVISION.
 INPUT-OUTPUT SECTION.
 FILE-CONTROL.
 COPY DCL12.
     SELECT INPUT-FILE ASSIGN TO DISK-INFILE.                       COPY
 DATA DIVISION.
 FILE SECTION.
 COPY DCL03.
 FD  INPUT-FILE EXTERNAL                                            COPY
     BLOCK CONTAINS 10 RECORDS                                      COPY
     LABEL RECORDS ARE STANDARD.                                    COPY
 COPY DCL01.
 01  INPUT-RECORD.                                                  COPY
     02  ITEM-NUMBER                      PICTURE X(4).             COPY
     02  FILLER                           PICTURE XX.               COPY
     02  TYPE-OF-SHIPMENT                 PICTURE X.                COPY
     02  FILLER                           PICTURE XX.               COPY
     02  QUANTITY                         PICTURE 9(6).             COPY
     02  FILLER                           PICTURE X.                COPY
 WORKING-STORAGE SECTION.
 77  VERSION-NUMBER                       PICTURE X(27) VALUE
     "VERSION 1      SEPT. 7, 1985".
 COPY DCL11.
 77  FIRST-TIME-IN-MODULE                 PICTURE XXX VALUE "YES".  COPY
 LINKAGE SECTION.
 COPY DCL05.
 77  DATA-STREAM-STATUS                   PICTURE X(10).            COPY
 COPY DCL08.
 77  NUMBER-OF-INPUT-RECORDS              PICTURE S9(7).            COPY
 COPY DCL10.
 77  CURRENT-ITEM-NUMBER                  PICTURE X(4).             COPY
 COPY DCL09.
 77  PREVIOUS-ITEM-NUMBER                 PICTURE X(4).             COPY
 01  LINKAGE-INPUT-RECORD                 PICTURE X(16).
****************************************************************
```

(a)

Figure 13.19. *Read input module in COBOL.*

```
/*****************************************************************

 PROCEDURE DIVISION USING DATA-STREAM-STATUS,
                          CURRENT-ITEM-NUMBER,
                          PREVIOUS-ITEM-NUMBER,
                          NUMBER-OF-INPUT-RECORDS,
                          LINKAGE-INPUT-RECORD.

     IF DATA-STREAM-STATUS = "AT END"
       THEN
         DISPLAY "PROGRAM READING PAST DATA END"
         STOP RUN
     END-IF.

     MOVE CURRENT-ITEM-NUMBER TO PREVIOUS-ITEM-NUMBER.

     READ INPUT-FILE RECORD
       AT END
         MOVE "AT END" TO DATA-STREAM-STATUS
         EXIT PROGRAM
     END-READ.

     MOVE INPUT-RECORD TO LINKAGE-INPUT-RECORD.
     ADD 1 TO NUMBER-OF-INPUT-RECORDS.
     MOVE ITEM-NUMBER TO CURRENT-ITEM-NUMBER.

     IF FIRST-TIME-IN-MODULE = "YES"
       THEN
         MOVE "NO " TO FIRST-TIME-IN-MODULE
         MOVE LOW-VALUES TO PREVIOUS-ITEM-NUMBER
         EXIT PROGRAM
     END-IF.

     IF CURRENT-ITEM-NUMBER LESS THAN PREVIOUS-ITEM-NUMBER
       THEN
         DISPLAY "PRINT PROGRAM ENDED ABNORMALLY"
         DISPLAY "INPUT FILE OUT OF SEQUENCE"
         DISPLAY "CURRENT ITEM NUMBER = ", CURRENT-ITEM-NUMBER
         DISPLAY "NUMBER OF INPUT RECORDS READ = ",
                 NUMBER-OF-INPUT-RECORDS
         STOP RUN
     END-IF.

 END PROGRAM PRREAD.
******************************************************************
```

(b)

```
/*****************************************************************
 IDENTIFICATION DIVISION.

 PROGRAM-ID.        PRPRT.

 AUTHOR.            G.R. ROGERS.

****************************************************************
*                                                              *
* WAREHOUSE PRINT PROGRAM                                      *
* MODULE - PRINT REPORT DETAILS                                *
*                                                              *
*--------------------------------------------------------------*
* CHANGE HISTORY                                               *
*   090785 NEW PROGRAM                                     GRR *
****************************************************************

 ENVIRONMENT DIVISION.

 INPUT-OUTPUT SECTION.

 FILE-CONTROL.

 COPY DCL13.
     SELECT PRINT-FILE ASSIGN TO PRINTER-PRFILE.                    COPY

 DATA DIVISION.

 FILE SECTION.

 COPY DCL04.
 FD  PRINT-FILE EXTERNAL                                            COPY
     LABEL RECORDS ARE OMITTED.                                     COPY

 COPY DCL02.
 01  PRINT-RECORD                        PICTURE X(132).            COPY

 WORKING-STORAGE SECTION.

 77  VERSION-NUMBER                      PICTURE X(27) VALUE
     "VERSION 1     SEPT. 7, 1985".

 01  HEADING-LINE-1.
     02  FILLER                          PICTURE X(17) VALUE
     "MANAGEMENT REPORT".
     02  FILLER                          PICTURE X(107) VALUE SPACES.
     02  FILLER                          PICTURE X(5) VALUE "PAGE ".
     02  HEADING-PAGE-NUMBER             PICTURE ZZ9.

 01  HEADING-LINE-2.
     02  FILLER                          PICTURE X(18) VALUE
     "ITEM     NET CHANGE".
     02  FILLER                          PICTURE X(104) VALUE SPACES.

 01  DETAIL-LINE.
     02  DETAIL-LINE-ITEM-NUMBER         PICTURE X(4).
     02  FILLER                          PICTURE X(3) VALUE SPACES.
     02  DETAIL-LINE-NET-CHANGE          PICTURE +(7)9.
     02  FILLER                          PICTURE X(117) VALUE SPACES.

 01  SUMMARY-LINE.
     02  FILLER                          PICTURE X(17) VALUE
     "NUMBER CHANGED = ".
     02  SUMMARY-QUANTITY                PICTURE Z(6)9.
     02  FILLER                          PICTURE X(108) VALUE SPACES.

 77  PAGE-NUMBER                         PICTURE S9(3) VALUE 0.

 77  LINE-NUMBER                         PICTURE S9(3) VALUE 999.

 77  PAGE-SIZE                           PICTURE S9(3) VALUE 25.

 LINKAGE SECTION.

 77  REPORT-LINE-TYPE                    PICTURE X(5).

 77  REPORT-ITEM-NUMBER                  PICTURE X(4).

 77  REPORT-QUANTITY                     PICTURE S9(7).

*****************************************************************
```

(a)

Figure 13.20. *Print report detail module in COBOL.*

```
/*****************************************************************

 PROCEDURE DIVISION USING REPORT-ITEM-NUMBER,
                          REPORT-QUANTITY, REPORT-LINE-TYPE.

     IF LINE-NUMBER GREATER THAN PAGE-SIZE
       THEN
         ADD 1 TO PAGE-NUMBER
         MOVE 0 TO LINE-NUMBER
         MOVE PAGE-NUMBER TO HEADING-PAGE-NUMBER
         WRITE PRINT-RECORD FROM HEADING-LINE-1
            AFTER ADVANCING PAGE
         WRITE PRINT-RECORD FROM HEADING-LINE-2
            AFTER ADVANCING 2 LINES
     END-IF.

     IF REPORT-LINE-TYPE = "GROUP"
       THEN
         MOVE REPORT-ITEM-NUMBER TO DETAIL-LINE-ITEM-NUMBER
         MOVE REPORT-QUANTITY TO DETAIL-LINE-NET-CHANGE
         WRITE PRINT-RECORD FROM DETAIL-LINE
            AFTER ADVANCING 2 LINES
     END-IF.

     IF REPORT-LINE-TYPE = "EOJ  "
       THEN
         MOVE REPORT-QUANTITY TO SUMMARY-QUANTITY
         WRITE PRINT-RECORD FROM SUMMARY-LINE
            AFTER ADVANCING 2 LINES
     END-IF.

     ADD 1 TO LINE-NUMBER.

 END PROGRAM PRPRT.

******************************************************************
```

(b)

```
/*****************************************************************
 IDENTIFICATION DIVISION.

 PROGRAM-ID.        PREOJ.

 AUTHOR.            G.R. ROGERS.

****************************************************************
*                                                              *
* WAREHOUSE PRINT PROGRAM                                      *
* MODULE - END OF JOB                                          *
*                                                              *
*--------------------------------------------------------------*
* CHANGE HISTORY                                               *
*   090785 NEW PROGRAM                                     GRR *
****************************************************************

 ENVIRONMENT DIVISION.

 INPUT-OUTPUT SECTION.

 FILE-CONTROL.

 COPY DCL12.
     SELECT INPUT-FILE ASSIGN TO DISK-INFILE.                         COPY
 COPY DCL13.
     SELECT PRINT-FILE ASSIGN TO PRINTER-PRFILE.                      COPY

 DATA DIVISION.

 FILE SECTION.

 COPY DCL03.
 FD  INPUT-FILE EXTERNAL                                              COPY
     BLOCK CONTAINS 10 RECORDS                                        COPY
     LABEL RECORDS ARE STANDARD.                                      COPY

 COPY DCL01.
 01  INPUT-RECORD.                                                    COPY
     02  ITEM-NUMBER                    PICTURE X(4).                 COPY
     02  FILLER                         PICTURE XX.                   COPY
     02  TYPE-OF-SHIPMENT               PICTURE X.                    COPY
     02  FILLER                         PICTURE XX.                   COPY
     02  QUANTITY                       PICTURE 9(6).                 COPY
     02  FILLER                         PICTURE X.                    COPY

 COPY DCL04.
 FD  PRINT-FILE EXTERNAL                                              COPY
     LABEL RECORDS ARE OMITTED.                                       COPY

 COPY DCL02.
 01  PRINT-RECORD                       PICTURE X(132).               COPY

 WORKING-STORAGE SECTION.

 77  VERSION-NUMBER                     PICTURE X(27) VALUE
     "VERSION 1     SEPT. 7, 1985".

 77  DUMMY-FIELD                        PICTURE X(4) VALUE SPACES.

 77  EOJ                                PICTURE X(5) VALUE "EOJ  ".

 LINKAGE SECTION.

 COPY DCL07.
 77  NUMBER-CHANGED                     PICTURE S9(7).                COPY

 COPY DCL08.
 77  NUMBER-OF-INPUT-RECORDS            PICTURE S9(7).                COPY
*****************************************************************

/*****************************************************************

 PROCEDURE DIVISION USING NUMBER-CHANGED,
                          NUMBER-OF-INPUT-RECORDS.

     CALL "PRPRT" USING DUMMY-FIELD, NUMBER-CHANGED, EOJ.
     DISPLAY "PRINT PROGRAM ENDED NORMALLY".
     DISPLAY "NUMBER OF INPUT RECORDS READ = ",
             NUMBER-OF-INPUT-RECORDS.
     CLOSE INPUT-FILE
           PRINT-FILE.

 END PROGRAM PREOJ.

*****************************************************************
```

Figure 13.21. *End of job module in COBOL.*

READ statement and AT END test are combined. In the design language we still keep the structures separate to provide flexibility for media changes. For example, we might want to change from a sequental file read to a call to a system data base access mechanism. The COBOL code may change but the structure of the design logic won't.

Also note that there are no labels in the program, and the code is indented in the same fashion as the design language. To go along with this, the use of periods is restricted. A programmer must be careful not confuse the end of a statement by both joint use of periods and scope terminators (END-IF, END-PERFORM, END-EVALUATE, etc.).

In business COBOL programs, most of the data traverses many modules of programs, and this print program is no different in that respect. This means that most data items appear more than once and are, thus, described by COPY members. Although this causes some additional compiler overhead, it doesn't affect execution performance.

14 Example Balance Line Program

PROBLEM DEFINITION

A brokerage house has a need for a daily update of its securities position master file. A computer program is to be designed to handle this function in a batch processing environment.

The securities position master file is a sequential disk file containing two types of records: customer records and security records. For each customer, there is one customer record followed by one security record for each security (stock, bond, gold, etc.) held by the customer.

Each customer record contains the following data elements:

Customer number,
Record type (always *C*),
Security number (always blank),
Customer name,
Customer address,
Salesperson name.

Each security record contains the following data elements:

Customer number,
Record type (always *S*),
Security number (nonblank),
Security name,
Number of shares held (can be negative, i.e., short).

The master file is in ascending sequence of security number within record type within customer number.

A sequential disk file of transactions updates the master file. The sequence of this file is the same as the master file, and the transaction file contains the following data elements:

Customer number,
Record type (always *S*),
Security number,
Trade code (*B*-buy, *S*-sell),
Security name,
Quantity.

Each input transaction is matched against the master file. For matching security records, the security name and number of shares held is updated. If no matching record exists, a new one is added to the file. If the number of securities held is zero, the security record is dropped from the master file.

The result of the match is a new sequential master file having the same data elements and sequence as the input master file.

This program does not update the customer master record and all input data fields on the transactions have been previously validated by an edit program (and do not have to be rechecked). However, transactions having no matching customer number of a customer record on the master file, will be printed on an error report and be rejected. The error report has the format shown in Figure 14.1.

	UPDATE ERROR REPORT	PAGE 1
CUSTOMER NUMBER	SECURITY NUMBER	SECURITY NAME
---------------------------------	-----------------------------	--------------------------------------
A0001	27534	COMPUTER SPECIALISTS
B2733	08745	BIG STEEL MAKER
H0041	88894	FAST AUTOS

Figure 14.1. *Update error report format.*

MODULE HIERARCHY

We must now complete the first phase of the design, which is to draw the hierarchical module relationships. As no mention was made of special software operating environments, assume that we will have to provide the main line module. As, in Chapter 13, the standard mainline logic of Figure 7.1 can do the job.

The mainline module calls decision logic at the next level below, and initialization and end of job modules at the support level. The result is the first design step of Figure 14.2.

The choice of decision logic is easy. The key is the mention of *batch processing* in the specification and the two sequential input files: the transaction file and the master file. These clues point to the balance line classical function for the decision logic to support this application.

Referring to Figure 8.2, we see that there are five modules called by this decision logic. Two modules are necessary at the support level to read the input files—one to read the input transaction file and one to read the input master file. There are also three detail processing modules called to handle the result of the key match testing: transaction key low, master key low, and keys equal. The second design step of Figure 14.3 is now completed.

We must now decide the modules that are to be invoked by the three detail processing modules. Chapter 2 can be used as a guide if there are any questions about the functional boundaries of the modules. The out-

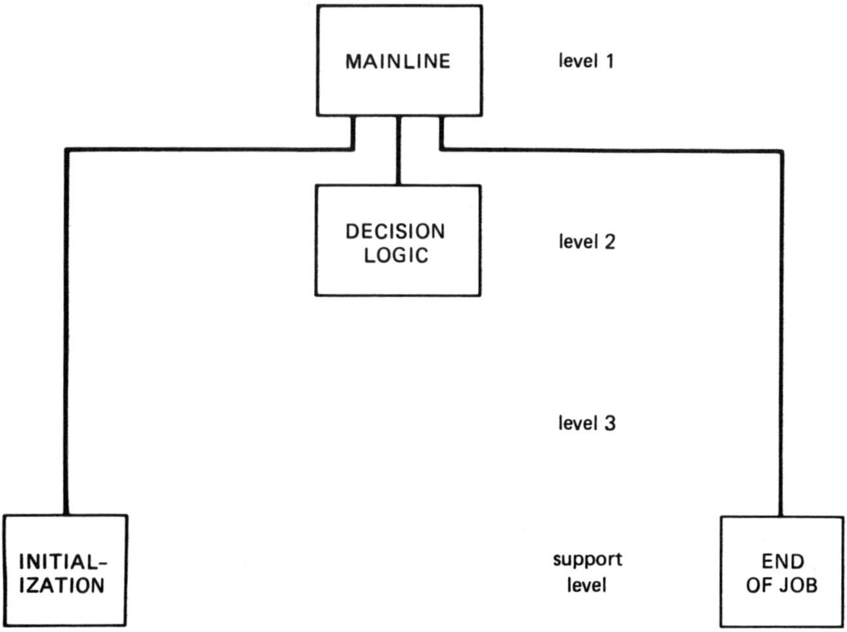

Figure 14.2. *First design step.*

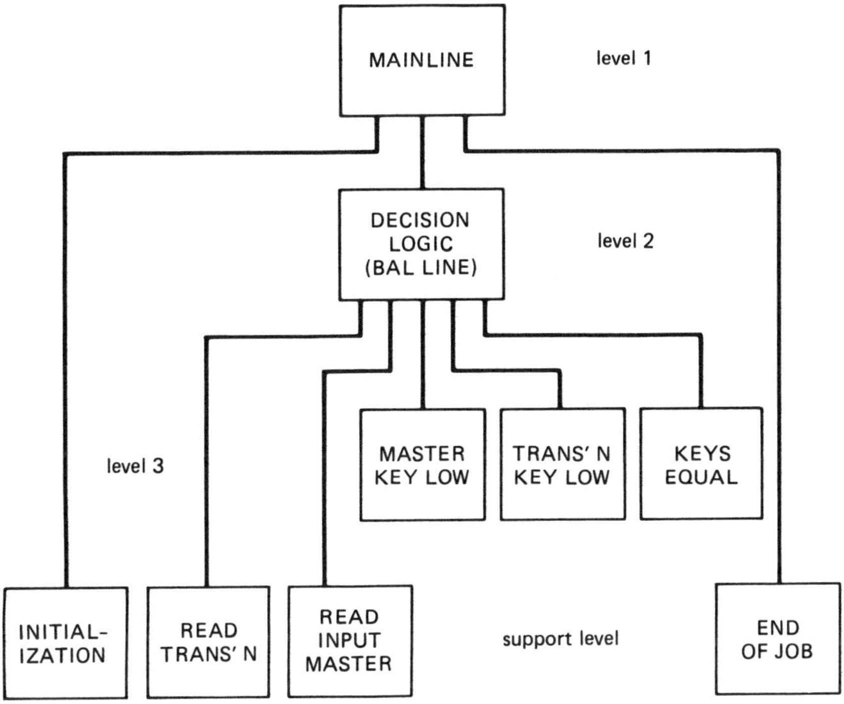

Figure 14.3. *Second design step.*

put master file will have to be created, through just passing records that are not updated from the input master, deleting records that have a zero total for number of shares, and records that are changed via input transactions. This means that all three detail processing modules will call a utility module to write output records.

The specifications define an error report that is to be produced when securities that have no associated customer record on the master file are processed. This situation can occur when the transaction file is unique or when there is security record on the master file but, somehow, the customer record has been deleted from the master. Therefore, a print report utility module is called by the transaction key low module and the keys equal module.

Looking over the problem statement, it becomes clear that there are no more utility functions in this program. The calculations could be candidates, but they are so uncomplicated that it is not worthwhile to collect them in a separate module. The third module hierarchy chart is pictured in Figure 14.4.

Of all four program types, balance line kinds are, typically, the most complex. A simple type of balance line problem would have one input transaction record matching one master file record. However, this problem is substantially more intricate, requiring that customer records be passed without change and allowing any number of trades transactions to update the securities records. To accommodate the multirecord case, a holding area must be provided. It is called *output security data* and is held in WORKING STORAGE until the last security transaction for each particular security number is processed. This means that the end of job module must check this holding area and call the write output master module to put the final accumulated security record out on to the output master file; therefore, the module hierarchy chart is modified with this last design refinement. The final module hierarchy chart appcars in Figure 14.5.

DETAIL DESIGN

We now begin the detail design. We want to eliminate as much reinvention as possible, so we examine the module hierarchy chart of Figure

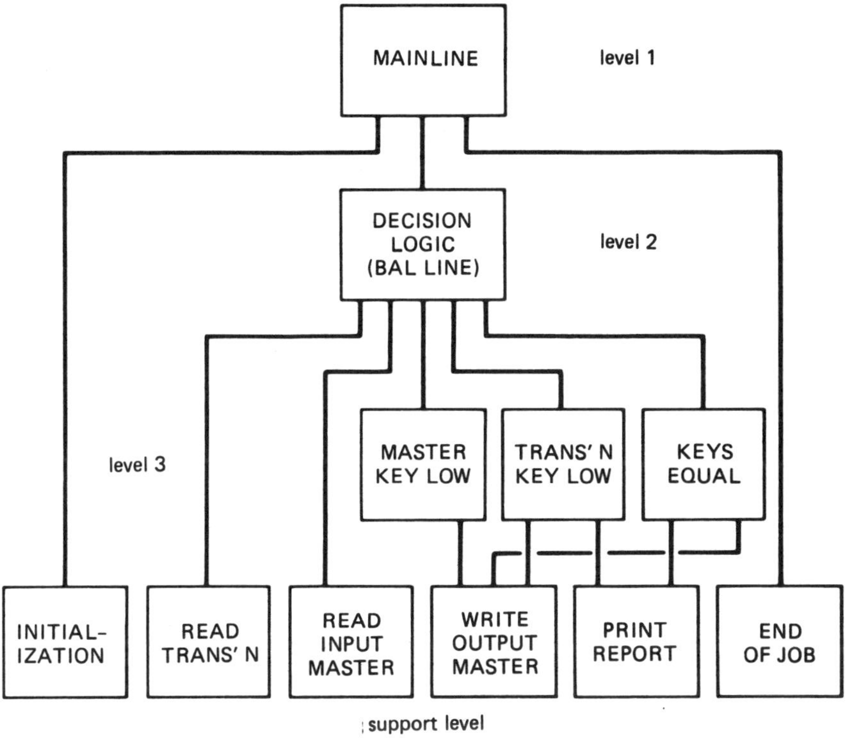

Figure 14.4. *Third design step.*

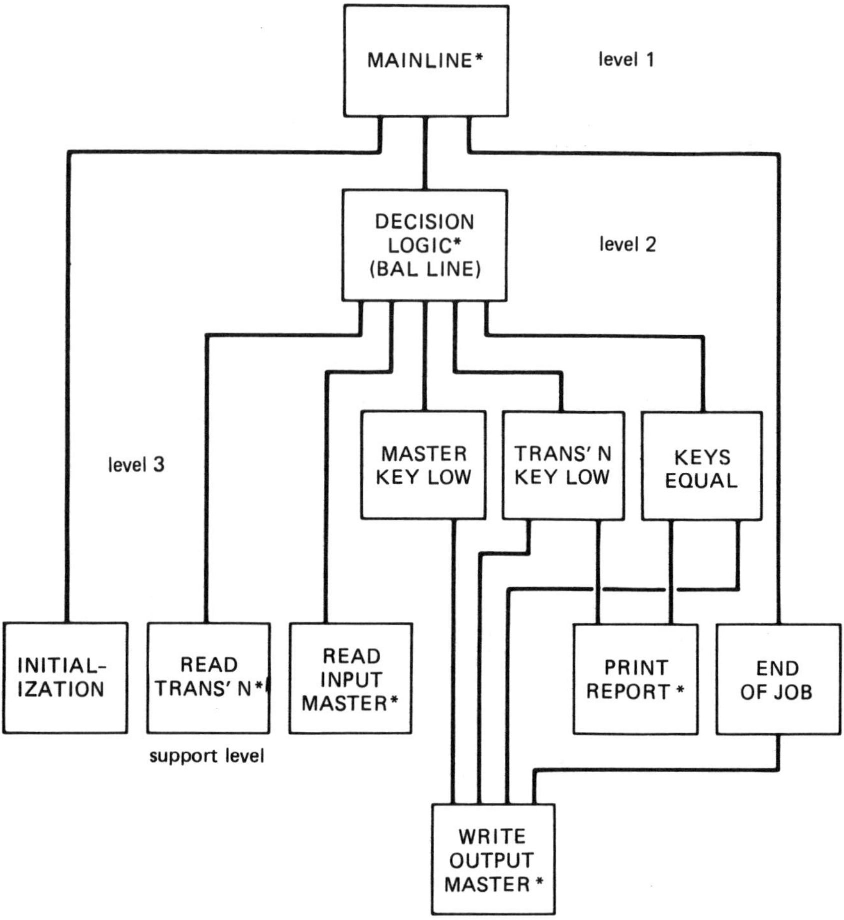

Figure 14.5. *Fourth design step.*

14.5 to identify those modules that are candidates for classical logic. Six of the eleven modules are suitable. These are mainline, decision logic, read transaction, read input master, write output master, and print report. They are marked in the diagram of Figure 14.5 with an asterisk (*).

Proceeding from the top of the module hierarchy, begin the detail design with the mainline module. The standard mainline module is adapted by using module names of our choosing for this program, and specifying the data that is specific to this program. Figure 14.6 portrays the logic after this has been done.

```
*               BROKERAGE TRADES UPDATE—MAINLINE MODULE

 PROGRAM-ID. brmain <MAIN>.

    CALL "brinit" USING data stream 1 status,
                        data stream 2 status,
                        key of last customer record,
                        number of input transactions,
                        number of input masters,
                        number of output masters,
                        output security data.

    PERFORM WITH TEST BEFORE UNTIL data stream 1 status = "at end"
         and data stream 2 status = "at end"
       CALL "brdec" USING data stream 1 status,
                          data stream 2 status,
                          key of last customer record,
                          number of input transactions,
                          number of input masters,
                          number of output masters,
                          output security data
    END-PERFORM.

    CALL "breoj" USING number of input transactions,
                       number of input masters,
                       output security data,
                       number of output masters.

 END PROGRAM brmain.
```

Figure 14.6. *Mainline module.*

```
*          BROKERAGE TRADES UPDATE—DECISION LOGIC MODULE

 PROGRAM-ID. brdec USING data stream 1 status,
                         data stream 2 status,
                         key of last customer record,
                         number of input transactions,
                         number of input masters,
                         number of output master,
                         output security data.

   IF first time in module
      THEN
         reset first time indicator
         CALL "brrd1" USING data stream 1 status,
                            current sequential key 1,
                            previous sequential key 1,
                            number of input transactions,
                            input transaction
         CALL "brrd2" USING data stream 2 status,
                            current sequential key 2,
                            previous sequential key 2,
                            number of input masters,
                            master data

         IF data stream 1 status = "at end" and
            data stream 2 status = "at end"
            THEN
               EXIT PROGRAM
         END-IF

   END-IF.

   IF data stream 2 status = "at end" or
      current sequential key 1 less than
      current sequential key 2
      THEN
         CALL "brk1lw" USING current sequential key 1,
                             key of last customer record,
                             input transaction,
                             number of output masters,
                             output security data
         CALL "brrd1" USING data stream 1 status,
                            current sequential key 1,
                            previous sequential key 1,
                            number of input transactions,
                            input transaction
         EXIT PROGRAM
   END-IF.
```

Figure 14.7. *Decision logic module.*

```
IF data stream 1 status = "at end" or
   current sequential key 2 less than
   current sequential key 1
    THEN
       CALL "brk2lw" USING current sequential key 2,
                           master data,
                           number of output masters,
                           output security data,
                           key of last customer record
       CALL "brrd2" USING data stream 2 status,
                          current sequential key 2,
                          previous sequential key 2,
                          number of input masters,
                          master data
       EXIT PROGRAM
END-IF.

CALL "brkeq" USING current sequential key 1,
                   key of last customer record,
                   input transaction, master data,
                   number of output master records,
                   output security data.
CALL "brrd1" USING data stream 1 status,
                   current sequential key 1,
                   previous sequential key 1,
                   number of input transactions,
                   input transaction.
CALL "brrd2" USING data stream 2 status,
                   current sequential key 2,
                   previous sequential key 2,
                   number of input masters,
                   master data.

END PROGRAM brdec.
```

The data that appears in this module is that which controls the execution of the decision logic (data stream 1 status, data stream 2 status), record counts for auditing, and the output security data that must be initialized at the beginning of program execution. Data stream 1 status and data stream 2 status are the end of file indicators for the input transaction and input master files respectively. They are initialized to *not at end* by the initialization module, and subsequently control the PERFORM statement in this mainline module.

We now consider the decision logic at the next level in the program's hierarchy. As this has been identified as a balance line classical function, the logic is taken and fitted with the data relevant to the brokerage problem as may be seen in Figure 14.7. Because the program updates, rather than selects, the last optional call in the logic of the classical function is left in the design.

Note, again, that the module names called in the classical logic have been changed to conform with the naming convention of this program. Decide becomes brdec, seqread1 becomes brrd1, seqread2 becomes brrd2, and so on. The data processed at this level in the program hierarchy now includes the input records that are read by the read transaction and read master modules along with the associated file keys.

The design process moves to the next level down in the hierarchy, the detail processing modules. All three must be designed by the programmer as there are no classical functions for them.

Module *brk1lw* performs the processing when the key in the transaction file is found to be lowest. It begins with a test comparing the key data values of the output security data with the key data values of the current transaction record. Remember that the output security data is a WORKING STORAGE area used to accumulate all transaction data for each security identified by a unique customer number and security number.

If the current transaction key matches the key of the output security data, the accumulated data is updated depending on whether the transaction is a buy or sell transaction. Control then leaves this module.

For a no-match situation, the previous security data must be written to the output file if there is valid data. The output security data is checked, and if not blank and there is a nonzero value in the number of shares held field, a security record will be written to the output master

```
* BROKERAGE TRADES UPDATE—TRANSACTION KEY LOW MODULE

 PROGRAM-ID. brk1lw USING current sequential key 1,
                          key of last customer record,
                          input transaction,
                          number of output masters,
                          output security data.

   IF current sequential key 1  = output security key
      THEN

         IF buy
            THEN
               add quantity in transaction to
                 number of shares held in output security data
            ELSE
               subtract quantity in transaction from
                 number of shares held in output security data
         END-IF

         EXIT PROGRAM
   END-IF.

   IF output security data = spaces or
      number of shares held in output security data = 0
      THEN
         continue
      ELSE
         CALL "brwrt" USING output security data,
                            number of output masters
   END-IF.

   move spaces to output security data.

   IF key of last customer record not =
      customer number in input transaction
      THEN
         CALL "brprt" USING input transaction
         EXIT PROGRAM
   END-IF.

   set up new output security data from input transaction.

 END PROGRAM brk1lw.
```

Figure 14.8. *Transaction key low module.*

file (via a call to module *brwrt*). The output security data area is then cleared, ready for setup of the new transaction data.

A check is taken to ascertain that a customer record did previously exist for this security transaction. If one did not, module *brprt* is called to print a notice on the error report, and control leaves this module.

Finally, if everything is correct, the transaction is employed to set up the output security data area. The processing for module *brk1lw*, shown in Figure 14.8 is finished.

The master key low module, *brk2lw*, handles the processing when the master file records have unique keys. The master file records may be either customer records (type *C*) or security records (type *S*).

Upon entry into this module, the output security data area is tested for the existence of previous security data having a nonzero value in the number of shares held field. If this condition is true, module *brwrt* is called to write the data to the output master file.

If the current master record being processed is a customer record, the key value is saved in key of last customer record data element to provide the value to determine if a customer record exists for subsequently processed input securities transactions.

At the end of this module, module *brwrt* is called to copy the record from the input master file to the output master file. The output security data area is then cleared to blanks to indicate no prior security record, and control leaves *brk2lw*. The logic for this master key low module is laid out in Figure 14.9.

As with the two prior detail processing modules, the keys equal module (*brkeq*) begins with a test for data in the output security data area having a nonzero value in the number of shares held field. If such data is present, a record is written to the output master file via module *brwrt*.

Because there is a master-transaction key match, the record under evaluation must be a security record; therefore, a new output security data area is created from the master data.

Before continuing, a check is made to verify that a customer record was previously processed. If not, module *brprt* is called to print an error message, and control leaves this module.

The newly created output security data area is updated with the transaction data. Processing for this module is now completed. The logic is displayed in Figure 14.10.

```
* BROKERAGE TRADES UPDATE—MASTER KEY LOW MODULE

  PROGRAM-ID. brk2lw USING current sequential key 2,
                           master data,
                           number of output masters,
                           output security data,
                           key of last customer record.

    IF output security data = spaces or
       number of shares held in output security data = 0
       THEN
          continue
       ELSE
          CALL "brwrt" USING output security data,
                             number of output masters
    END-IF.

    IF record type in master data = "c"
       THEN
          move customer number in master data to
               key of last customer record
    END-IF.

    CALL "brwrt" USING master data,
                       number of output masters.
    move spaces to output security data.

  END PROGRAM brk2lw.
```

Figure 14.9. *Master key low module.*

```
*   BROKERAGE TRADES UPDATE—KEYS EQUAL MODULE

 PROGRAM-ID. brkeq USING current sequential key 1,
                         key of last customer record,
                         input transaction, master data,
                         number of output masters,
                         output security data.

   IF output security data = spaces or
      number of shares held in output security data = 0
      THEN
         continue
      ELSE
         CALL "brwrt" USING output security data,
                            number of output masters
   END-IF.

   set up new output security data from master data.

   IF key of last customer record not =
      customer number in input transaction
      THEN
         CALL "brprt" USING input transaction
         EXIT PROGRAM
   END-IF.

   IF buy
      THEN
         add quantity in transaction to
            number of shares held in output security data
      ELSE
         subtract quantity in transaction from
            number of shares held in output security data
   END-IF.

 END PROGRAM brkeq.
```

Figure 14.10. *Keys equal module.*

Having finished with the design of the detail processing modules, we can concentrate on the utility functions. We begin with the initialization module, which must be designed by the programmer.

Initialization consists of setting starting values for both data stream status indicators, initializing auditing record counts, and blanking the key of last customer record and output security data areas. The final function in this module is the opening of the files. Details of the logic are displayed in Figure 14.11.

The read transaction module is designed next. This is the classical sequential read function of Figure 9.2. That logic is modified by incorporating the data to be read in this program. Also, the module name is changed from *seqread* to *brrd1*.

The sequence test is retained because the matching logic of the balance line will fall apart if the records are processed in a random sequence. Sequence errors will cause the program to stop immediately. Note that in the resulting logic of Figure 14.12, all key data elements are suffixed with 1 to indicate the transaction file values.

```
* BROKERAGE TRADES UPDATE—INITIALIZATION MODULE

  PROGRAM-ID. brinit USING data stream 1 status,
                           data stream 2 status,
                           key of last customer record,
                           number of input transactions,
                           number of input masters,
                           number of output masters,
                           output security data.

     move "not at end" to data stream 1 status.
     move "not at end" to data stream 2 status.
     move 0 to all file record counts.
     move spaces to key of last customer record.
     move spaces to output security data.
     open the files.

  END PROGRAM brinit.
```

Figure 14.11. *Initialization module.*

```
* BROKERAGE TRADES UPDATE—READ TRANSACTION MODULE

PROGRAM-ID. brrd1 USING data stream 1 status,
                        current sequential key 1,
                        previous sequential key 1,
                        number of input transactions,
                        transaction data.

   IF data stream 1 status = "at end"
      THEN
         display message - "program reading past data end"
         stop the program
   END-IF.

   move current sequential key 1 to previous sequential key 1.
   read file sequentially to get transaction data.

   IF end of data reached
      THEN
         move "at end" to data stream 1 status
         EXIT PROGRAM
   END-IF.

   add 1 to number of input transactions.
   set up current sequential key 1.

   IF first time in module
      THEN
         reset first time indicator
         move low values to previous sequential key 1
         EXIT PROGRAM
   END-IF.

   IF current sequential key 1 less than
      previous sequential key 1
      THEN
         display message and error information on system printer
         stop the program
   END-IF.

END PROGRAM brrd1.
```

Figure 4.12. *Read transaction module.*

```
*     BROKERAGE TRADES UPDATE—READ MASTER MODULE

  PROGRAM-ID. brrd2 USING data stream 2 status,
                          current sequential key 2,
                          previous sequential key 2,
                          number of input masters,
                          master data.

     IF data stream 2 status = "at end"
        THEN
           display message - "program reading past master end"
           stop the program
     END-IF.

     move current sequential key 2 to previous sequential key 2.
     read file sequentially to get master data.

     IF end of data reached
        THEN
           move "at end" to data stream 2 status
           EXIT PROGRAM
     END-IF.

     add 1 to number of input masters.
     set up current sequential key 2.

     IF first time in module
        THEN
           reset first time indicator
           move low values to previous sequential key 2
           EXIT PROGRAM
     END-IF.

     IF current sequential key 2 not greater than
       previous sequential key 2
        THEN
           display message and error information on system printer
           stop the program
     END-IF.

  END PROGRAM brrd2.
```

Figure 14.13. *Read master module.*

The read master module is also a classical read sequential function. It is very similar to the read transaction module, except it processes master file records.

Its name is *brrd2* and the appropriate master file data is processed. Where the read transaction module used *1* as a suffix for key data elements, this module uses *2* to notate the master file connection. Again, the logic will stop the program if an out-of-sequence condition is detected. An unsequenced master file points to severe data difficulties that should be investigated by the programmers who maintain the brokerage application. The design developed is portrayed in Figure 14.13.

The write output module (*brwrt*) is, likewise, a classical function. It is the classical sequential write of Figure 9.5 and is adapted with the data to be written in this program. The resulting logic appears in Figure 14.14.

The print error report module creates the report of figure 14.1. It is the classical function of Figure 9.1 with the data to be printed by this update program. Figure 14.15 displays the logic.

The final module in the module hierarchy is the end of job module. No classical function is available, so the functions must be designed by the programmer.

The output security data WORKING STORAGE area accumulates transactions for the security trades (buys and sells). It is very likely that an end of file will occur without the accumulated transactions for the last security number being written to the output master file. Check the output security data for blanks; if not blank, the accumulated data has not been written, and if the number of shares held is not zero, module *brwrt* is called to write the output master record.

The last things to be done in this end of job module is to display the record counts on the system printer (a different file than the error report) and close the files. We then have the end of job module design of Figure 14.16.

THE COBOL CODE

With a complete logic design specified in the design language, we can now code the program in COBOL. The design and the data COPYs

```
*           BROKERAGE TRADES UPDATE—WRITE OUTPUT MODULE

  PROGRAM-ID. brwrt USING master data,
                              number of output masters.

     write output master file sequentially.
     add 1 to number of output masters.

  END PROGRAM brwrt.
```

Figure 14.14. *Write output module.*

```
*         BROKERAGE TRADES UPDATE—PRINT ERROR REPORT MODULE

  PROGRAM-ID. brprt USING input transaction.

           《 page number should have an initial value of zero 》
           《 line number should have an initial value of 999   》
           《 page size is initialized to 50                     》

     IF line number greater than page size
        THEN
           add 1 to page number
           move 0 to line number
           print page headings
     END-IF.

     set up detail line.
     print detail line.
     add 1 to line number.

  END PROGRAM brprt.
```

Figure 14.15. *Print error report module.*

```
*   BROKERAGE TRADES UPDATE—END OF JOB MODULE

  PROGRAM-ID. breoj USING number of input transactions,
                          number of input masters,
                          output security data,
                          number of output masters.

     IF output security data = blanks    « data to be written »
        or number of shares held in output security data = 0
        THEN                             « at end of file     »
           continue
        ELSE
           CALL "brwrt" USING output security data,
                              number of output masters
     END-IF.

     display count fields on system printer with identifier
       messages.
     close the files.

  END PROGRAM breoj.
```

Figure 14.16. *End of job module.*

are put together in the COBOL modules of Figures 14.17 through 14.27. The COBOL modules must match the logic structures of the equivalent design language modules.

The coding is again a mechanical operation. This example program is larger than the previous printing program, and the ratio of COBOL code to design language is correspondingly larger.

```
/*****************************************************************
 IDENTIFICATION DIVISION.

 PROGRAM-ID.        BRMAIN.

 AUTHOR.            G.R. ROGERS.

****************************************************************
*                                                              *
* BROKERAGE TRADES UPDATE PROGRAM                              *
* MODULE - MAINLINE                                            *
*                                                              *
*--------------------------------------------------------------*
* CHANGE HISTORY                                               *
*   090785 NEW PROGRAM                                     GRR *
****************************************************************

 DATA DIVISION.

 WORKING-STORAGE SECTION.

 77  VERSION-NUMBER                     PICTURE X(27) VALUE
     "VERSION 1     SEPT. 7, 1985".

 COPY DCL19.
 77  DATA-STREAM-1-STATUS               PICTURE X(10).            COPY

 COPY DCL20.
 77  DATA-STREAM-2-STATUS               PICTURE X(10).            COPY

 COPY DCL30.
 77  KEY-OF-LAST-CUSTOMER-RECORD        PICTURE X(5).             COPY

 COPY DCL21.
 77  NUMBER-OF-INPUT-MASTERS            PICTURE S9(7).            COPY

 COPY DCL22.
 77  NUMBER-OF-OUTPUT-MASTERS           PICTURE S9(7).            COPY

 COPY DCL23.
 77  NUMBER-OF-INPUT-TRANSACTIONS       PICTURE S9(7).            COPY

 COPY DCL24.
 01  OUTPUT-SECURITY-DATA.                                        COPY
     02  OUTPUT-SECURITY-KEY.                                     COPY
         03  CUSTOMER-NUMBER            PICTURE X(5).             COPY
         03  RECORD-TYPE                PICTURE X.                COPY
         03  SECURITY-NUMBER            PICTURE X(5).             COPY
     02  SECURITY-NAME                  PICTURE X(30).            COPY
     02  NUMBER-OF-SHARES-HELD          PICTURE S9(15).           COPY
     02  FILLER                         PICTURE X(5).             COPY
     02  FILLER                         PICTURE X.                COPY

****************************************************************

/***************************************************************

 PROCEDURE DIVISION.

     CALL "BRINIT" USING DATA-STREAM-1-STATUS,
                         DATA-STREAM-2-STATUS,
                         KEY-OF-LAST-CUSTOMER-RECORD,
                         NUMBER-OF-INPUT-TRANSACTIONS,
                         NUMBER-OF-INPUT-MASTERS,
                         NUMBER-OF-OUTPUT-MASTERS,
                         OUTPUT-SECURITY-DATA.

     PERFORM WITH TEST BEFORE UNTIL
        DATA-STREAM-1-STATUS = "AT END" AND
        DATA-STREAM-2-STATUS = "AT END"
       CALL "BRDEC" USING DATA-STREAM-1-STATUS,
                          DATA-STREAM-2-STATUS,
                          KEY-OF-LAST-CUSTOMER-RECORD,
                          NUMBER-OF-INPUT-TRANSACTIONS,
                          NUMBER-OF-INPUT-MASTERS,
                          NUMBER-OF-OUTPUT-MASTERS,
                          OUTPUT-SECURITY-DATA
     END-PERFORM.

     CALL "BREOJ" USING NUMBER-OF-INPUT-TRANSACTIONS,
                        NUMBER-OF-INPUT-MASTERS,
                        OUTPUT-SECURITY-DATA,
                        NUMBER-OF-OUTPUT-MASTERS.

     STOP RUN.

 END PROGRAM BRMAIN.

****************************************************************
```

Figure 14.17. *Mainline module in COBOL.*

```
/****************************************************************
 IDENTIFICATION DIVISION.

 PROGRAM-ID.        BRDEC.

 AUTHOR.            G.R. ROGERS.

***************************************************************
*                                                             *
* BROKERAGE TRADES UPDATE PROGRAM                             *
* MODULE - DECISION LOGIC                                     *
*                                                             *
*-------------------------------------------------------------*
* CHANGE HISTORY                                              *
*   090785 NEW PROGRAM                                    GRR *
***************************************************************

 DATA DIVISION.

 WORKING-STORAGE SECTION.

 77  VERSION-NUMBER                      PICTURE X(27) VALUE
     "VERSION 1     SEPT. 7, 1985".

 COPY DCL25.
 77  CURRENT-SEQUENTIAL-KEY-1            PICTURE X(11).           COPY

 COPY DCL26.
 77  PREVIOUS-SEQUENTIAL-KEY-1           PICTURE X(11).           COPY

 COPY DCL27.
 77  CURRENT-SEQUENTIAL-KEY-2            PICTURE X(11).           COPY

 COPY DCL28.
 77  PREVIOUS-SEQUENTIAL-KEY-2           PICTURE X(11).           COPY

 COPY DCL11.
 77  FIRST-TIME-IN-MODULE                PICTURE XXX VALUE "YES".  COPY

 COPY DCL15.
 01  INPUT-TRANSACTION.                                           COPY
     02  TRANSACTION-KEY.                                         COPY
         03  CUSTOMER-NUMBER             PICTURE X(5).            COPY
         03  RECORD-TYPE                 PICTURE X.               COPY
         03  SECURITY-NUMBER             PICTURE X(5).            COPY
     02  TRADE-CODE                      PICTURE X.               COPY
     02  SECURITY-NAME                   PICTURE X(20).           COPY
     02  QUANTITY                        PICTURE 9(9).            COPY
     02  FILLER                          PICTURE X.               COPY

 COPY DCL16.
 01  MASTER-DATA.                                                 COPY
     02  MASTER-KEY.                                              COPY
         03  CUSTOMER-NUMBER             PICTURE X(5).            COPY
         03  RECORD-TYPE                 PICTURE X.               COPY
         03  SECURITY-NUMBER             PICTURE X(5).            COPY
     02  CUSTOMER-DATA.                                           COPY
         03  CUSTOMER-NAME               PICTURE X(20).           COPY
         03  CUSTOMER-ADDRESS            PICTURE X(20).           COPY
         03  SALESMAN-NAME               PICTURE X(10).           COPY
     02  SECURITY-DATA  REDEFINES  CUSTOMER-DATA.                 COPY
         03  SECURITY-NAME               PICTURE X(30).           COPY
         03  NUMBER-OF-SHARES-HELD       PICTURE S9(15).          COPY
         03  FILLER                      PICTURE X(5).            COPY
     02  FILLER                          PICTURE X.               COPY

 LINKAGE SECTION.

 COPY DCL19.
 77  DATA-STREAM-1-STATUS                PICTURE X(10).           COPY

 COPY DCL20.
 77  DATA-STREAM-2-STATUS                PICTURE X(10).           COPY

 COPY DCL30.
 77  KEY-OF-LAST-CUSTOMER-RECORD         PICTURE X(5).            COPY

 COPY DCL23.
 77  NUMBER-OF-INPUT-TRANSACTIONS        PICTURE S9(7).           COPY

 COPY DCL21.
 77  NUMBER-OF-INPUT-MASTERS             PICTURE S9(7).           COPY

 COPY DCL22.
 77  NUMBER-OF-OUTPUT-MASTERS            PICTURE S9(7).           COPY

 COPY DCL24.
 01  OUTPUT-SECURITY-DATA.                                        COPY
     02  OUTPUT-SECURITY-KEY.                                     COPY
         03  CUSTOMER-NUMBER             PICTURE X(5).            COPY
         03  RECORD-TYPE                 PICTURE X.               COPY
         03  SECURITY-NUMBER             PICTURE X(5).            COPY
     02  SECURITY-NAME                   PICTURE X(30).           COPY
     02  NUMBER-OF-SHARES-HELD           PICTURE S9(15).          COPY
     02  FILLER                          PICTURE X(5).            COPY
     02  FILLER                          PICTURE X.               COPY
***************************************************************
```

(a)

Figure 14.18. *Decision logic module in COBOL.*

```
/*************************************************************

PROCEDURE DIVISION USING DATA-STREAM-1-STATUS,
                         DATA-STREAM-2-STATUS,
                         KEY-OF-LAST-CUSTOMER-RECORD,
                         NUMBER-OF-INPUT-TRANSACTIONS,
                         NUMBER-OF-INPUT-MASTERS,
                         NUMBER-OF-OUTPUT-MASTERS,
                         OUTPUT-SECURITY-DATA.

    IF FIRST-TIME-IN-MODULE = "YES"
      THEN
        MOVE "NO " TO FIRST-TIME-IN-MODULE
        CALL "BRRD1" USING DATA-STREAM-1-STATUS,
                           CURRENT-SEQUENTIAL-KEY-1,
                           PREVIOUS-SEQUENTIAL-KEY-1,
                           NUMBER-OF-INPUT-TRANSACTIONS,
                           INPUT-TRANSACTION
        CALL "BRRD2" USING DATA-STREAM-2-STATUS,
                           CURRENT-SEQUENTIAL-KEY-2,
                           PREVIOUS-SEQUENTIAL-KEY-2,
                           NUMBER-OF-INPUT-MASTERS,
                           MASTER-DATA

        IF DATA-STREAM-1-STATUS = "AT END" AND
           DATA-STREAM-2-STATUS = "AT END"
          THEN
            EXIT PROGRAM
        END-IF

    END-IF.

    IF DATA-STREAM-2-STATUS = "AT END" OR
       CURRENT-SEQUENTIAL-KEY-1 LESS THAN
       CURRENT-SEQUENTIAL-KEY-2
      THEN
        CALL "BRK1LW" USING CURRENT-SEQUENTIAL-KEY-1,
                            KEY-OF-LAST-CUSTOMER-RECORD,
                            INPUT-TRANSACTION,
                            NUMBER-OF-OUTPUT-MASTERS,
                            OUTPUT-SECURITY-DATA
        CALL "BRRD1" USING DATA-STREAM-1-STATUS,
                           CURRENT-SEQUENTIAL-KEY-1,
                           PREVIOUS-SEQUENTIAL-KEY-1,
                           NUMBER-OF-INPUT-TRANSACTIONS,
                           INPUT-TRANSACTION
        EXIT PROGRAM
    END-IF.

    IF DATA-STREAM-1-STATUS = "AT END" OR
       CURRENT-SEQUENTIAL-KEY-2 LESS THAN
       CURRENT-SEQUENTIAL-KEY-1
      THEN
        CALL "BRK2LW" USING CURRENT-SEQUENTIAL-KEY-2,
                            MASTER-DATA,
                            NUMBER-OF-OUTPUT-MASTERS,
                            OUTPUT-SECURITY-DATA,
                            KEY-OF-LAST-CUSTOMER-RECORD
        CALL "BRRD2" USING DATA-STREAM-2-STATUS,
                           CURRENT-SEQUENTIAL-KEY-2,
                           PREVIOUS-SEQUENTIAL-KEY-2,
                           NUMBER-OF-INPUT-MASTERS,
                           MASTER-DATA
        EXIT PROGRAM
    END-IF.

    CALL "BRKEQ" USING CURRENT-SEQUENTIAL-KEY-1,
                       KEY-OF-LAST-CUSTOMER-RECORD,
                       INPUT-TRANSACTION,
                       MASTER-DATA,
                       NUMBER-OF-OUTPUT-MASTERS,
                       OUTPUT-SECURITY-DATA.
    CALL "BRRD1" USING DATA-STREAM-1-STATUS,
                       CURRENT-SEQUENTIAL-KEY-1,
                       PREVIOUS-SEQUENTIAL-KEY-1,
                       NUMBER-OF-INPUT-TRANSACTIONS,
                       INPUT-TRANSACTION.
    CALL "BRRD2" USING DATA-STREAM-2-STATUS,
                       CURRENT-SEQUENTIAL-KEY-2,
                       PREVIOUS-SEQUENTIAL-KEY-2,
                       NUMBER-OF-INPUT-MASTERS,
                       MASTER-DATA.

END PROGRAM BRDEC.
**************************************************************
```

(b)

```
/*************************************************************************
 IDENTIFICATION DIVISION.

 PROGRAM-ID.        BRK1LW.

 AUTHOR.            G.R. ROGERS.

************************************************************************
*                                                                      *
* BROKERAGE TRADES UPDATE PROGRAM                                       *
* MODULE - DETAIL PROCESSING FOR LOW TRANSACTION FILE KEY              *
*                                                                      *
*----------------------------------------------------------------------*
* CHANGE HISTORY                                                       *
*   090785 NEW PROGRAM                                              GRR *
************************************************************************

 DATA DIVISION.

 WORKING-STORAGE SECTION.

 77  VERSION-NUMBER                      PICTURE X(27) VALUE
     "VERSION 1      SEPT. 7, 1985".

 LINKAGE SECTION.

 COPY DCL25.
 77  CURRENT-SEQUENTIAL-KEY-1            PICTURE X(11).              COPY

 COPY DCL30.
 77  KEY-OF-LAST-CUSTOMER-RECORD         PICTURE X(5).               COPY

 COPY DCL22.
 77  NUMBER-OF-OUTPUT-MASTERS            PICTURE S9(7).              COPY

 COPY DCL15.
 01  INPUT-TRANSACTION.                                              COPY
     02  TRANSACTION-KEY.                                            COPY
         03  CUSTOMER-NUMBER             PICTURE X(5).               COPY
         03  RECORD-TYPE                 PICTURE X.                  COPY
         03  SECURITY-NUMBER             PICTURE X(5).               COPY
     02  TRADE-CODE                      PICTURE X.                  COPY
     02  SECURITY-NAME                   PICTURE X(20).              COPY
     02  QUANTITY                        PICTURE 9(9).               COPY
     02  FILLER                          PICTURE X.                  COPY

 COPY DCL24.
 01  OUTPUT-SECURITY-DATA.                                           COPY
     02  OUTPUT-SECURITY-KEY.                                        COPY
         03  CUSTOMER-NUMBER             PICTURE X(5).               COPY
         03  RECORD-TYPE                 PICTURE X.                  COPY
         03  SECURITY-NUMBER             PICTURE X(5).               COPY
     02  SECURITY-NAME                   PICTURE X(30).              COPY
     02  NUMBER-OF-SHARES-HELD           PICTURE S9(15).             COPY
     02  FILLER                          PICTURE X(5).               COPY
     02  FILLER                          PICTURE X.                  COPY

*************************************************************************
```

(a)

Figure 14.19. *Transaction key low module in COBOL.*

```
/*****************************************************************

 PROCEDURE DIVISION USING CURRENT-SEQUENTIAL-KEY-1,
                          KEY-OF-LAST-CUSTOMER-RECORD,
                          INPUT-TRANSACTION,
                          NUMBER-OF-OUTPUT-MASTERS,
                          OUTPUT-SECURITY-DATA.

     IF CURRENT-SEQUENTIAL-KEY-1 = OUTPUT-SECURITY-KEY
       THEN

         IF TRADE-CODE = "B"
           THEN
             ADD QUANTITY TO NUMBER-OF-SHARES-HELD IN
                 OUTPUT-SECURITY-DATA
             EXIT PROGRAM
           ELSE
             SUBTRACT QUANTITY FROM NUMBER-OF-SHARES-HELD IN
                 OUTPUT-SECURITY-DATA
             EXIT PROGRAM
         END-IF

     END-IF.

     IF OUTPUT-SECURITY-DATA = SPACES OR
        NUMBER-OF-SHARES-HELD IN OUTPUT-SECURITY-DATA = 0
       THEN
         CONTINUE
       ELSE
         CALL "BRWRT" USING OUTPUT-SECURITY-DATA,
                            NUMBER-OF-OUTPUT-MASTERS
     END-IF.

     MOVE SPACES TO OUTPUT-SECURITY-DATA.

     IF KEY-OF-LAST-CUSTOMER-RECORD NOT = CUSTOMER-NUMBER
        IN INPUT-TRANSACTION
       THEN
         CALL "BRPRT" USING INPUT-TRANSACTION
         EXIT PROGRAM
     END-IF.

     MOVE TRANSACTION-KEY TO OUTPUT-SECURITY-KEY.
     MOVE SECURITY-NAME IN INPUT-TRANSACTION TO
          SECURITY-NAME IN OUTPUT-SECURITY-DATA.

     IF TRADE-CODE = "B"
       THEN
         MOVE QUANTITY TO NUMBER-OF-SHARES-HELD
            IN OUTPUT-SECURITY-DATA
       ELSE
         COMPUTE NUMBER-OF-SHARES-HELD IN OUTPUT-SECURITY-DATA =
            - QUANTITY
     END-IF.

 END PROGRAM BRK1LW.
*****************************************************************
```

(b)

```
/****************************************************************
 IDENTIFICATION DIVISION.

 PROGRAM-ID.        BRK2LW.

 AUTHOR.            G.R. ROGERS.

****************************************************************
*                                                              *
* BROKERAGE TRADES UPDATE PROGRAM                              *
* MODULE - DETAIL PROCESSING FOR LOW MASTER FILE KEY           *
*                                                              *
*--------------------------------------------------------------*
* CHANGE HISTORY                                               *
*   090785 NEW PROGRAM                                     GRR *
****************************************************************

 DATA DIVISION.

 WORKING-STORAGE SECTION.

 77  VERSION-NUMBER                    PICTURE X(27) VALUE
     "VERSION 1      SEPT. 7, 1985".

 LINKAGE SECTION.

 COPY DCL27.
 77  CURRENT-SEQUENTIAL-KEY-2          PICTURE X(11).              COPY

 COPY DCL30.
 77  KEY-OF-LAST-CUSTOMER-RECORD       PICTURE X(5).               COPY

 COPY DCL22.
 77  NUMBER-OF-OUTPUT-MASTERS          PICTURE S9(7).              COPY

 COPY DCL16.
 01  MASTER-DATA.                                                  COPY
     02  MASTER-KEY.                                               COPY
         03  CUSTOMER-NUMBER           PICTURE X(5).               COPY
         03  RECORD-TYPE               PICTURE X.                  COPY
         03  SECURITY-NUMBER           PICTURE X(5).               COPY
     02  CUSTOMER-DATA.                                            COPY
         03  CUSTOMER-NAME             PICTURE X(20).              COPY
         03  CUSTOMER-ADDRESS          PICTURE X(20).              COPY
         03  SALESMAN-NAME             PICTURE X(10).              COPY
     02  SECURITY-DATA  REDEFINES   CUSTOMER-DATA.                 COPY
         03  SECURITY-NAME             PICTURE X(30).              COPY
         03  NUMBER-OF-SHARES-HELD     PICTURE S9(15).             COPY
         03  FILLER                    PICTURE X(5).               COPY
     02  FILLER                        PICTURE X.                  COPY

 COPY DCL24.
 01  OUTPUT-SECURITY-DATA.                                         COPY
     02  OUTPUT-SECURITY-KEY.                                      COPY
         03  CUSTOMER-NUMBER           PICTURE X(5).               COPY
         03  RECORD-TYPE               PICTURE X.                  COPY
         03  SECURITY-NUMBER           PICTURE X(5).               COPY
     02  SECURITY-NAME                 PICTURE X(30).              COPY
     02  NUMBER-OF-SHARES-HELD         PICTURE S9(15).             COPY
     02  FILLER                        PICTURE X(5).               COPY
     02  FILLER                        PICTURE X.                  COPY
****************************************************************
/***************************************************************

 PROCEDURE DIVISION USING CURRENT-SEQUENTIAL-KEY-2,
                          MASTER-DATA,
                          NUMBER-OF-OUTPUT-MASTERS,
                          OUTPUT-SECURITY-DATA,
                          KEY-OF-LAST-CUSTOMER-RECORD.

     IF OUTPUT-SECURITY-DATA  = SPACES OR
        NUMBER-OF-SHARES-HELD IN OUTPUT-SECURITY-DATA = 0
       THEN
         CONTINUE
       ELSE
         CALL "BRWRT" USING OUTPUT-SECURITY-DATA,
                            NUMBER-OF-OUTPUT-MASTERS
     END-IF.

     IF RECORD-TYPE IN MASTER-DATA = "C"
       THEN
         MOVE CUSTOMER-NUMBER IN MASTER-DATA TO
           KEY-OF-LAST-CUSTOMER-RECORD
     END-IF.

     CALL "BRWRT" USING MASTER-DATA,
                        NUMBER-OF-OUTPUT-MASTERS.
     MOVE SPACES TO OUTPUT-SECURITY-DATA.

 END PROGRAM BRK2LW.

****************************************************************
```


Figure 14.20. *Master key low module in COBOL.*

```
/************************************************************************
 IDENTIFICATION DIVISION.

 PROGRAM-ID.        BRKEQ.

 AUTHOR.            G.R. ROGERS.

***********************************************************************
*                                                                     *
* BROKERAGE TRADES UPDATE PROGRAM                                     *
* MODULE - DETAIL PROCESSING FOR MATCHING MASTER AND                  *
*          TRANSACTION FILES KEYS                                     *
*                                                                     *
*---------------------------------------------------------------------*
* CHANGE HISTORY                                                      *
*   090785 NEW PROGRAM                                            GRR *
***********************************************************************

 DATA DIVISION.

 WORKING-STORAGE SECTION.

 77  VERSION-NUMBER                  PICTURE X(27) VALUE
     "VERSION 1     SEPT. 7, 1985".

 LINKAGE SECTION.

 COPY DCL25.
 77  CURRENT-SEQUENTIAL-KEY-1        PICTURE X(11).              COPY

 COPY DCL30.
 77  KEY-OF-LAST-CUSTOMER-RECORD     PICTURE X(5).               COPY

 COPY DCL22.
 77  NUMBER-OF-OUTPUT-MASTERS        PICTURE S9(7).              COPY

 COPY DCL15.
 01  INPUT-TRANSACTION.                                          COPY
     02  TRANSACTION-KEY.                                        COPY
         03  CUSTOMER-NUMBER         PICTURE X(5).               COPY
         03  RECORD-TYPE             PICTURE X.                  COPY
         03  SECURITY-NUMBER         PICTURE X(5).               COPY
     02  TRADE-CODE                  PICTURE X.                  COPY
     02  SECURITY-NAME               PICTURE X(20).              COPY
     02  QUANTITY                    PICTURE 9(9).               COPY
     02  FILLER                      PICTURE X.                  COPY

 COPY DCL16.
 01  MASTER-DATA.                                                COPY
     02  MASTER-KEY.                                             COPY
         03  CUSTOMER-NUMBER         PICTURE X(5).               COPY
         03  RECORD-TYPE             PICTURE X.                  COPY
         03  SECURITY-NUMBER         PICTURE X(5).               COPY
     02  CUSTOMER-DATA.                                          COPY
         03  CUSTOMER-NAME           PICTURE X(20).              COPY
         03  CUSTOMER-ADDRESS        PICTURE X(20).              COPY
         03  SALESMAN-NAME           PICTURE X(10).              COPY
     02  SECURITY-DATA  REDEFINES  CUSTOMER-DATA.                COPY
         03  SECURITY-NAME           PICTURE X(30).              COPY
         03  NUMBER-OF-SHARES-HELD   PICTURE S9(15).             COPY
         03  FILLER                  PICTURE X(5).               COPY
     02  FILLER                      PICTURE X.                  COPY

 COPY DCL24.
 01  OUTPUT-SECURITY-DATA.                                       COPY
     02  OUTPUT-SECURITY-KEY.                                    COPY
         03  CUSTOMER-NUMBER         PICTURE X(5).               COPY
         03  RECORD-TYPE             PICTURE X.                  COPY
         03  SECURITY-NUMBER         PICTURE X(5).               COPY
     02  SECURITY-NAME               PICTURE X(30).              COPY
     02  NUMBER-OF-SHARES-HELD       PICTURE S9(15).             COPY
     02  FILLER                      PICTURE X(5).               COPY
     02  FILLER                      PICTURE X.                  COPY

***********************************************************************
```

(a)

Figure 14.21. *Keys equal module in COBOL.*

(continued on next page)

```
/*****************************************************************
 PROCEDURE DIVISION USING CURRENT-SEQUENTIAL-KEY-1,
                          KEY-OF-LAST-CUSTOMER-RECORD,
                          INPUT-TRANSACTION,
                          MASTER-DATA,
                          NUMBER-OF-OUTPUT-MASTERS,
                          OUTPUT-SECURITY-DATA.

     IF OUTPUT-SECURITY-DATA = SPACES OR
        NUMBER-OF-SHARES-HELD IN OUTPUT-SECURITY-DATA = 0
       THEN
         CONTINUE
       ELSE
         CALL "BRWRT" USING OUTPUT-SECURITY-DATA,
                            NUMBER-OF-OUTPUT-MASTERS
     END-IF.

     MOVE MASTER-DATA TO OUTPUT-SECURITY-DATA.

     IF KEY-OF-LAST-CUSTOMER-RECORD NOT = CUSTOMER-NUMBER
        IN INPUT-TRANSACTION
       THEN
         CALL "BRPRT" USING INPUT-TRANSACTION
         EXIT PROGRAM
     END-IF.

     IF TRADE-CODE = "B"
       THEN
         ADD QUANTITY TO NUMBER-OF-SHARES-HELD IN
             OUTPUT-SECURITY-DATA
       ELSE
         SUBTRACT QUANTITY FROM NUMBER-OF-SHARES-HELD IN
             OUTPUT-SECURITY-DATA
     END-IF.

 END PROGRAM BRKEQ.
******************************************************************
```

(b)

Figure 14.21. *(Continued)*

```
/*****************************************************************
 IDENTIFICATION DIVISION.

 PROGRAM-ID.         BRINIT.

 AUTHOR.             G.R. ROGERS.

*****************************************************************
*                                                               *
* BROKERAGE TRADES UPDATE PROGRAM                               *
* MODULE - INITIALIZATION                                       *
*                                                               *
*---------------------------------------------------------------*
* CHANGE HISTORY                                                *
*   090785 NEW PROGRAM                                      GRR *
*****************************************************************

 ENVIRONMENT DIVISION.

 INPUT-OUTPUT SECTION.

 FILE-CONTROL.

 COPY DCL58.
     SELECT INPUT-FILE ASSIGN TO DISK-INFILE.                      COPY
 COPY DCL60.
     SELECT INPUT-MASTER-FILE ASSIGN TO DISK-INMAST.               COPY
 COPY DCL13.
     SELECT PRINT-FILE ASSIGN TO PRINTER-PRFILE.                   COPY
 COPY DCL62.
     SELECT OUTPUT-MASTER-FILE ASSIGN TO DISK-OUMAST.              COPY

 DATA DIVISION.

 FILE SECTION.

 COPY DCL59.
 FD  INPUT-FILE EXTERNAL                                           COPY
     BLOCK CONTAINS 10 RECORDS                                     COPY
     LABEL RECORDS ARE STANDARD.                                   COPY

 COPY DCL15.
 01  INPUT-TRANSACTION.                                            COPY
     02  TRANSACTION-KEY.                                          COPY
         03  CUSTOMER-NUMBER           PICTURE X(5).               COPY
         03  RECORD-TYPE               PICTURE X.                  COPY
         03  SECURITY-NUMBER           PICTURE X(5).               COPY
     02  TRADE-CODE                    PICTURE X.                  COPY
     02  SECURITY-NAME                 PICTURE X(20).              COPY
     02  QUANTITY                      PICTURE 9(9).               COPY
     02  FILLER                        PICTURE X.                  COPY

 COPY DCL61.
 FD  INPUT-MASTER-FILE EXTERNAL                                    COPY
     BLOCK CONTAINS 10 RECORDS                                     COPY
     LABEL RECORDS ARE STANDARD.                                   COPY

 COPY DCL16.
 01  MASTER-DATA.                                                  COPY
     02  MASTER-KEY.                                               COPY
         03  CUSTOMER-NUMBER           PICTURE X(5).               COPY
         03  RECORD-TYPE               PICTURE X.                  COPY
         03  SECURITY-NUMBER           PICTURE X(5).               COPY
     02  CUSTOMER-DATA.                                            COPY
         03  CUSTOMER-NAME             PICTURE X(20).              COPY
         03  CUSTOMER-ADDRESS          PICTURE X(20).              COPY
         03  SALESMAN-NAME             PICTURE X(10).              COPY
     02  SECURITY-DATA  REDEFINES   CUSTOMER-DATA.                 COPY
         03  SECURITY-NAME             PICTURE X(30).              COPY
         03  NUMBER-OF-SHARES-HELD     PICTURE S9(15).             COPY
         03  FILLER                    PICTURE X(5).               COPY
     02  FILLER                        PICTURE X.                  COPY

 COPY DCL04.
 FD  PRINT-FILE EXTERNAL                                           COPY
     LABEL RECORDS ARE OMITTED.                                    COPY

 COPY DCL02.
 01  PRINT-RECORD                      PICTURE X(132).             COPY
```

(a)

Figure 14.22. *Initialization module in COBOL.*

(continued on next page)

```
COPY DCL63.
FD  OUTPUT-MASTER-FILE EXTERNAL                                    COPY
    BLOCK CONTAINS 10 RECORDS                                      COPY
    LABEL RECORDS ARE STANDARD.                                    COPY

COPY DCL16.
01  MASTER-DATA.                                                   COPY
    02  MASTER-KEY.                                                COPY
        03  CUSTOMER-NUMBER          PICTURE X(5).                 COPY
        03  RECORD-TYPE              PICTURE X.                    COPY
        03  SECURITY-NUMBER          PICTURE X(5).                 COPY
    02  CUSTOMER-DATA.                                             COPY
        03  CUSTOMER-NAME            PICTURE X(20).                COPY
        03  CUSTOMER-ADDRESS         PICTURE X(20).                COPY
        03  SALESMAN-NAME            PICTURE X(10).                COPY
    02  SECURITY-DATA  REDEFINES  CUSTOMER-DATA.                   COPY
        03  SECURITY-NAME            PICTURE X(30).                COPY
        03  NUMBER-OF-SHARES-HELD    PICTURE S9(15).               COPY
        03  FILLER                   PICTURE X(5).                 COPY
    02  FILLER                       PICTURE X.                    COPY

WORKING-STORAGE SECTION.

77  VERSION-NUMBER                   PICTURE X(27) VALUE
    "VERSION 1      SEPT. 7, 1985".

LINKAGE SECTION.

COPY DCL19.
77  DATA-STREAM-1-STATUS             PICTURE X(10).                COPY

COPY DCL20.
77  DATA-STREAM-2-STATUS             PICTURE X(10).                COPY

COPY DCL30.
77  KEY-OF-LAST-CUSTOMER-RECORD      PICTURE X(5).                 COPY

COPY DCL23.
77  NUMBER-OF-INPUT-TRANSACTIONS     PICTURE S9(7).                COPY

COPY DCL21.
77  NUMBER-OF-INPUT-MASTERS          PICTURE S9(7).                COPY

COPY DCL22.
77  NUMBER-OF-OUTPUT-MASTERS         PICTURE S9(7).                COPY

COPY DCL24.
01  OUTPUT-SECURITY-DATA.                                          COPY
    02  OUTPUT-SECURITY-KEY.                                       COPY
        03  CUSTOMER-NUMBER          PICTURE X(5).                 COPY
        03  RECORD-TYPE              PICTURE X.                    COPY
        03  SECURITY-NUMBER          PICTURE X(5).                 COPY
    02  SECURITY-NAME                PICTURE X(30).                COPY
    02  NUMBER-OF-SHARES-HELD        PICTURE S9(15).               COPY
    02  FILLER                       PICTURE X(5).                 COPY
    02  FILLER                       PICTURE X.                    COPY
*****************************************************************

/****************************************************************

 PROCEDURE DIVISION USING DATA-STREAM-1-STATUS,
                          DATA-STREAM-2-STATUS,
                          KEY-OF-LAST-CUSTOMER-RECORD,
                          NUMBER-OF-INPUT-TRANSACTIONS,
                          NUMBER-OF-INPUT-MASTERS,
                          NUMBER-OF-OUTPUT-MASTERS,
                          OUTPUT-SECURITY-DATA.

     MOVE "NOT AT END" TO DATA-STREAM-1-STATUS.
     MOVE "NOT AT END" TO DATA-STREAM-2-STATUS.
     MOVE 0 TO NUMBER-OF-INPUT-TRANSACTIONS.
     MOVE 0 TO NUMBER-OF-INPUT-MASTERS.
     MOVE 0 TO NUMBER-OF-OUTPUT-MASTERS.
     MOVE SPACES TO KEY-OF-LAST-CUSTOMER-RECORD.
     MOVE SPACES TO OUTPUT-SECURITY-DATA.
     OPEN INPUT INPUT-FILE
                INPUT-MASTER-FILE
          OUTPUT PRINT-FILE
                 OUTPUT-MASTER-FILE.

 END PROGRAM BRINIT.

*****************************************************************
```

(b)

Figure 14.22. *(Continued)*

```
/***************************************************************
 IDENTIFICATION DIVISION.
 PROGRAM-ID.        BRRD1.
 AUTHOR.            G.R. ROGERS.
**************************************************************
*                                                            *
* BROKERAGE TRADES UPDATE PROGRAM                            *
* MODULE - READ INPUT TRADES TRANSACTION FILE                *
*                                                            *
*------------------------------------------------------------*
* CHANGE HISTORY                                             *
*   090785 NEW PROGRAM                                   GRR *
**************************************************************
 ENVIRONMENT DIVISION.
 INPUT-OUTPUT SECTION.
 FILE-CONTROL.
 COPY DCL58.
     SELECT INPUT-FILE ASSIGN TO DISK-INFILE.                     COPY
 DATA DIVISION.
 FILE SECTION.
 COPY DCL59.
 FD  INPUT-FILE EXTERNAL                                          COPY
     BLOCK CONTAINS 10 RECORDS                                    COPY
     LABEL RECORDS ARE STANDARD.                                  COPY
 COPY DCL15.
 01  INPUT-TRANSACTION.                                           COPY
     02  TRANSACTION-KEY.                                         COPY
         03  CUSTOMER-NUMBER            PICTURE X(5).             COPY
         03  RECORD-TYPE                PICTURE X.                COPY
         03  SECURITY-NUMBER            PICTURE X(5).             COPY
     02  TRADE-CODE                     PICTURE X.                COPY
     02  SECURITY-NAME                  PICTURE X(20).            COPY
     02  QUANTITY                       PICTURE 9(9).             COPY
     02  FILLER                         PICTURE X.                COPY
 WORKING-STORAGE SECTION.
 77  VERSION-NUMBER                     PICTURE X(27) VALUE
     "VERSION 1      SEPT. 7, 1985".
 COPY DCL11.
 77  FIRST-TIME-IN-MODULE               PICTURE XXX VALUE "YES".  COPY
 LINKAGE SECTION.
 COPY DCL19.
 77  DATA-STREAM-1-STATUS               PICTURE X(10).            COPY
 COPY DCL23.
 77  NUMBER-OF-INPUT-TRANSACTIONS       PICTURE S9(7).            COPY
 COPY DCL25.
 77  CURRENT-SEQUENTIAL-KEY-1           PICTURE X(11).            COPY
 COPY DCL26.
 77  PREVIOUS-SEQUENTIAL-KEY-1          PICTURE X(11).            COPY
 01  LINKAGE-INPUT-TRANSACTION          PICTURE X(42).
***************************************************************
```

(a)

Figure 14.23. *Read transaction module in COBOL.*

(*continued on next page*)

```
/*****************************************************************

 PROCEDURE DIVISION USING DATA-STREAM-1-STATUS,
                          CURRENT-SEQUENTIAL-KEY-1,
                          PREVIOUS-SEQUENTIAL-KEY-1,
                          NUMBER-OF-INPUT-TRANSACTIONS,
                          LINKAGE-INPUT-TRANSACTION.

     IF DATA-STREAM-1-STATUS = "AT END"
       THEN
         DISPLAY "PROGRAM READING PAST DATA END"
         STOP RUN
     END-IF.

     MOVE CURRENT-SEQUENTIAL-KEY-1 TO PREVIOUS-SEQUENTIAL-KEY-1.

     READ INPUT-FILE RECORD
        AT END
          MOVE "AT END" TO DATA-STREAM-1-STATUS
          EXIT PROGRAM
     END-READ.

     MOVE INPUT-TRANSACTION TO LINKAGE-INPUT-TRANSACTION.
     ADD 1 TO NUMBER-OF-INPUT-TRANSACTIONS.
     MOVE TRANSACTION-KEY TO CURRENT-SEQUENTIAL-KEY-1.

     IF FIRST-TIME-IN-MODULE = "YES"
       THEN
         MOVE "NO " TO FIRST-TIME-IN-MODULE
         MOVE LOW-VALUES TO PREVIOUS-SEQUENTIAL-KEY-1
         EXIT PROGRAM
     END-IF.

     IF CURRENT-SEQUENTIAL-KEY-1 LESS THAN
        PREVIOUS-SEQUENTIAL-KEY-1
       THEN
         DISPLAY "BROKERAGE UPDATE PROGRAM ENDED ABNORMALLY"
         DISPLAY "TRANSACTION FILE OUT OF SEQUENCE"
         DISPLAY "CURRENT KEY = ", CURRENT-SEQUENTIAL-KEY-1
         DISPLAY "PREVIOUS KEY = ", PREVIOUS-SEQUENTIAL-KEY-1
         DISPLAY "NUMBER OF INPUT TRANSACTIONS READ = ",
                 NUMBER-OF-INPUT-TRANSACTIONS
         STOP RUN
     END-IF.

 END PROGRAM BRRD1.

*****************************************************************
```

(b)

Figure 14.23. *(Continued)*

```
/*************************************************************

 IDENTIFICATION DIVISION.

 PROGRAM-ID.       BRRD2.

*************************************************************
*                                                           *
* BROKERAGE TRADES UPDATE PROGRAM                           *
* MODULE - READ INPUT MASTER FILE                           *
*                                                           *
*-----------------------------------------------------------*
* CHANGE HISTORY                                            *
*   090785 NEW PROGRAM                                  GRR *
*************************************************************

 AUTHOR.           G.R. ROGERS.

 ENVIRONMENT DIVISION.

 INPUT-OUTPUT SECTION.

 FILE-CONTROL.

 COPY DCL60.
     SELECT INPUT-MASTER-FILE ASSIGN TO DISK-INMAST.              COPY

 DATA DIVISION.

 FILE SECTION.

 COPY DCL61.
 FD  INPUT-MASTER-FILE EXTERNAL                                   COPY
     BLOCK CONTAINS 10 RECORDS                                    COPY
     LABEL RECORDS ARE STANDARD.                                  COPY

 COPY DCL16.
 01  MASTER-DATA.                                                 COPY
     02  MASTER-KEY.                                              COPY
         03  CUSTOMER-NUMBER           PICTURE X(5).              COPY
         03  RECORD-TYPE               PICTURE X.                 COPY
         03  SECURITY-NUMBER           PICTURE X(5).              COPY
     02  CUSTOMER-DATA.                                           COPY
         03  CUSTOMER-NAME             PICTURE X(20).             COPY
         03  CUSTOMER-ADDRESS          PICTURE X(20).             COPY
         03  SALESMAN-NAME             PICTURE X(10).             COPY
     02  SECURITY-DATA  REDEFINES  CUSTOMER-DATA.                 COPY
         03  SECURITY-NAME             PICTURE X(30).             COPY
         03  NUMBER-OF-SHARES-HELD     PICTURE S9(15).            COPY
         03  FILLER                    PICTURE X(5).              COPY
     02  FILLER                        PICTURE X.                 COPY

 WORKING-STORAGE SECTION.

 77  VERSION-NUMBER                    PICTURE X(27) VALUE
     "VERSION 1     SEPT. 7, 1985".

 COPY DCL11.
 77  FIRST-TIME-IN-MODULE              PICTURE XXX VALUE "YES".   COPY

 LINKAGE SECTION.

 COPY DCL20.
 77  DATA-STREAM-2-STATUS              PICTURE X(10).             COPY

 COPY DCL21.
 77  NUMBER-OF-INPUT-MASTERS           PICTURE S9(7).             COPY

 COPY DCL27.
 77  CURRENT-SEQUENTIAL-KEY-2          PICTURE X(11).             COPY

 COPY DCL28.
 77  PREVIOUS-SEQUENTIAL-KEY-2         PICTURE X(11).             COPY

 01  LINKAGE-MASTER-DATA               PICTURE X(62).

*************************************************************
```

(a)

Figure 14.24. Read master module in COBOL.

(*continued on next page*)

```
/*****************************************************************

 PROCEDURE DIVISION USING DATA-STREAM-2-STATUS,
                          CURRENT-SEQUENTIAL-KEY-2,
                          PREVIOUS-SEQUENTIAL-KEY-2,
                          NUMBER-OF-INPUT-MASTERS,
                          LINKAGE-MASTER-DATA.

     IF DATA-STREAM-2-STATUS = "AT END"
       THEN
         DISPLAY "PROGRAM READING PAST DATA END"
         STOP RUN
     END-IF.

     MOVE CURRENT-SEQUENTIAL-KEY-2 TO PREVIOUS-SEQUENTIAL-KEY-2.

     READ INPUT-MASTER-FILE RECORD
        AT END
          MOVE "AT END" TO DATA-STREAM-2-STATUS
          EXIT PROGRAM
     END-READ.

     MOVE MASTER-DATA TO LINKAGE-MASTER-DATA.
     ADD 1 TO NUMBER-OF-INPUT-MASTERS.
     MOVE MASTER-KEY TO CURRENT-SEQUENTIAL-KEY-2.

     IF FIRST-TIME-IN-MODULE = "YES"
       THEN
         MOVE "NO " TO FIRST-TIME-IN-MODULE
         MOVE LOW-VALUES TO PREVIOUS-SEQUENTIAL-KEY-2
         EXIT PROGRAM
     END-IF.

     IF CURRENT-SEQUENTIAL-KEY-2 NOT GREATER THAN
        PREVIOUS-SEQUENTIAL-KEY-2
       THEN
         DISPLAY "BROKERAGE UPDATE PROGRAM ENDED ABNORMALLY"
         DISPLAY "MASTER FILE OUT OF SEQUENCE"
         DISPLAY "CURRENT KEY = ", CURRENT-SEQUENTIAL-KEY-2
         DISPLAY "PREVIOUS KEY = ", PREVIOUS-SEQUENTIAL-KEY-2
         DISPLAY "NUMBER OF INPUT MASTERS READ = ",
                 NUMBER-OF-INPUT-MASTERS
         STOP RUN
     END-IF.

 END PROGRAM BRRD2.

*****************************************************************
```

(b)

Figure 14.24. *(Continued)*

```
/*************************************************************

 IDENTIFICATION DIVISION.

 PROGRAM-ID.       BRWRT.

*************************************************************
*                                                           *
* BROKERAGE TRADES UPDATE PROGRAM                           *
* MODULE - WRITE OUTPUT MASTER FILE                         *
*                                                           *
*-----------------------------------------------------------*
* CHANGE HISTORY                                            *
*   090785 NEW PROGRAM                                  GRR *
*************************************************************

 AUTHOR.           G.R. ROGERS.

 ENVIRONMENT DIVISION.

 INPUT-OUTPUT SECTION.

 FILE-CONTROL.

 COPY DCL62.
     SELECT OUTPUT-MASTER-FILE ASSIGN TO DISK-OUMAST.           COPY

 DATA DIVISION.

 FILE SECTION.

 COPY DCL63.
 FD  OUTPUT-MASTER-FILE EXTERNAL                                COPY
     BLOCK CONTAINS 10 RECORDS                                  COPY
     LABEL RECORDS ARE STANDARD.                                COPY

 COPY DCL16.
 01  MASTER-DATA.                                               COPY
     02  MASTER-KEY.                                            COPY
         03  CUSTOMER-NUMBER         PICTURE X(5).              COPY
         03  RECORD-TYPE             PICTURE X.                 COPY
         03  SECURITY-NUMBER         PICTURE X(5).              COPY
     02  CUSTOMER-DATA.                                         COPY
         03  CUSTOMER-NAME           PICTURE X(20).             COPY
         03  CUSTOMER-ADDRESS        PICTURE X(20).             COPY
         03  SALESMAN-NAME           PICTURE X(10).             COPY
     02  SECURITY-DATA  REDEFINES  CUSTOMER-DATA.               COPY
         03  SECURITY-NAME           PICTURE X(30).             COPY
         03  NUMBER-OF-SHARES-HELD   PICTURE S9(15).            COPY
         03  FILLER                  PICTURE X(5).              COPY
     02  FILLER                      PICTURE X.                 COPY

 WORKING-STORAGE SECTION.

 77  VERSION-NUMBER                  PICTURE X(27) VALUE
     "VERSION 1     SEPT. 7, 1985".

 LINKAGE SECTION.

 COPY DCL22.
 77  NUMBER-OF-OUTPUT-MASTERS        PICTURE S9(7).             COPY

 01  LINKAGE-MASTER-DATA             PICTURE X(62).

**************************************************************

/*************************************************************

 PROCEDURE DIVISION USING LINKAGE-MASTER-DATA,
                          NUMBER-OF-OUTPUT-MASTERS.

     WRITE MASTER-DATA FROM LINKAGE-MASTER-DATA.
     ADD 1 TO NUMBER-OF-OUTPUT-MASTERS.

 END PROGRAM BRWRT.

**************************************************************
```

Figure 14.25. *Write output module in COBOL.*

```
/*****************************************************************
 IDENTIFICATION DIVISION.

 PROGRAM-ID.        BRPRT.

 AUTHOR.            G.R. ROGERS.

****************************************************************
*                                                              *
* BROKERAGE TRADES UPDATE PROGRAM                              *
* MODULE - PRINT ERROR REPORT                                  *
*                                                              *
*--------------------------------------------------------------*
* CHANGE HISTORY                                               *
*   090785 NEW PROGRAM                                     GRR *
****************************************************************

 ENVIRONMENT DIVISION.

 INPUT-OUTPUT SECTION.

 FILE-CONTROL.

 COPY DCL13.
     SELECT PRINT-FILE ASSIGN TO PRINTER-PRFILE.                COPY

 DATA DIVISION.

 FILE SECTION.

 COPY DCL04.
 FD  PRINT-FILE EXTERNAL                                         COPY
     LABEL RECORDS ARE OMITTED.                                  COPY

 COPY DCL02.
 01  PRINT-RECORD                    PICTURE X(132).             COPY

 WORKING-STORAGE SECTION.

 77  VERSION-NUMBER                  PICTURE X(27) VALUE
     "VERSION 1     SEPT. 7, 1985".

 01  HEADING-LINE-1.
     02  FILLER                      PICTURE X(42) VALUE
     "                        UPDATE ERROR REPORT".
     02  FILLER                      PICTURE X(82) VALUE SPACES.
     02  FILLER                      PICTURE X(5) VALUE "PAGE ".
     02  HEADING-PAGE-NUMBER         PICTURE ZZ9.

 01  HEADING-LINE-2.
     02  FILLER                      PICTURE X(50) VALUE
     "CUSTOMER NUMBER          SECURITY NUMBER         ".
     02  FILLER                      PICTURE X(13) VALUE
     "SECURITY NAME".
     02  FILLER                      PICTURE X(69) VALUE SPACES.

 01  HEADING-LINE-3.
     02  FILLER                      PICTURE X(50) VALUE
     "---------------          ---------------         ".
     02  FILLER                      PICTURE X(13) VALUE
     "-------------".
     02  FILLER                      PICTURE X(69) VALUE SPACES.

 01  DETAIL-LINE.
     02  FILLER                      PICTURE X(5) VALUE SPACES.
     02  DETAIL-CUSTOMER-NUMBER      PICTURE X(5).
     02  FILLER                      PICTURE X(20) VALUE SPACES.
     02  DETAIL-SECURITY-NUMBER      PICTURE X(4).
     02  FILLER                      PICTURE X(16) VALUE SPACES.
     02  DETAIL-SECURITY-NAME        PICTURE X(20).
     02  FILLER                      PICTURE X(62) VALUE SPACES.

 77  PAGE-NUMBER                     PICTURE S9(3) VALUE 0.

 77  LINE-NUMBER                     PICTURE S9(3) VALUE 999.

 77  PAGE-SIZE                       PICTURE S9(3) VALUE 50.

 LINKAGE SECTION.

 COPY DCL15.
 01  INPUT-TRANSACTION.                                          COPY
     02  TRANSACTION-KEY.                                        COPY
         03  CUSTOMER-NUMBER         PICTURE X(5).               COPY
         03  RECORD-TYPE             PICTURE X.                  COPY
         03  SECURITY-NUMBER         PICTURE X(5).               COPY
     02  TRADE-CODE                  PICTURE X.                  COPY
     02  SECURITY-NAME               PICTURE X(20).              COPY
     02  QUANTITY                    PICTURE 9(9).               COPY
     02  FILLER                      PICTURE X.                  COPY

*****************************************************************
```

(a)

Figure 14.26. *Print error report module in COBOL.*

```
/*****************************************************************

 PROCEDURE DIVISION USING INPUT-TRANSACTION.

     IF LINE-NUMBER GREATER THAN PAGE-SIZE
       THEN
         ADD 1 TO PAGE-NUMBER
         MOVE 0 TO LINE-NUMBER
         MOVE PAGE-NUMBER TO HEADING-PAGE-NUMBER
         WRITE PRINT-RECORD FROM HEADING-LINE-1
            AFTER ADVANCING PAGE
         WRITE PRINT-RECORD FROM HEADING-LINE-2
            AFTER ADVANCING 2 LINES
         WRITE PRINT-RECORD FROM HEADING-LINE-3
            AFTER ADVANCING 2 LINES
     END-IF.

     MOVE CUSTOMER-NUMBER TO DETAIL-CUSTOMER-NUMBER.
     MOVE SECURITY-NUMBER TO DETAIL-SECURITY-NUMBER.
     MOVE SECURITY-NAME TO DETAIL-SECURITY-NAME.
     WRITE PRINT-RECORD FROM DETAIL-LINE
        AFTER ADVANCING 2 LINES.
     ADD 1 TO LINE-NUMBER.

 END PROGRAM BRPRT.

******************************************************************
```

(b)

```
/***************************************************************
 IDENTIFICATION DIVISION.

 PROGRAM-ID.        BREOJ.

 AUTHOR.            G.R. ROGERS.

**************************************************************
*                                                            *
* BROKERAGE TRADES UPDATE PROGRAM                            *
* MODULE - END OF JOB                                        *
*                                                            *
*------------------------------------------------------------*
* CHANGE HISTORY                                             *
*   090785 NEW PROGRAM                                  GRR  *
**************************************************************

 ENVIRONMENT DIVISION.

 INPUT-OUTPUT SECTION.

 FILE-CONTROL.

 COPY DCL58.
     SELECT INPUT-FILE ASSIGN TO DISK-INFILE.                    COPY
 COPY DCL60.
     SELECT INPUT-MASTER-FILE ASSIGN TO DISK-INMAST.             COPY
 COPY DCL13.
     SELECT PRINT-FILE ASSIGN TO PRINTER-PRFILE.                 COPY
 COPY DCL62.
     SELECT OUTPUT-MASTER-FILE ASSIGN TO DISK-OUMAST.            COPY

 DATA DIVISION.

 FILE SECTION.

 COPY DCL59.
 FD  INPUT-FILE EXTERNAL                                         COPY
     BLOCK CONTAINS 10 RECORDS                                   COPY
     LABEL RECORDS ARE STANDARD.                                 COPY

 COPY DCL15.
 01  INPUT-TRANSACTION.                                          COPY
     02  TRANSACTION-KEY.                                        COPY
         03  CUSTOMER-NUMBER         PICTURE X(5).               COPY
         03  RECORD-TYPE             PICTURE X.                  COPY
         03  SECURITY-NUMBER         PICTURE X(5).               COPY
     02  TRADE-CODE                  PICTURE X.                  COPY
     02  SECURITY-NAME               PICTURE X(20).              COPY
     02  QUANTITY                    PICTURE 9(9).               COPY
     02  FILLER                      PICTURE X.                  COPY

 COPY DCL61.
 FD  INPUT-MASTER-FILE EXTERNAL                                  COPY
     BLOCK CONTAINS 10 RECORDS                                   COPY
     LABEL RECORDS ARE STANDARD.                                 COPY

 COPY DCL16.
 01  MASTER-DATA.                                                COPY
     02  MASTER-KEY.                                             COPY
         03  CUSTOMER-NUMBER         PICTURE X(5).               COPY
         03  RECORD-TYPE             PICTURE X.                  COPY
         03  SECURITY-NUMBER         PICTURE X(5).               COPY
     02  CUSTOMER-DATA.                                          COPY
         03  CUSTOMER-NAME           PICTURE X(20).              COPY
         03  CUSTOMER-ADDRESS        PICTURE X(20).              COPY
         03  SALESMAN-NAME           PICTURE X(10).              COPY
     02  SECURITY-DATA  REDEFINES  CUSTOMER-DATA.                COPY
         03  SECURITY-NAME           PICTURE X(30).              COPY
         03  NUMBER-OF-SHARES-HELD   PICTURE S9(15).             COPY
         03  FILLER                  PICTURE X(5).               COPY
     02  FILLER                      PICTURE X.                  COPY

 COPY DCL04.
 FD  PRINT-FILE EXTERNAL                                         COPY
     LABEL RECORDS ARE OMITTED.                                  COPY

 COPY DCL02.
 01  PRINT-RECORD                    PICTURE X(132).             COPY
```

(a)

Figure 14.27. *End of job module in COBOL.*

```
COPY DCL63.
FD  OUTPUT-MASTER-FILE EXTERNAL                                          COPY
    BLOCK CONTAINS 10 RECORDS                                            COPY
    LABEL RECORDS ARE STANDARD.                                          COPY

COPY DCL16.
01  MASTER-DATA.                                                         COPY
    02  MASTER-KEY.                                                      COPY
        03  CUSTOMER-NUMBER           PICTURE X(5).                      COPY
        03  RECORD-TYPE               PICTURE X.                         COPY
        03  SECURITY-NUMBER           PICTURE X(5).                      COPY
    02  CUSTOMER-DATA.                                                   COPY
        03  CUSTOMER-NAME             PICTURE X(20).                     COPY
        03  CUSTOMER-ADDRESS          PICTURE X(20).                     COPY
        03  SALESMAN-NAME             PICTURE X(10).                     COPY
    02  SECURITY-DATA  REDEFINES   CUSTOMER-DATA.                        COPY
        03  SECURITY-NAME             PICTURE X(30).                     COPY
        03  NUMBER-OF-SHARES-HELD     PICTURE S9(15).                    COPY
        03  FILLER                    PICTURE X(5).                      COPY
    02  FILLER                        PICTURE X.                         COPY

WORKING-STORAGE SECTION.

77  VERSION-NUMBER                    PICTURE X(27) VALUE
    "VERSION 1     SEPT. 7, 1985".

LINKAGE SECTION.

COPY DCL23.
77  NUMBER-OF-INPUT-TRANSACTIONS      PICTURE S9(7).                     COPY

COPY DCL21.
77  NUMBER-OF-INPUT-MASTERS           PICTURE S9(7).                     COPY

COPY DCL22.
77  NUMBER-OF-OUTPUT-MASTERS          PICTURE S9(7).                     COPY

COPY DCL24.
01  OUTPUT-SECURITY-DATA.                                                COPY
    02  OUTPUT-SECURITY-KEY.                                             COPY
        03  CUSTOMER-NUMBER           PICTURE X(5).                      COPY
        03  RECORD-TYPE               PICTURE X.                         COPY
        03  SECURITY-NUMBER           PICTURE X(5).                      COPY
    02  SECURITY-NAME                 PICTURE X(30).                     COPY
    02  NUMBER-OF-SHARES-HELD         PICTURE S9(15).                    COPY
    02  FILLER                        PICTURE X(5).                      COPY
    02  FILLER                        PICTURE X.                         COPY

*****************************************************************

/****************************************************************

PROCEDURE DIVISION USING NUMBER-OF-INPUT-TRANSACTIONS,
                         NUMBER-OF-INPUT-MASTERS,
                         OUTPUT-SECURITY-DATA,
                         NUMBER-OF-OUTPUT-MASTERS.

    IF OUTPUT-SECURITY-DATA = SPACES OR
       NUMBER-OF-SHARES-HELD IN OUTPUT-SECURITY-DATA = 0
      THEN
        CONTINUE
      ELSE
        CALL "BRWRT" USING OUTPUT-SECURITY-DATA,
                           NUMBER-OF-OUTPUT-MASTERS
    END-IF.

    DISPLAY "BROKERAGE UPDATE PROGRAM ENDED NORMALLY".
    DISPLAY "NUMBER OF INPUT TRANSACTIONS READ = ",
            NUMBER-OF-INPUT-TRANSACTIONS.
    DISPLAY "NUMBER OF INPUT MASTERS READ      = ",
            NUMBER-OF-INPUT-MASTERS.
    DISPLAY "NUMBER OF OUTPUT MASTERS WRITTEN  = ",
            NUMBER-OF-OUTPUT-MASTERS.
    CLOSE INPUT-FILE
          INPUT-MASTER-FILE
          PRINT-FILE
          OUTPUT-MASTER-FILE.

END PROGRAM BREOJ.

*****************************************************************
```

(b)

15 Example Single Panel Interactive Program

PROBLEM DEFINITION

An interactive credit authorization program is to be designed for a chain of stores. The program will be run by a single operator at head office on a small business computer.

Sales personnel in the different stores telephone the operator for credit purchase authorizations. They give merchant number (to identify the store in the chain), credit card number, and amount or value of purchase. The operator enters the data and the program responds with an authorization number, or a message showing one of: invalid merchant number, outdated card, stolen card, or ineligible for credit.

The program uses four master files.

1. an indexed credit master with fields: credit card number (numeric key field), holder name and address, and credit status (G—GOOD, S—stolen, O—outdated, I—neligible)
2. an indexed merchant master with fields: merchant number (numeric key field), merchant name and address
3. running authorization number incremented by one for each authorized purchase

4. sequential activity log, for recovery and auditing purposes, with fields: card number, holder name and address, merchant number, merchant name, amount of purchase, authorization number, and credit status reply. A record is written to this log for each acknowledged input transaction

System security is provided via a key lock The format of the operator display is shown in Figure 15.1.

To end the program, the operator enters a nonblank character in the bottom right END field.

The small computer does not use a special software manager for the program and, therefore, the program will operate under the provided operating system. Usually, it is more practical to run in an environment that provides automatic file backup and recovery facilities for software, hardware, and power failures. However, this is a simple one-terminal setup and recovery can be obtained by reapplying the log records to the master file, as necessary. In Chapter 16, we will look at a complex environment requiring more sophisticated techniques.

The computer system comes with a formatting tool which enables a programmer to specify display formats. In the COBOL program, a call is made to this formatting tool to pass data that is displayed upon, and read from, the terminal device.

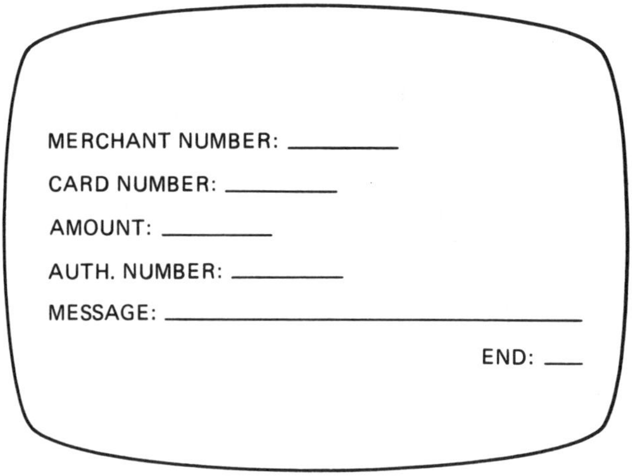

Figure 15.1. *Operator display.*

MODULE HIERARCHY

The problem definition has already stated that the program will not run under any special environment but, under the operating system provided. This means that the classical mainline module can be used for this problem. As with the previous warehouse print and brokerage trades update programs, the first design step is described with the module hierarchy chart of Figure 15.2.

Because the program is to support interactive data entry and there is only one type of display panel, the decision logic for the program is classified as single panel interactive. For reference, look at the classical logic of Figure 8.3 which shows that the single panel interactive module calls five lower level modules: get data and update data at the detail

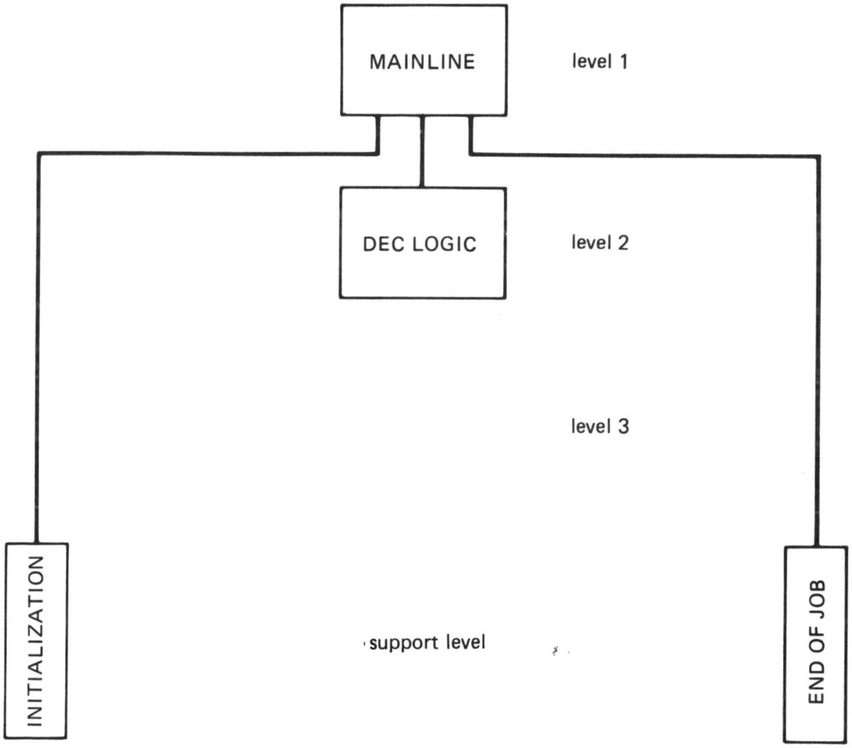

Figure 15.2. *First design step.*

processing level, and prompt, send data, and receive data utility modules at the support level in the hierarchy. This completes the second step of the module hierarchy design as pictured in Figure 15.3.

We now move to complete the module hierarchy design by showing the modules that are called by the two detail processing modules (get data and update data). Looking first at the get data module and the problem definition, consider that a number of the key fields and an amount field are numeric. Since it is not specified that the display formatter automatically right justifies these fields, a right justify function should be provided to simplify operator data entry. (Many systems

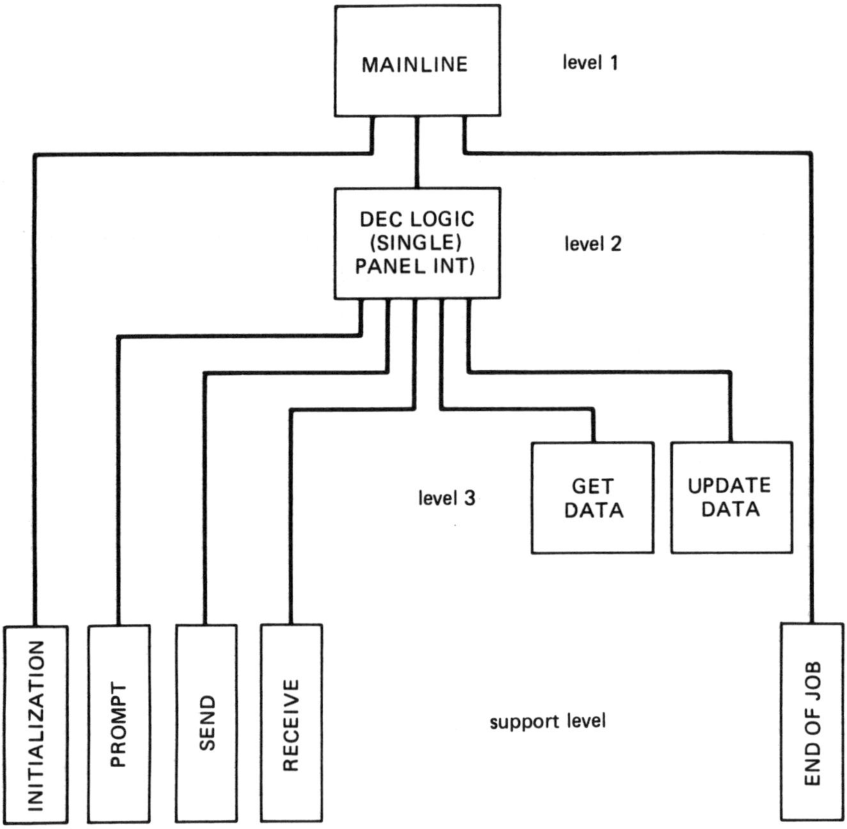

Figure 15.3. *Second design step.*

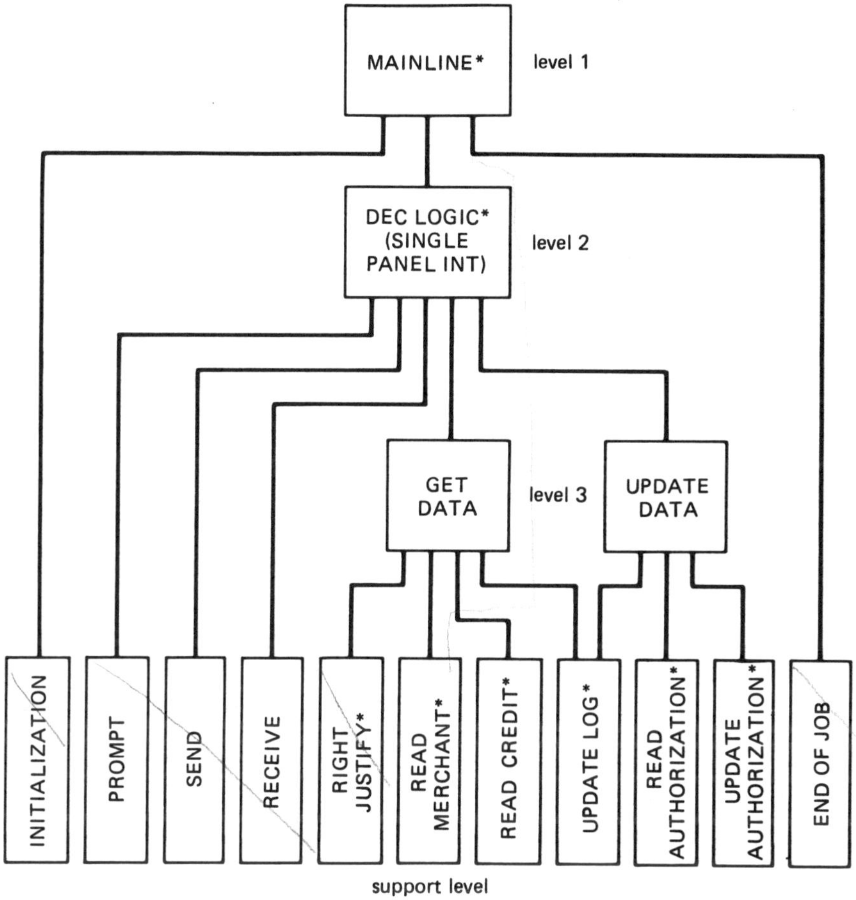

Figure 15.4. *Third design step.*

have display formatters that handle justification, field padding, and simple validation checks. If these functions are provided and do not detract from operator data entry performance, they should be used as they simplify the program logic.)

The get data module has to validate the data entered by the operator. This includes checking for valid merchant and credit card numbers; therefore, a read merchant master module and a read credit master module are called by the get data module.

Because credit authorization information is processed, a log is needed to report the status of both credit checks and credit authorizations. If a log was not kept, fraud losses due to unauthorized purchases could be substantial. In the program this requires an update log module to be invoked by the get data module.

Moving to the update data module, we analyze the specification to discover that a running authorization number must be provided and updated for each authorized credit transaction. This requires a read authorization master module and an update authorization master module to be called by the update data module.

Since it has been previously stated that all authorizations will be logged, the update log utility module will also be called by the update data module. This completes the third design step and the resulting module hierarchy chart as shown in Figure 15.4.

The chart can now be reviewed to see if it can be refined and any of the modules further subdivided. We look to Chapter 2 for guidance and find that no further subdivision can be accomplished.

DETAIL DESIGN

Begin the detail design by reviewing the module chart to identify those modules that can utilize classical functions for their operations. In Figure 15.4 they are each marked with an asterisk. The mainline, decision logic, right justify, read merchant master, read credit master, update log, read authorization data, and update authorization data are the modules identified.

Starting from the top of the module hierarchy, we adapt the classical mainline logic to this credit authorization problem. Because the program operates under the normal operating system, it is the type that *sees* the whole terminal session rather than just one transaction at a time. The iteration logic in the mainline operates until the end of program indicator is set to *yes* as a result of a nonblank value entered on the bottom right of the input data panel.

The only data that appears in this module is the end of program indicator that controls program iteration. The other adaption to this (and other modules in the program) is to give the module a name that conforms to the program naming convention. Figure 15.5 shows the mainline module design.

Next in the module hierarchy of the program is the decision logic. For it, we take the single panel interactive decision logic of Figure 8.3 and add the data for this program. The data is mainly the credit display data and associated key data elements identifying the current data that is being displayed.

Because we are updating the authorization number and log files, the update options of the classical function are chosen. We also dispense with the optional security profile check as there is only one terminal operator, and the terminal security is controlled via a key lock. The resulting design for the decision log appears in Figure 15.6.

```
*          CREDIT AUTHORIZATION—MAINLINE MODULE

     PROGRAM-ID. crmain <MAIN>.

        CALL "crinit" USING end of program.

        PERFORM WITH TEST BEFORE UNTIL end of program = "yes"
           CALL "crdec" USING end of program
        END-PERFORM.

        CALL "creoj".

     END PROGRAM crmain.
```

Figure 15.5. *Mainline module.*

```
*       CREDIT AUTHORIZATION—DECISION LOGIC MODULE

    PROGRAM-ID. crdec USING end of program.

        IF first time in module
            THEN
                reset first time indicator
                CALL "crprom" USING credit display data
                make current and previous display keys different
                CALL "crsend" USING credit display data
                EXIT PROGRAM
        END-IF.

        CALL "crrecv" USING credit display data.

        IF current display key not = previous display key
            THEN
                CALL "crgtda" USING end of program, credit display data
                move current display key to previous display key
                CALL "crsend" USING credit display data
                EXIT PROGRAM
        END-IF.

        CALL "crdaup" USING end of program, credit display data.
        move current display key to previous display key.
        CALL "crsend" USING credit display data.

    END PROGRAM crdec.
```

Figure 15.6. *Decision logic module.*

The next module to be designed is the get data module at the detail processing level of the program. This module has to be designed by the programmer as there is no classical logic to perform its functions.

Upon entry into this module, the logic first checks to see if the input end indicator is not blank. If it is not, the end of program data item is set to *yes,* and control exits from the module.

Note that a field called *force recheck* is included in the current and previous data display keys. The purpose of this data item is to ensure that data reentered at the terminal is rechecked for valid values. It is very easy at a display terminal to accidently depress the enter key when an error message has been displayed. At this point in the logic, the force recheck field is given a nonblank value to ensure that a recheck will occur if invalid data is simply reentered.

The amount field is also part of the display keys as a customer may use the credit card for purchases in different departments of one store.

The right justify module is called to justify the input merchant number. A nonblank returned message field indicates a problem with the merchant number. Such a case will cause control to leave the module.

After justification, the merchant number is tested for zero decimal places and numeric data. If these conditions are not met, an appropriate error message is set up, and control exits from the module.

The final check for merchant number is verification that the merchant record exists in the merchant master file. The read merchant master module (crrdmr) is called to handle the read function. The read module will return a nonblank error message if the record can not be found. This causes control to be given up.

Next, the right justify module is called again to justify the credit card number. Any encountered problems cause the returned message field to contain nonblank values and result in control leaving this module.

As with the merchant number, the credit card number is tested for zero decimal places and numeric data. If these conditions are not met, an invalid card number message is set up, and control exits from this module.

The last test of credit card number is validation that the associated credit record exists on the credit master file. The read credit master module (crrdcr) is called to enact this function and return the card holder's credit status. If the record does not exist, the returned error message will not be blank causing control to leave the get data module.

```
*                  CREDIT AUTHORIZATION—GET DATA MODULE

 PROGRAM-ID. crgtda USING end of program, credit display data.

    IF end indicator in credit display data not = spaces
       THEN
          move "yes" to end of program
          move "good bye" to message in credit display data
          EXIT PROGRAM
    END-IF.

    move "y" to force recheck.
    CALL "crrtjs" USING merchant number array,
                        justified merchant number array,
                        number of decimal places,
                        message in display data, 9, 9.

    IF message not = spaces
       THEN
          EXIT PROGRAM
    END-IF.

    IF number of decimal places not = 0 or
      justified merchant number array not numeric
       THEN
          move "invalid merchant number" to message
                in credit display data
          EXIT PROGRAM
    END-IF.

    put justified merchant number in credit display data.
    CALL "crrdmr" USING merchant master data,
                         message in display data.

    IF message in display data not = spaces
       THEN
          EXIT PROGRAM
    END-IF.

    CALL "crrtjs" USING card number array,
                        justified card number array,
                        number of decimal places,
                        message in display data, 9, 9.

    IF message not = spaces
       THEN
          EXIT PROGRAM
    END-IF.

    IF number of decimal places not = 0 or
      justified card number array not numeric
       THEN
          move "invalid card number" to message
                in credit display data
          EXIT PROGRAM
    END-IF.
```

Figure 15.7. *Get data module.*

```
put justified card number in credit display data.
CALL "crrdcr" USING credit master data,
                    message in credit display data.

IF message in credit display data not = spaces
   THEN
      EXIT PROGRAM
END-IF.

CALL "crrtjs" USING amount array,
                    justified amount array,
                    number of decimal places,
                    message in display data, 9, 9.

IF message not = spaces
   THEN
      EXIT PROGRAM
END-IF.

IF number of decimal places not = 2 or
  justified amount array not numeric
   THEN
      move "invalid amount" to message in credit display data
      EXIT PROGRAM
END-IF.

put justified amount in credit display data.

EVALUATE credit status in credit master data
   WHEN good
      move "status OK" to message in credit display data
      move spaces to force recheck
   WHEN stolen
      move "stolen card" to message in credit display data
   WHEN outdated
      move "outdated card" to message in credit display data
   WHEN ineligible
      move "ineligible" to message in credit display data
   WHEN OTHER
      move "system problem" to message in credit display data
END-EVALUATE.

set up activity log data.
CALL "cruplg" USING activity log data.

END PROGRAM crgtda.
```

The input purchase amount field is now validated. It must be numeric and have two decimal place. To start the validation, the right justify module (crrtjs) is called to provide a justified amount field. The justify module will return a nonblank message field if problems are encountered justifying the amount. Such a condition causes control to exit from the get data module.

The justified amount is checked to see that it has two decimal places and is numeric. If not, an invalid amount message is set up, and control leaves this module.

In all of the preceding checks, the justified validated data replaces the equivalent input fields. This reaffirms, for the person entering the data, that the data has been accepted.

After the input fields have been checked, the credit status field on the credit master record is examined to ensure that the card holder is entitled to credit. If the status is good, the message field shows *status OK*, and the force recheck field is blanked to allow the data to pass to the data update module. For other status conditions, the appropriate message is placed in the message field. If the status is not good, stolen, outdated, or ineligible, there is some type of system problem with the master file, and a programmer will have to investigate the cause (likely a data entry problem with the credit master file contents).

After the credit status has been determined, the results are logged via a call to the update log module (cruplg). This is necessary to track problems that may be associated with refusing credit. The design for the get data module is displayed in Figure 15.7.

The other detail processing module is the data update module. This must also be designed by the programmer as there is no classical function available.

In a manner similar to the get data module, this update data module first checks the input end indicator field. If it does not contain blanks, the end of program field is set to *yes*, and control exits from the module.

Next, the force recheck data element is given a nonblank value to ensure that subsequently entered data is validated by the get data module. Then, the read authorization module (crrdau) is called to get the authorization number. There is only one record in the authorization number file and it contains the running number that is returned to the sales personnel for valid credit conditions. If the attempted read of the authorization record is unsuccessful, the returned message field will show the problem, causing control to leave the module.

The authorization number is incremented by one and the authorization record is written back to the authorization file via module *crupau.*

At the end of the data update, the update log module (cruplg) is invoked to save the authorization number. The record written shows that the purchase was authorized and holds the last valid authorization number for program recovery purposes. The design language for the update data module is portrayed in Figure 15.8.

```
*        CREDIT AUTHORIZATION—DATA UPDATE MODULE

 PROGRAM-ID. crdaup USING end of ppogram, credit display data.

    IF end indicator in credit display data not = spaces
       THEN
          move "yes" to end of program
          move "good bye" to message in credit display data
          EXIT PROGRAM
    END-IF.

    move "y" to force recheck.
    move "001" to authorization key.
    CALL "crrdau" authorization data,
                  message in credit display data.

    IF message in credit display not = spaces
       THEN
          EXIT PROGRAM
    END-IF.

    add 1 to authorization number in authorization data.
    CALL "crupau" USING authorization data,
                        message in credit display data.

    set up activity log data.
    CALL "cruplg" USING activity log data.

 END PROGRAM crdaup.
```

Figure 15.8. *Data update module.*

We now move to the support level in the module hierarchy and design the initialization module.

The module must be designed by the programmer without reference to any classical functions. However, the design is very simple, requiring only the end of program indicator to be set to *no* and the files to be opened. This is seen in Figure 15.9.

The prompt module is next in sequence for design. It must also be designed by the programmer. For this application, it is straightforward, having only to blank the data display areas and set up the message to prompt the terminal operator for input data. Figure 15.10 shows this.

The receive data from the terminal module is designed by the programmer as it is specific to the particular computer environment. Figure 15.11 shows the logic. In our system, terminal input and output is accomplished with calls to the system module named *trans1*. The data is read from the terminal device, and the force recheck field in the current data display key is set to blanks. The message area is also blanked as a starting point for terminal transaction processing.

There is no classical function to support the module that sends transactions to the terminal. Because, a system operation handles terminal formatting, we simply have to write the data to the terminal as shown in Figure 15.12.

Now consider the file input and output utility modules. All can be adapted from the appropriate classical functions. The read authorization data is an adaptation of the direct read classical logic of Figure 9.4. Note that locking indicators are not required for any file access modules as only one user accesses the program at a time. The classical logic has the data for this program incorporated into it as portrayed in Figure 15.13.

The design for the read credit master module of Figure 15.14 also utilizes the classical logic of Figure 9.4. It is similarly adapted with data for this credit authorization application.

The read merchant master module is, likewise, an adaptation of the classical direct read function of Figure 9.4. The design appears in Figure 15.15.

For the update authorization master module designed in Figure 15.16, take the classical logic of Figure 9.7 and make it fit our programming problem. Here, also, record locking is not necessary due to the one-user-at-a-time environment.

```
*              CREDIT AUTHORIZATION—INITIALIZATION MODULE

  PROGRAM-ID. crinit USING end of program.

     move "no" to end of program.
     open the files.

  END PROGRAM crinit.
```

Figure 15.9. *Initialization module.*

```
*                 CREDIT AUTHORIZATION—PROMPT MODULE

  PROGRAM-ID. crprom USING credit display data.

     move spaces to credit display data.
     move "enter merchant number, card number, amount" to
          message in credit display data.

  END PROGRAM crprom.
```

Figure 15.10. *Prompt module.*

```
*           CREDIT AUTHORIZATION—RECEIVE TRANSACTION MODULE

  PROGRAM-ID. crrecv USING credit display data.

     read the display data from the terminal.
     move spaces to force recheck in credit display data.
     move spaces to message in credit display data.

  END PROGRAM crrecv.
```

Figure 5.11. *Receive transaction module.*

```
*         CREDIT AUTHORIZATION—SEND TRANSACTION MODULE

 PROGRAM-ID. crsend USING credit display data.

    write the display data to the terminal.

 END PROGRAM crsend.
```

Figure 15.12. *Send transaction module.*

```
*         CREDIT AUTHORIZATION—READ AUTH. DATA MODULE

 PROGRAM-ID. crrdau USING aurhorization data, message.

    set up parameters to read authorization record.
    read record with authorization key.

    IF record found
       THEN
          move spaces to message
          set up data fields from record
       ELSE
          move "can't get authorization record-call support"
              to message
    END-IF.

 END PROGRAM crrdau.
```

Figure 15.13. *Read authorization data module.*

```
*         CREDIT AUTHORIZATION—READ CREDIT MASTER MODULE

 PROGRAM-ID. crrdcr USING credit master data, message.

     set up parameters to access credit record.
     read record with card number key.

     IF record found
        THEN
           move spaces to message
           set up data fields from record
        ELSE
           move "credit master not found" to message
     END-IF.

 END PROGRAM crrdcr.
```

Figure 15.14. *Read credit master module.*

```
*       CREDIT AUTHORIZATION—READ MERCHANT MASTER MODULE

 PROGRAM-ID. crrdmr USING merchant master data, message.

     set up parameters to access merchant record.
     read record with merchant number key.

     IF record found
        THEN
           move spaces to message
           set up data fields from record
        ELSE
           move "merchant master record not found" to message
     END-IF.

 END PROGRAM crrdmr.
```

Figure 15.15. *Read merchant master module.*

```
*         CREDIT AUTHORIZATION—UPDATE AUTH. MASTER MODULE

 PROGRAM-ID. crupau USING authorization data, message.

    set up parameters to access authorization record.
    replace record.

    IF replace is successful
       THEN
          move "credit authorized-enter next transaction"
               to message
       ELSE
          move "can't get authorization record-call support"
               to message
    END-IF.

 END PROGRAM crupau.
```

Figure 15.16. *Update authorization master module.*

```
*              CREDIT AUTHORIZATION—UPDATE LOG MODULE

 PROGRAM-ID. cruplg USING activity log data.

    write activity log data.

 END PROGRAM cruplg.
```

Figure 15.17. *Update log module.*

The last file access module to be designed is the update log module. As this module sequentially writes the log records, we can utilize the sequential write classical logic of Figure 9.5 to arrive at the design portrayed in Figure 15.17.

The design for the right justify module of Figure 15.18 allows us to directly use the classical logic of Figure 9.9 without changing any data names. All we do is name the module *crrtjs* to conform to our program module naming convention.

The final module to be designed for this program is the end of job module. We must design this ourselves, rather than utilize classical logic. The module has no parameters; its only function is to close the files. The resulting design is that of Figure 15.19.

THE COBOL CODE

The program is coded in the COBOL programming language. The code appears in Figures 15.20 through 15.34. Once more, we see that the code is a direct image of the design as expressed in the design language.

Note that a number of messages appear in the various modules. If the program was a production program in your organization, you might consider having all messages for this program, and, possibly, others in the credit application, combined in a single module. The module would be called with message number as an input parameter. The module would then return the message contents. This could provide consistent numbering and easier maintenance of the messages. For this particular problem, we have elected to leave the messages in the modules where they are used.

```
*            CREDIT AUTHORIZATION—RIGHT JUSTIFY MODULE

 PROGRAM-ID. crrtjs USING input array,
                           output array,
                           number of decimal places, message,
                           number of input characters,
                           number of output characters.

    IF number of output characters less than
       number of input characters
       THEN
          move "output array too small" to message
          EXIT PROGRAM
    END-IF.

    move 0 to location of first nonblank character.
    set output data array to all zeros.
    move 0 to location of decimal point.
    move 0 to location of last blank after a character.
    move number of input characters to input array index.
    move number of output characters to output array index.

    PERFORM WITH TEST BEFORE UNTIL input array index less than 1

       EVALUATE input array (input array index)
          WHEN spaces

             IF location of first nonblank character not = 0
                THEN
                   move input array index to
                        location of last blank after a character
             END-IF

          WHEN "."

             IF location of decimal point not = 0
                THEN
                   move "multiple decimal points" to message
                   EXIT PROGRAM
             END-IF

             move output array index to location of decimal point
          WHEN OTHER
```

Figure 15.18. *Right justify module.*

```
            IF location of last blank after a character not = 0
               THEN
                  move "imbedded blanks" to message
                  move spaces to output array
                  EXIT PROGRAM
            END-IF

            IF location of first nonblank character = 0
               THEN
                  move input array index to
                        location of first nonblank character
            END-IF

            move input array (input array index) to
                  output array (output array index)
            subtract 1 from output array index
        END-EVALUATE

        subtract 1 from input array index
    END-PERFORM.

    IF location of decimal point = 0
        THEN
            move 0 to number of decimal places
        ELSE
            compute number of decimal places =
              location of first character
                - location of decimal place.
    END-IF.

    move spaces to message.

END PROGRAM crrtjs.
```

```
*              CREDIT AUTHORIZATION—END OF JOB MODULE

 PROGRAM-ID. creoj.

    close the files.

 END PROGRAM creoj.
```

Figure 15.19. *End of job module.*

```
/*****************************************************************
 IDENTIFICATION DIVISION.
 PROGRAM-ID.        CRMAIN.
 AUTHOR.            G.R. ROGERS.
*****************************************************************
*                                                               *
* CREDIT AUTHORIZATION PROGRAM                                  *
* MODULE - MAINLINE                                             *
*                                                               *
*---------------------------------------------------------------*
* CHANGE HISTORY                                                *
*    090785 NEW PROGRAM                                     GRR *
*****************************************************************
 DATA DIVISION.
 WORKING-STORAGE SECTION.
 77  VERSION-NUMBER                     PICTURE X(27) VALUE
     "VERSION 1      SEPT. 7, 1985".
 COPY DCL31.
 77  END-OF-PROGRAM                     PICTURE X(3).             COPY
*****************************************************************
/*****************************************************************
 PROCEDURE DIVISION.
     CALL "CRINIT" USING END-OF-PROGRAM.
     PERFORM WITH TEST BEFORE UNTIL END-OF-PROGRAM = "YES"
       CALL "CRDEC" USING END-OF-PROGRAM
     END-PERFORM.
     CALL "CREOJ".
     STOP RUN.
 END PROGRAM CRMAIN.
*****************************************************************
```

Figure 15.20. *Mainline module in COBOL.*

```
/*************************************************************

 IDENTIFICATION DIVISION.

 PROGRAM-ID.        CRDEC.

 AUTHOR.            G.R. ROGERS.

*************************************************************
*                                                           *
* CREDIT AUTHORIZATION PROGRAM                              *
* MODULE - DECISION LOGIC                                   *
*                                                           *
*-----------------------------------------------------------*
* CHANGE HISTORY                                            *
*   090785 NEW PROGRAM                                  GRR *
*************************************************************

 DATA DIVISION.

 WORKING-STORAGE SECTION.

 77  VERSION-NUMBER                   PICTURE X(27) VALUE
     "VERSION 1     SEPT. 7, 1985".

 COPY DCL11.
 77  FIRST-TIME-IN-MODULE             PICTURE XXX VALUE "YES".     COPY

 COPY DCL33.
 01  CREDIT-DISPLAY-DATA.                                          COPY
     02  CURRENT-DISPLAY-KEY.                                      COPY
         03  MERCHANT-NUMBER          PICTURE X(9).                COPY
         03  CARD-NUMBER              PICTURE X(9).                COPY
         03  AMOUNT                   PICTURE X(9).                COPY
         03  NUMERIC-AMOUNT REDEFINES AMOUNT                       COPY
                                      PICTURE 9(6).99.             COPY
         03  FORCE-RECHECK            PICTURE X.                   COPY
     02  ALIGNED-AMOUNT               PICTURE 9(6)V99.             COPY
     02  AUTHORIZATION-NUMBER         PICTURE X(9).                COPY
     02  MESSAGE                      PICTURE X(50).               COPY
     02  END-INDICATOR                PICTURE X.                   COPY
     02  FILLER                       PICTURE X.                   COPY

 COPY DCL44.
 01  PREVIOUS-DISPLAY-KEY.                                         COPY
     02  MERCHANT-NUMBER              PICTURE X(9).                COPY
     02  CARD-NUMBER                  PICTURE X(9).                COPY
     02  AMOUNT                       PICTURE X(9).                COPY
     02  FORCE-RECHECK                PICTURE X.                   COPY

 LINKAGE SECTION.

 COPY DCL31.
 77  END-OF-PROGRAM                   PICTURE X(3).                COPY

*************************************************************

/*************************************************************

 PROCEDURE DIVISION USING END-OF-PROGRAM.

     IF FIRST-TIME-IN-MODULE = "YES"
       THEN
         MOVE "NO " TO FIRST-TIME-IN-MODULE
         CALL "CRPROM" USING CREDIT-DISPLAY-DATA
         MOVE SPACES TO CURRENT-DISPLAY-KEY
         MOVE LOW-VALUES TO PREVIOUS-DISPLAY-KEY
         CALL "CRSEND" USING CREDIT-DISPLAY-DATA
         EXIT PROGRAM
     END-IF.

     CALL "CRRECV" USING CREDIT-DISPLAY-DATA.

     IF CURRENT-DISPLAY-KEY NOT = PREVIOUS-DISPLAY-KEY
       THEN
         CALL "CRGTDA" USING END-OF-PROGRAM, CREDIT-DISPLAY-DATA
         MOVE CURRENT-DISPLAY-KEY TO PREVIOUS-DISPLAY-KEY
         CALL "CRSEND" USING CREDIT-DISPLAY-DATA
         EXIT PROGRAM
     END-IF.

     CALL "CRDAUP" USING END-OF-PROGRAM, CREDIT-DISPLAY-DATA.
     MOVE CURRENT-DISPLAY-KEY TO PREVIOUS-DISPLAY-KEY.
     CALL "CRSEND" USING CREDIT-DISPLAY-DATA.

 END PROGRAM CRDEC.

*************************************************************
```

Figure 15.21. *Decision logic module in COBOL.*

```
/*****************************************************************
 IDENTIFICATION DIVISION.

 PROGRAM-ID.        CRGTDA.

 AUTHOR.            G.R. ROGERS.

*****************************************************************
*                                                               *
* CREDIT AUTHORIZATION PROGRAM                                  *
* MODULE - GET DATA                                             *
*                                                               *
*---------------------------------------------------------------*
* CHANGE HISTORY                                                *
*   090785 NEW PROGRAM                                      GRR *
*****************************************************************

 DATA DIVISION.

 WORKING-STORAGE SECTION.

 77  VERSION-NUMBER                   PICTURE X(27) VALUE
     "VERSION 1     SEPT. 7, 1985".

 77  GOOD-BYE-MESSAGE                 PICTURE X(8) VALUE
     "GOOD BYE".
 77  STATUS-OK-MESSAGE                PICTURE X(48) VALUE
     "STATUS IS OK - ENTER TO GET AUTHORIZATION NUMBER".
 77  STOLEN-MESSAGE                   PICTURE X(11) VALUE
     "STOLEN CARD".
 77  OUTDATED-MESSAGE                 PICTURE X(13) VALUE
     "OUTDATED CARD".
 77  INELIGIBLE-MESSAGE               PICTURE X(21) VALUE
     "INELIGIBLE FOR CREDIT".
 77  SYSTEM-PROBLEM-MESSAGE           PICTURE X(35) VALUE
     "SYSTEM PROBLEM - CALL ADMINISTRATOR".
 77  INVALID-MERCHANT-MESSAGE         PICTURE X(23) VALUE
     "INVALID MERCHANT NUMBER".
 77  INVALID-CARD-MESSAGE             PICTURE X(19) VALUE
     "INVALID CARD NUMBER".
 77  INVALID-AMOUNT-MESSAGE           PICTURE X(14) VALUE
     "INVALID AMOUNT".

 77  NINE                             PICTURE S99 VALUE 9.

 77  AMOUNT-1                         PICTURE X(9).
 77  AMOUNT-2 REDEFINES AMOUNT-1      PICTURE 9(7)V99.

 COPY DCL38.
 77  NUMBER-OF-DECIMAL-PLACES         PICTURE S99.              COPY

 COPY DCL35.
 01  INPUT-DATA-ARRAY.                                          COPY
     02  INPUT-ELEMENT                PICTURE X OCCURS 9 TIMES. COPY

 COPY DCL36.
 01  OUTPUT-DATA-ARRAY.                                         COPY
     02  OUTPUT-ELEMENT               PICTURE X OCCURS 9 TIMES. COPY

 COPY DCL34.
 01  CREDIT-MASTER-DATA.                                        COPY
     02  CREDIT-KEY.                                            COPY
         03  CARD-NUMBER              PICTURE X(9).             COPY
     02  HOLDER-NAME                  PICTURE X(30).            COPY
     02  HOLDER-ADDRESS               PICTURE X(30).            COPY
     02  CREDIT-STATUS                PICTURE X.                COPY
         88  GOOD                     VALUE "G".                COPY
         88  STOLEN                   VALUE "S".                COPY
         88  OUTDATED                 VALUE "O".                COPY
         88  INELIGIBLE               VALUE "I".                COPY
     02  FILLER                       PICTURE X.                COPY

 COPY DCL40.
 01  MERCHANT-MASTER-DATA.                                      COPY
     02  MERCHANT-KEY.                                          COPY
         03  MERCHANT-NUMBER          PICTURE X(9).             COPY
     02  MERCHANT-NAME                PICTURE X(30).            COPY
     02  MERCHANT-ADDRESS             PICTURE X(30).            COPY
     02  FILLER                       PICTURE X.                COPY

 COPY DCL42.
 01  ACTIVITY-LOG-DATA.                                         COPY
     02  AUTHORIZATION-NUMBER         PICTURE X(9).             COPY
     02  CARD-NUMBER                  PICTURE X(9).             COPY
     02  HOLDER-NAME                  PICTURE X(30).            COPY
     02  HOLDER-ADDRESS               PICTURE X(30).            COPY
     02  MERCHANT-NUMBER              PICTURE X(9).             COPY
     02  MERCHANT-NAME                PICTURE X(30).            COPY
     02  AMOUNT                       PICTURE 9(6)V99.          COPY
     02  CREDIT-STATUS                PICTURE X.                COPY
         88  GOOD                     VALUE "G".                COPY
         88  STOLEN                   VALUE "S".                COPY
         88  OUTDATED                 VALUE "O".                COPY
         88  INELIGIBLE               VALUE "I".                COPY
     02  FILLER                       PICTURE X.                COPY
```

(a)

Figure 15.22. Get data module in COBOL.

```
LINKAGE SECTION.

COPY DCL31.
77  END-OF-PROGRAM                    PICTURE X(3).          COPY

COPY DCL33.
01  CREDIT-DISPLAY-DATA.                                     COPY
    02  CURRENT-DISPLAY-KEY.                                 COPY
        03  MERCHANT-NUMBER           PICTURE X(9).          COPY
        03  CARD-NUMBER               PICTURE X(9).          COPY
        03  AMOUNT                    PICTURE X(9).          COPY
        03  NUMERIC-AMOUNT REDEFINES  AMOUNT                 COPY
                                      PICTURE 9(6).99.       COPY
        03  FORCE-RECHECK             PICTURE X.             COPY
    02  ALIGNED-AMOUNT                PICTURE 9(6)V99.       COPY
    02  AUTHORIZATION-NUMBER          PICTURE X(9).          COPY
    02  MESSAGE                       PICTURE X(50).         COPY
    02  END-INDICATOR                 PICTURE X.             COPY
    02  FILLER                        PICTURE X.             COPY
***************************************************************

/**************************************************************

PROCEDURE DIVISION USING END-OF-PROGRAM, CREDIT-DISPLAY-DATA.

    IF END-INDICATOR IN CREDIT-DISPLAY-DATA NOT = SPACES
      THEN
        MOVE "YES" TO END-OF-PROGRAM
        MOVE GOOD-BYE-MESSAGE TO MESSAGE
        EXIT PROGRAM
    END-IF.

    MOVE "Y" TO FORCE-RECHECK.
    MOVE MERCHANT-NUMBER IN CREDIT-DISPLAY-DATA TO
       INPUT-DATA-ARRAY.
    CALL "CRRTJS" USING INPUT-DATA-ARRAY,
                        OUTPUT-DATA-ARRAY,
                        NUMBER-OF-DECIMAL-PLACES, MESSAGE,
                        NINE, NINE.

    IF MESSAGE NOT = SPACES
      THEN
        EXIT PROGRAM
    END-IF.

    IF NUMBER-OF-DECIMAL-PLACES NOT = 0 OR
       OUTPUT-DATA-ARRAY NOT NUMERIC
      THEN
        MOVE INVALID-MERCHANT-MESSAGE TO MESSAGE
        EXIT PROGRAM
    END-IF.

    MOVE OUTPUT-DATA-ARRAY TO MERCHANT-NUMBER IN
       CREDIT-DISPLAY-DATA.
    MOVE OUTPUT-DATA-ARRAY TO MERCHANT-NUMBER IN
       MERCHANT-MASTER-DATA.
    CALL "CRRDMR" USING MERCHANT-MASTER-DATA, MESSAGE.

    IF MESSAGE NOT = SPACES
      THEN
        EXIT PROGRAM
    END-IF.

    MOVE CARD-NUMBER IN CREDIT-DISPLAY-DATA TO
       INPUT-DATA-ARRAY.
    CALL "CRRTJS" USING INPUT-DATA-ARRAY,
                        OUTPUT-DATA-ARRAY,
                        NUMBER-OF-DECIMAL-PLACES, MESSAGE,
                        NINE, NINE.

    IF MESSAGE NOT = SPACES
      THEN
        EXIT PROGRAM
    END-IF.

    IF NUMBER-OF-DECIMAL-PLACES NOT = 0 OR
       OUTPUT-DATA-ARRAY NOT NUMERIC
      THEN
        MOVE INVALID-CARD-MESSAGE TO MESSAGE
        EXIT PROGRAM
    END-IF.

    MOVE OUTPUT-DATA-ARRAY TO CARD-NUMBER IN
       CREDIT-DISPLAY-DATA.
    MOVE OUTPUT-DATA-ARRAY TO CARD-NUMBER IN
       CREDIT-MASTER-DATA.
    CALL "CRRDCR" USING CREDIT-MASTER-DATA, MESSAGE.

    IF MESSAGE NOT = SPACES
      THEN
        EXIT PROGRAM
    END-IF.
```

(b)

(*continued on next page*)

```
     MOVE AMOUNT IN CREDIT-DISPLAY-DATA TO INPUT-DATA-ARRAY.
     CALL "CRRTJS" USING INPUT-DATA-ARRAY,
                         OUTPUT-DATA-ARRAY,
                         NUMBER-OF-DECIMAL-PLACES, MESSAGE,
                         NINE, NINE.

     IF MESSAGE NOT = SPACES
       THEN
         EXIT PROGRAM
     END-IF.

     MOVE OUTPUT-DATA-ARRAY TO AMOUNT-1.

     IF NUMBER-OF-DECIMAL-PLACES NOT = 2 OR
        AMOUNT-1 NOT NUMERIC
       THEN
         MOVE INVALID-AMOUNT-MESSAGE TO MESSAGE
         EXIT PROGRAM
     END-IF.

     MOVE AMOUNT-2 TO NUMERIC-AMOUNT ALIGNED-AMOUNT.

     EVALUATE CREDIT-STATUS IN CREDIT-MASTER-DATA
       WHEN GOOD
         MOVE STATUS-OK-MESSAGE TO MESSAGE
         MOVE SPACES TO FORCE-RECHECK
       WHEN STOLEN
         MOVE STOLEN-MESSAGE TO MESSAGE
       WHEN OUTDATED
         MOVE OUTDATED-MESSAGE TO MESSAGE
       WHEN INELIGIBLE
         MOVE INELIGIBLE-MESSAGE TO MESSAGE
       WHEN OTHER
         MOVE SYSTEM-PROBLEM-MESSAGE TO MESSAGE
     END-EVALUATE.

     MOVE SPACES TO ACTIVITY-LOG-DATA.
     MOVE MERCHANT-NUMBER IN CREDIT-DISPLAY-DATA TO
        MERCHANT-NUMBER IN ACTIVITY-LOG-DATA.
     MOVE MERCHANT-NAME IN MERCHANT-MASTER-DATA TO
        MERCHANT-NAME IN ACTIVITY-LOG-DATA.
     MOVE CARD-NUMBER IN CREDIT-DISPLAY-DATA TO
        CARD-NUMBER IN ACTIVITY-LOG-DATA.
     MOVE HOLDER-NAME IN CREDIT-MASTER-DATA TO
        HOLDER-NAME IN ACTIVITY-LOG-DATA.
     MOVE HOLDER-ADDRESS IN CREDIT-MASTER-DATA TO
        HOLDER-ADDRESS IN ACTIVITY-LOG-DATA.
     MOVE ALIGNED-AMOUNT IN CREDIT-DISPLAY-DATA TO
        AMOUNT IN ACTIVITY-LOG-DATA.
     MOVE CREDIT-STATUS IN CREDIT-MASTER-DATA TO
        CREDIT-STATUS IN ACTIVITY-LOG-DATA.
     CALL "CRUPLG" USING ACTIVITY-LOG-DATA.

 END PROGRAM CRGTDA.

*****************************************************************
```

(c)

Figure 15.22. *(Continued)*

```
/*****************************************************************
 IDENTIFICATION DIVISION.

 PROGRAM-ID.       CRDAUP.

*****************************************************************
*                                                               *
* CREDIT AUTHORIZATION PROGRAM                                  *
* MODULE - UPDATE DATA                                          *
*                                                               *
*---------------------------------------------------------------*
* CHANGE HISTORY                                                *
*   090785 NEW PROGRAM                                      GRR *
*****************************************************************

 AUTHOR.           G.R. ROGERS.

 DATA DIVISION.

 WORKING-STORAGE SECTION.

 77  VERSION-NUMBER                    PICTURE X(27) VALUE
     "VERSION 1     SEPT. 7, 1985".

 77  GOOD-BYE-MESSAGE                  PICTURE X(8) VALUE
     "GOOD BYE".

 COPY DCL41.
 01  AUTHORIZATION-DATA.                                     COPY
     02  AUTHORIZATION-KEY             PICTURE X(3).         COPY
     02  AUTHORIZATION-NUMBER          PICTURE X(9).         COPY
     02  NUMERIC-AUTHORIZATION-NUMBER REDEFINES              COPY
              AUTHORIZATION-NUMBER     PICTURE 9(9).         COPY
     02  FILLER                        PICTURE X.            COPY

 COPY DCL42.
 01  ACTIVITY-LOG-DATA.                                      COPY
     02  AUTHORIZATION-NUMBER          PICTURE X(9).         COPY
     02  CARD-NUMBER                   PICTURE X(9).         COPY
     02  HOLDER-NAME                   PICTURE X(30).        COPY
     02  HOLDER-ADDRESS                PICTURE X(30).        COPY
     02  MERCHANT-NUMBER               PICTURE X(9).         COPY
     02  MERCHANT-NAME                 PICTURE X(30).        COPY
     02  AMOUNT                        PICTURE 9(6)V99.      COPY
     02  CREDIT-STATUS                 PICTURE X.            COPY
         88  GOOD                      VALUE "G".            COPY
         88  STOLEN                    VALUE "S".            COPY
         88  OUTDATED                  VALUE "O".            COPY
         88  INELIGIBLE                VALUE "I".            COPY
     02  FILLER                        PICTURE X.            COPY

 LINKAGE SECTION.

 COPY DCL31.
 77  END-OF-PROGRAM                    PICTURE X(3).         COPY

 COPY DCL33.
 01  CREDIT-DISPLAY-DATA.                                    COPY
     02  CURRENT-DISPLAY-KEY.                                COPY
         03  MERCHANT-NUMBER           PICTURE X(9).         COPY
         03  CARD-NUMBER               PICTURE X(9).         COPY
         03  AMOUNT                    PICTURE X(9).         COPY
         03  NUMERIC-AMOUNT REDEFINES  AMOUNT                COPY
                                       PICTURE 9(6).99.      COPY
         03  FORCE-RECHECK             PICTURE X.            COPY
     02  ALIGNED-AMOUNT                PICTURE 9(6)V99.      COPY
     02  AUTHORIZATION-NUMBER          PICTURE X(9).         COPY
     02  MESSAGE                       PICTURE X(50).        COPY
     02  END-INDICATOR                 PICTURE X.            COPY
     02  FILLER                        PICTURE X.            COPY

*****************************************************************
```

(a)

Figure 15.23. Data update module in COBOL.

(continued on next page)

```
/*****************************************************************

 PROCEDURE DIVISION USING END-OF-PROGRAM, CREDIT-DISPLAY-DATA.

     IF END-INDICATOR IN CREDIT-DISPLAY-DATA NOT = SPACES
       THEN
         MOVE "YES" TO END-OF-PROGRAM
         MOVE GOOD-BYE-MESSAGE TO MESSAGE
         EXIT PROGRAM
     END-IF.

     MOVE "Y" TO FORCE-RECHECK.
     MOVE "001" TO AUTHORIZATION-KEY.
     CALL "CRRDAU" USING AUTHORIZATION-DATA, MESSAGE.

     IF MESSAGE NOT = SPACES
       THEN
         EXIT PROGRAM
     END-IF.

     MOVE AUTHORIZATION-NUMBER IN AUTHORIZATION-DATA TO
        AUTHORIZATION-NUMBER IN CREDIT-DISPLAY-DATA.
     ADD 1 TO NUMERIC-AUTHORIZATION-NUMBER.
     CALL "CRUPAU" USING AUTHORIZATION-DATA, MESSAGE.

     MOVE SPACES TO ACTIVITY-LOG-DATA.
     MOVE AUTHORIZATION-NUMBER IN CREDIT-DISPLAY-DATA TO
        AUTHORIZATION-NUMBER IN ACTIVITY-LOG-DATA.
     MOVE MERCHANT-NUMBER IN CREDIT-DISPLAY-DATA TO
        MERCHANT-NUMBER IN ACTIVITY-LOG-DATA.
     MOVE CARD-NUMBER IN CREDIT-DISPLAY-DATA TO
        CARD-NUMBER IN ACTIVITY-LOG-DATA.
     MOVE ALIGNED-AMOUNT IN CREDIT-DISPLAY-DATA TO
        AMOUNT IN ACTIVITY-LOG-DATA.
     CALL "CRUPLG" USING ACTIVITY-LOG-DATA.

 END PROGRAM CRDAUP.

*****************************************************************
```

(b)

Figure 15.23. *(Continued)*

```
/*******************************************************************

 IDENTIFICATION DIVISION.

 PROGRAM-ID.       CRINIT.

*****************************************************************
*                                                               *
* CREDIT AUTHORIZATION PROGRAM                                  *
* MODULE - INITIALIZATION                                       *
*                                                               *
*---------------------------------------------------------------*
* CHANGE HISTORY                                                *
*   090785 NEW PROGRAM                                      GRR *
*****************************************************************

 AUTHOR.            G.R. ROGERS.

 ENVIRONMENT DIVISION.

 INPUT-OUTPUT SECTION.

 FILE-CONTROL.

 COPY DCL64.
     SELECT CREDIT-FILE ASSIGN TO DISK-CRFILE                   COPY
                        ACCESS IS RANDOM                        COPY
                        ORGANIZATION IS INDEXED                 COPY
                        RECORD KEY IS CREDIT-KEY.               COPY
 COPY DCL65.
     SELECT MERCHANT-FILE ASSIGN TO DISK-MRFILE                 COPY
                          ACCESS IS RANDOM                      COPY
                          ORGANIZATION IS INDEXED               COPY
                          RECORD KEY IS MERCHANT-KEY.           COPY
 COPY DCL66.
     SELECT ACTIVITY-LOG-FILE ASSIGN TO DISK-LOG.               COPY
 COPY DCL67.
     SELECT AUTHORIZATION-FILE ASSIGN TO DISK-AUTH              COPY
                               ACCESS IS RANDOM                 COPY
                               ORGANIZATION IS INDEXED          COPY
                               RECORD KEY IS AUTHORIZATION-KEY. COPY

 DATA DIVISION.

 FILE SECTION.

 COPY DCL46.
 FD  CREDIT-FILE EXTERNAL                                       COPY
     BLOCK CONTAINS 10 RECORDS                                  COPY
     LABEL RECORDS ARE STANDARD.                                COPY

 COPY DCL34.
 01  CREDIT-MASTER-DATA.                                        COPY
     02  CREDIT-KEY.                                            COPY
         03  CARD-NUMBER              PICTURE X(9).             COPY
     02  HOLDER-NAME                  PICTURE X(30).            COPY
     02  HOLDER-ADDRESS               PICTURE X(30).            COPY
     02  CREDIT-STATUS                PICTURE X.                COPY
         88  GOOD                     VALUE "G".                COPY
         88  STOLEN                   VALUE "S".                COPY
         88  OUTDATED                 VALUE "O".                COPY
         88  INELIGIBLE               VALUE "I".                COPY
     02  FILLER                       PICTURE X.                COPY

 COPY DCL47.
 FD  MERCHANT-FILE EXTERNAL                                     COPY
     BLOCK CONTAINS 10 RECORDS                                  COPY
     LABEL RECORDS ARE STANDARD.                                COPY

 COPY DCL40.
 01  MERCHANT-MASTER-DATA.                                      COPY
     02  MERCHANT-KEY.                                          COPY
         03  MERCHANT-NUMBER          PICTURE X(9).             COPY
     02  MERCHANT-NAME                PICTURE X(30).            COPY
     02  MERCHANT-ADDRESS             PICTURE X(30).            COPY
     02  FILLER                       PICTURE X.                COPY

 COPY DCL48.
 FD  ACTIVITY-LOG-FILE EXTERNAL                                 COPY
     BLOCK CONTAINS 10 RECORDS                                  COPY
     LABEL RECORDS ARE STANDARD.                                COPY
```

(a)

Figure 15.24. *Initialization module in COBOL.*

(*continued on next page*)

```
COPY DCL42.
01  ACTIVITY-LOG-DATA.                                                    COPY
    02  AUTHORIZATION-NUMBER            PICTURE X(9).                     COPY
    02  CARD-NUMBER                     PICTURE X(9).                     COPY
    02  HOLDER-NAME                     PICTURE X(30).                    COPY
    02  HOLDER-ADDRESS                  PICTURE X(30).                    COPY
    02  MERCHANT-NUMBER                 PICTURE X(9).                     COPY
    02  MERCHANT-NAME                   PICTURE X(30).                    COPY
    02  AMOUNT                          PICTURE 9(6)V99.                  COPY
    02  CREDIT-STATUS                   PICTURE X.                        COPY
        88  GOOD                        VALUE "G".                        COPY
        88  STOLEN                      VALUE "S".                        COPY
        88  OUTDATED                    VALUE "O".                        COPY
        88  INELIGIBLE                  VALUE "I".                        COPY
    02  FILLER                          PICTURE X.                        COPY

COPY DCL49.
FD  AUTHORIZATION-FILE EXTERNAL                                           COPY
    BLOCK CONTAINS 10 RECORDS                                             COPY
    LABEL RECORDS ARE STANDARD.                                           COPY

COPY DCL41.
01  AUTHORIZATION-DATA.                                                   COPY
    02  AUTHORIZATION-KEY               PICTURE X(3).                     COPY
    02  AUTHORIZATION-NUMBER            PICTURE X(9).                     COPY
    02  NUMERIC-AUTHORIZATION-NUMBER REDEFINES                            COPY
            AUTHORIZATION-NUMBER        PICTURE 9(9).                     COPY
    02  FILLER                          PICTURE X.                        COPY

WORKING-STORAGE SECTION.

77  VERSION-NUMBER                      PICTURE X(27) VALUE
    "VERSION 1      SEPT. 7, 1985".

77  OPEN-VALUE                          PICTURE X(5) VALUE
    "OPEN ".

COPY DCL33.
01  CREDIT-DISPLAY-DATA.                                                  COPY
    02  CURRENT-DISPLAY-KEY.                                              COPY
        03  MERCHANT-NUMBER             PICTURE X(9).                     COPY
        03  CARD-NUMBER                 PICTURE X(9).                     COPY
        03  AMOUNT                      PICTURE X(9).                     COPY
        03  NUMERIC-AMOUNT REDEFINES    AMOUNT                            COPY
                                        PICTURE 9(6).99.                  COPY
        03  FORCE-RECHECK               PICTURE X.                        COPY
    02  ALIGNED-AMOUNT                  PICTURE 9(6)V99.                  COPY
    02  AUTHORIZATION-NUMBER            PICTURE X(9).                     COPY
    02  MESSAGE                         PICTURE X(50).                    COPY
    02  END-INDICATOR                   PICTURE X.                        COPY
    02  FILLER                          PICTURE X.                        COPY

LINKAGE SECTION.

COPY DCL31.
77  END-OF-PROGRAM                      PICTURE X(3).                     COPY
******************************************************************
/*****************************************************************

PROCEDURE DIVISION USING END-OF-PROGRAM.

    MOVE "NO" TO END-OF-PROGRAM.
    CALL "TRANS1" USING CREDIT-DISPLAY-DATA, OPEN-VALUE.
    OPEN INPUT MERCHANT-FILE
               CREDIT-FILE
         OUTPUT ACTIVITY-LOG-FILE
         I-O AUTHORIZATION-FILE.

END PROGRAM CRINIT.

******************************************************************
```

(b)

Figure 15.24. *(Continued)*

```
/**************************************************************

 IDENTIFICATION DIVISION.

 PROGRAM-ID.        CRPROM.

 AUTHOR.            G.R. ROGERS.

**************************************************************
*                                                            *
* CREDIT AUTHORIZATION PROGRAM                               *
* MODULE - BUILD PROMPT DATA                                 *
*                                                            *
*------------------------------------------------------------*
* CHANGE HISTORY                                             *
*   090785 NEW PROGRAM                                   GRR *
**************************************************************

 DATA DIVISION.

 WORKING-STORAGE SECTION.

 77  VERSION-NUMBER                    PICTURE X(27) VALUE
     "VERSION 1     SEPT. 7, 1985".

 77  PROMPT-MESSAGE                    PICTURE X(42) VALUE
     "ENTER MERCHANT NUMBER, CARD NUMBER, AMOUNT".

 LINKAGE SECTION.

 COPY DCL33.
 01  CREDIT-DISPLAY-DATA.                                          COPY
     02  CURRENT-DISPLAY-KEY.                                      COPY
         03  MERCHANT-NUMBER           PICTURE X(9).               COPY
         03  CARD-NUMBER               PICTURE X(9).               COPY
         03  AMOUNT                    PICTURE X(9).               COPY
         03  NUMERIC-AMOUNT REDEFINES AMOUNT                       COPY
                                       PICTURE 9(6).99.            COPY
         03  FORCE-RECHECK             PICTURE X.                  COPY
     02  ALIGNED-AMOUNT                PICTURE 9(6)V99.            COPY
     02  AUTHORIZATION-NUMBER          PICTURE X(9).               COPY
     02  MESSAGE                       PICTURE X(50).              COPY
     02  END-INDICATOR                 PICTURE X.                  COPY
     02  FILLER                        PICTURE X.                  COPY

**************************************************************

/**************************************************************

 PROCEDURE DIVISION USING CREDIT-DISPLAY-DATA.

     MOVE SPACES TO CREDIT-DISPLAY-DATA.
     MOVE PROMPT-MESSAGE TO MESSAGE.

 END PROGRAM CRPROM.

**************************************************************
```

Figure 15.25. *Prompt module in COBOL.*

```
/*************************************************************
 IDENTIFICATION DIVISION.

 PROGRAM-ID.        CRRECV.

 AUTHOR.            G.R. ROGERS.

*************************************************************
*                                                           *
* CREDIT AUTHORIZATION PROGRAM                              *
* MODULE - RECEIVE DATA FROM TERMINAL                       *
*                                                           *
*-----------------------------------------------------------*
* CHANGE HISTORY                                            *
*   090785 NEW PROGRAM                                  GRR *
*************************************************************

 DATA DIVISION.

 WORKING-STORAGE SECTION.

 77  VERSION-NUMBER                     PICTURE X(27) VALUE
     "VERSION 1     SEPT. 7, 1985".

 77  READ-VALUE                         PICTURE X(5) VALUE
     "READ ".

 LINKAGE SECTION.

 COPY DCL33.
 01  CREDIT-DISPLAY-DATA.                                       COPY
     02  CURRENT-DISPLAY-KEY.                                   COPY
         03  MERCHANT-NUMBER            PICTURE X(9).           COPY
         03  CARD-NUMBER                PICTURE X(9).           COPY
         03  AMOUNT                     PICTURE X(9).           COPY
         03  NUMERIC-AMOUNT REDEFINES AMOUNT                    COPY
                                        PICTURE 9(6).99.        COPY
         03  FORCE-RECHECK              PICTURE X.              COPY
     02  ALIGNED-AMOUNT                 PICTURE 9(6)V99.        COPY
     02  AUTHORIZATION-NUMBER           PICTURE X(9).           COPY
     02  MESSAGE                        PICTURE X(50).          COPY
     02  END-INDICATOR                  PICTURE X.              COPY
     02  FILLER                         PICTURE X.              COPY

**************************************************************

/*************************************************************

 PROCEDURE DIVISION USING CREDIT-DISPLAY-DATA.

     CALL "TRANS1" USING CREDIT-DISPLAY-DATA, READ-VALUE.
     MOVE SPACES TO FORCE-RECHECK IN CREDIT-DISPLAY-DATA.
     MOVE SPACES TO MESSAGE IN CREDIT-DISPLAY-DATA.

 END PROGRAM CRRECV.

**************************************************************
```

Figure 15.26. *Receive transaction module in COBOL.*

```
/*****************************************************************
 IDENTIFICATION DIVISION.
 PROGRAM-ID.        CRSEND.
 AUTHOR.            G.R. ROGERS.
*****************************************************************
*                                                               *
* CREDIT AUTHORIZATION PROGRAM                                  *
* MODULE - SEND DATA TO TERMINAL                                *
*                                                               *
*---------------------------------------------------------------*
* CHANGE HISTORY                                                *
*   090785 NEW PROGRAM                                      GRR *
*****************************************************************
 DATA DIVISION.
 WORKING-STORAGE SECTION.
 77  VERSION-NUMBER                      PICTURE X(27) VALUE
     "VERSION 1      SEPT. 7, 1985".
 77  WRITE-VALUE                         PICTURE X(5) VALUE
     "WRITE".
 LINKAGE SECTION.
 COPY DCL33.
 01  CREDIT-DISPLAY-DATA.                                       COPY
     02  CURRENT-DISPLAY-KEY.                                   COPY
         03  MERCHANT-NUMBER             PICTURE X(9).          COPY
         03  CARD-NUMBER                 PICTURE X(9).          COPY
         03  AMOUNT                      PICTURE X(9).          COPY
         03  NUMERIC-AMOUNT REDEFINES AMOUNT                    COPY
                                         PICTURE 9(6).99.       COPY
         03  FORCE-RECHECK               PICTURE X.             COPY
     02  ALIGNED-AMOUNT                  PICTURE 9(6)V99.       COPY
     02  AUTHORIZATION-NUMBER            PICTURE X(9).          COPY
     02  MESSAGE                         PICTURE X(50).         COPY
     02  END-INDICATOR                   PICTURE X.             COPY
     02  FILLER                          PICTURE X.             COPY
*****************************************************************
/*****************************************************************
 PROCEDURE DIVISION USING CREDIT-DISPLAY-DATA.
     CALL "TRANS1" USING CREDIT-DISPLAY-DATA, WRITE-VALUE.
 END PROGRAM CRSEND.
*****************************************************************
```

Figure 15.27. *Send transaction module in COBOL.*

```
/*************************************************************
 IDENTIFICATION DIVISION.

 PROGRAM-ID.        CRRDAU.

 AUTHOR.            G.R. ROGERS.

*************************************************************
*                                                           *
* CREDIT AUTHORIZATION PROGRAM                              *
* MODULE - READ AUTHORIZATION FILE                          *
*                                                           *
*-----------------------------------------------------------*
* CHANGE HISTORY                                            *
*   090785 NEW PROGRAM                                  GRR *
*************************************************************

 ENVIRONMENT DIVISION.

 INPUT-OUTPUT SECTION.

 FILE-CONTROL.

 COPY DCL67.
     SELECT AUTHORIZATION-FILE ASSIGN TO DISK-AUTH             COPY
                               ACCESS IS RANDOM                COPY
                               ORGANIZATION IS INDEXED         COPY
                               RECORD KEY IS AUTHORIZATION-KEY. COPY

 DATA DIVISION.

 FILE SECTION.

 COPY DCL49.
 FD  AUTHORIZATION-FILE EXTERNAL                               COPY
     BLOCK CONTAINS 10 RECORDS                                 COPY
     LABEL RECORDS ARE STANDARD.                               COPY

 COPY DCL41.
 01  AUTHORIZATION-DATA.                                       COPY
     02  AUTHORIZATION-KEY            PICTURE X(3).            COPY
     02  AUTHORIZATION-NUMBER         PICTURE X(9).            COPY
     02  NUMERIC-AUTHORIZATION-NUMBER REDEFINES                COPY
             AUTHORIZATION-NUMBER     PICTURE 9(9).            COPY
     02  FILLER                       PICTURE X.               COPY

 WORKING-STORAGE SECTION.

 77  VERSION-NUMBER                   PICTURE X(27) VALUE
     "VERSION 1     SEPT. 7, 1985".

 77  FILE-PROBLEM-MESSAGE             PICTURE X(46) VALUE
     "CAN'T GET AUTHORIZATION RECORD - CALL SUPPORT".

 LINKAGE SECTION.

 01  LINKAGE-AUTHORIZATION-DATA       PICTURE X(13).

 COPY DCL39.
 77  MESSAGE                          PICTURE X(50).           COPY
*************************************************************

/*************************************************************
 PROCEDURE DIVISION USING AUTHORIZATION-DATA, MESSAGE.

     MOVE LINKAGE-AUTHORIZATION-DATA TO AUTHORIZATION-DATA.

     READ AUTHORIZATION-FILE RECORD
       INVALID KEY
         MOVE FILE-PROBLEM-MESSAGE TO MESSAGE
         EXIT PROGRAM
     END-READ.

     MOVE AUTHORIZATION-DATA TO LINKAGE-AUTHORIZATION-DATA.
     MOVE SPACES TO MESSAGE.

 END PROGRAM CRRDAU.

*************************************************************
```

Figure 15.28. *Read authorization data module in COBOL.*

```
/*****************************************************************

 IDENTIFICATION DIVISION.

 PROGRAM-ID.        CRRDCR.

 AUTHOR.            G.R. ROGERS.

*****************************************************************
*                                                               *
* CREDIT AUTHORIZATION PROGRAM                                  *
* MODULE - READ CREDIT MASTER FILE                              *
*                                                               *
*---------------------------------------------------------------*
* CHANGE HISTORY                                                *
*   090785 NEW PROGRAM                                      GRR *
*****************************************************************

 ENVIRONMENT DIVISION.

 INPUT-OUTPUT SECTION.

 FILE-CONTROL.

 COPY DCL64.
     SELECT CREDIT-FILE ASSIGN TO DISK-CRFILE                   COPY
                        ACCESS IS RANDOM                        COPY
                        ORGANIZATION IS INDEXED                 COPY
                        RECORD KEY IS CREDIT-KEY.               COPY

 DATA DIVISION.

 FILE SECTION.

 COPY DCL46.
 FD  CREDIT-FILE EXTERNAL                                       COPY
     BLOCK CONTAINS 10 RECORDS                                  COPY
     LABEL RECORDS ARE STANDARD.                                COPY

 COPY DCL34.
 01  CREDIT-MASTER-DATA.                                        COPY
     02  CREDIT-KEY.                                            COPY
         03  CARD-NUMBER           PICTURE X(9).                COPY
     02  HOLDER-NAME               PICTURE X(30).               COPY
     02  HOLDER-ADDRESS            PICTURE X(30).               COPY
     02  CREDIT-STATUS             PICTURE X.                   COPY
         88  GOOD                  VALUE "G".                   COPY
         88  STOLEN                VALUE "S".                   COPY
         88  OUTDATED              VALUE "O".                   COPY
         88  INELIGIBLE            VALUE "I".                   COPY
     02  FILLER                    PICTURE X.                   COPY

 WORKING-STORAGE SECTION.

 77  VERSION-NUMBER                PICTURE X(27) VALUE
     "VERSION 1     SEPT. 7, 1985".

 77  NOT-FOUND-MESSAGE             PICTURE X(30) VALUE
     "CREDIT MASTER RECORD NOT FOUND".

 LINKAGE SECTION.

 COPY DCL39.
 77  MESSAGE                       PICTURE X(50).               COPY

 01  LINKAGE-CREDIT-MASTER-DATA    PICTURE X(71).

*****************************************************************

/*****************************************************************

 PROCEDURE DIVISION USING CREDIT-MASTER-DATA, MESSAGE.

     MOVE LINKAGE-CREDIT-MASTER-DATA TO CREDIT-MASTER-DATA.

     READ CREDIT-FILE RECORD
       INVALID KEY
         MOVE NOT-FOUND-MESSAGE TO MESSAGE
         EXIT PROGRAM
     END-READ.

     MOVE CREDIT-MASTER-DATA TO LINKAGE-CREDIT-MASTER-DATA.
     MOVE SPACES TO MESSAGE.

 END PROGRAM CRRDCR.

*****************************************************************
```

Figure 15.29. *Read credit master module in COBOL.*

```
/*****************************************************************
 IDENTIFICATION DIVISION.

 PROGRAM-ID.        CRRDMR.

 AUTHOR.            G.R. ROGERS.

****************************************************************
*                                                              *
* CREDIT AUTHORIZATION PROGRAM                                 *
* MODULE - READ MERCHANT MASTER FILE                           *
*                                                              *
*--------------------------------------------------------------*
* CHANGE HISTORY                                               *
*   090785 NEW PROGRAM                                   GRR   *
****************************************************************

 ENVIRONMENT DIVISION.

 INPUT-OUTPUT SECTION.

 FILE-CONTROL.

 COPY DCL65.
     SELECT MERCHANT-FILE ASSIGN TO DISK-MRFILE                    COPY
                          ACCESS IS RANDOM                         COPY
                          ORGANIZATION IS INDEXED                  COPY
                          RECORD KEY IS MERCHANT-KEY.              COPY

 DATA DIVISION.

 FILE SECTION.

 COPY DCL47.
 FD  MERCHANT-FILE EXTERNAL                                        COPY
     BLOCK CONTAINS 10 RECORDS                                     COPY
     LABEL RECORDS ARE STANDARD.                                   COPY

 COPY DCL40.
 01  MERCHANT-MASTER-DATA.                                         COPY
     02  MERCHANT-KEY.                                             COPY
         03  MERCHANT-NUMBER              PICTURE X(9).            COPY
     02  MERCHANT-NAME                    PICTURE X(30).           COPY
     02  MERCHANT-ADDRESS                 PICTURE X(30).           COPY
     02  FILLER                           PICTURE X.               COPY

 WORKING-STORAGE SECTION.

 77  VERSION-NUMBER                       PICTURE X(27) VALUE
     "VERSION 1       SEPT. 7, 1985".

 77  NOT-FOUND-MESSAGE                    PICTURE X(32) VALUE
     "MERCHANT MASTER RECORD NOT FOUND".

 LINKAGE SECTION.

 01  LINKAGE-MERCHANT-MASTER-DATA         PICTURE X(70).

 COPY DCL39.
 77  MESSAGE                              PICTURE X(50).           COPY
****************************************************************
/***************************************************************
 PROCEDURE DIVISION USING MERCHANT-MASTER-DATA, MESSAGE.

     MOVE LINKAGE-MERCHANT-MASTER-DATA TO MERCHANT-MASTER-DATA.

     READ MERCHANT-FILE RECORD
       INVALID KEY
         MOVE NOT-FOUND-MESSAGE TO MESSAGE
         EXIT PROGRAM
     END-READ.

     MOVE MERCHANT-MASTER-DATA TO LINKAGE-MERCHANT-MASTER-DATA.
     MOVE SPACES TO MESSAGE.

 END PROGRAM CRRDMR.

****************************************************************
```

Figure 15.30. *Read merchant master module in COBOL.*

```
/*************************************************************
 IDENTIFICATION DIVISION.

 PROGRAM-ID.        CRUPAU.

 AUTHOR.            G.R. ROGERS.

*************************************************************
*                                                           *
* CREDIT AUTHORIZATION PROGRAM                              *
* MODULE - UPDATE AUTHORIZATION FILE                        *
*                                                           *
*-----------------------------------------------------------*
* CHANGE HISTORY                                            *
*   090785 NEW PROGRAM                                  GRR *
*************************************************************

 ENVIRONMENT DIVISION.

 INPUT-OUTPUT SECTION.

 FILE-CONTROL.

 COPY DCL67.
     SELECT AUTHORIZATION-FILE ASSIGN TO DISK-AUTH              COPY
                               ACCESS IS RANDOM                 COPY
                               ORGANIZATION IS INDEXED          COPY
                               RECORD KEY IS AUTHORIZATION-KEY. COPY

 DATA DIVISION.

 FILE SECTION.

 COPY DCL49.
 FD  AUTHORIZATION-FILE EXTERNAL                                COPY
     BLOCK CONTAINS 10 RECORDS                                  COPY
     LABEL RECORDS ARE STANDARD.                                COPY

 COPY DCL41.
 01  AUTHORIZATION-DATA.                                        COPY
     02  AUTHORIZATION-KEY          PICTURE X(3).               COPY
     02  AUTHORIZATION-NUMBER       PICTURE X(9).               COPY
     02  NUMERIC-AUTHORIZATION-NUMBER REDEFINES                 COPY
              AUTHORIZATION-NUMBER  PICTURE 9(9).               COPY
     02  FILLER                     PICTURE X.                  COPY

 WORKING-STORAGE SECTION.

 77  VERSION-NUMBER                 PICTURE X(27) VALUE
     "VERSION 1     SEPT. 7, 1985".

 77  AUTHORIZED-MESSAGE             PICTURE X(42) VALUE
     "CREDIT AUTHORIZED - ENTER NEXT TRANSACTION".
 77  FILE-PROBLEM-MESSAGE           PICTURE X(46) VALUE
     "CAN'T GET AUTHORIZATION RECORD - CALL SUPPORT".

 LINKAGE SECTION.

 01  LINKAGE-AUTHORIZATION-DATA     PICTURE X(13).

 COPY DCL39.
 77  MESSAGE                        PICTURE X(50).              COPY
*************************************************************

/*************************************************************

 PROCEDURE DIVISION USING AUTHORIZATION-DATA, MESSAGE.

     MOVE LINKAGE-AUTHORIZATION-DATA TO AUTHORIZATION-DATA.

     REWRITE AUTHORIZATION-DATA
       INVALID KEY
         MOVE FILE-PROBLEM-MESSAGE TO MESSAGE
         EXIT PROGRAM
     END-REWRITE.

     MOVE AUTHORIZED-MESSAGE TO MESSAGE.

 END PROGRAM CRUPAU.

*************************************************************
```

Figure 15.31. *Update authorization master module in COBOL.*

```
/****************************************************************

 IDENTIFICATION DIVISION.

 PROGRAM-ID.        CRUPLG.

 AUTHOR.            G.R. ROGERS.

***************************************************************
*                                                             *
* CREDIT AUTHORIZATION PROGRAM                                *
* MODULE - UPDATE LOG FILE                                    *
*                                                             *
*-------------------------------------------------------------*
* CHANGE HISTORY                                              *
*   090785 NEW PROGRAM                                    GRR *
***************************************************************

 ENVIRONMENT DIVISION.

 INPUT-OUTPUT SECTION.

 FILE-CONTROL.

 COPY DCL66.
     SELECT ACTIVITY-LOG-FILE ASSIGN TO DISK-LOG.                    COPY

 DATA DIVISION.

 FILE SECTION.

 COPY DCL48.
 FD  ACTIVITY-LOG-FILE EXTERNAL                                      COPY
     BLOCK CONTAINS 10 RECORDS                                       COPY
     LABEL RECORDS ARE STANDARD.                                     COPY

 COPY DCL42.
 01  ACTIVITY-LOG-DATA.                                              COPY
     02  AUTHORIZATION-NUMBER          PICTURE X(9).                 COPY
     02  CARD-NUMBER                   PICTURE X(9).                 COPY
     02  HOLDER-NAME                   PICTURE X(30).                COPY
     02  HOLDER-ADDRESS                PICTURE X(30).                COPY
     02  MERCHANT-NUMBER               PICTURE X(9).                 COPY
     02  MERCHANT-NAME                 PICTURE X(30).                COPY
     02  AMOUNT                        PICTURE 9(6)V99.              COPY
     02  CREDIT-STATUS                 PICTURE X.                    COPY
         88  GOOD                      VALUE "G".                    COPY
         88  STOLEN                    VALUE "S".                    COPY
         88  OUTDATED                  VALUE "O".                    COPY
         88  INELIGIBLE                VALUE "I".                    COPY
     02  FILLER                        PICTURE X.                    COPY

 DATA DIVISION.

 WORKING-STORAGE SECTION.

 77  VERSION-NUMBER                    PICTURE X(27) VALUE
     "VERSION 1     SEPT. 7, 1985".

 LINKAGE SECTION.

 01  LINKAGE-ACTIVITY-LOG-DATA         PICTURE X(127).

****************************************************************

/***************************************************************

 PROCEDURE DIVISION USING ACTIVITY-LOG-DATA.

     MOVE LINKAGE-ACTIVITY-LOG-DATA TO ACTIVITY-LOG-DATA.
     WRITE ACTIVITY-LOG-DATA.

 END PROGRAM CRUPLG.

****************************************************************
```

Figure 15.32. *Update log module in COBOL.*

```
/*************************************************************
 IDENTIFICATION DIVISION.
 PROGRAM-ID.        CRRTJS.
 AUTHOR.            G.R. ROGERS.
*************************************************************
*                                                           *
* CREDIT AUTHORIZATION PROGRAM                              *
* MODULE - LEFT JUSTIFY                                     *
*                                                           *
*-----------------------------------------------------------*
* CHANGE HISTORY                                            *
*   090785 NEW PROGRAM                                  GRR *
*************************************************************
 DATA DIVISION.
 WORKING-STORAGE SECTION.
 77  VERSION-NUMBER                      PICTURE X(27) VALUE
     "VERSION 1     SEPT. 7, 1985".
 77  LOCATION-OF-FIRST-NON-BLANK         PICTURE S99.
 77  LOCATION-OF-LAST-BLANK              PICTURE S99.
 77  LOCATION-OF-DECIMAL-POINT           PICTURE S99.
 77  INPUT-ARRAY-INDEX                   PICTURE S99.
 77  OUTPUT-ARRAY-INDEX                  PICTURE S99.
 LINKAGE SECTION.
 COPY DCL37.
 77  NUMBER-OF-INPUT-CHARACTERS          PICTURE S99.              COPY
                                                                   COPY
 77  NUMBER-OF-OUTPUT-CHARACTERS         PICTURE S99.              COPY
 COPY DCL38.
 77  NUMBER-OF-DECIMAL-PLACES            PICTURE S99.              COPY
 COPY DCL39.
 77  MESSAGE                             PICTURE X(50).            COPY
 COPY DCL35.
 01  INPUT-DATA-ARRAY.                                             COPY
     02  INPUT-ELEMENT                   PICTURE X OCCURS 9 TIMES. COPY
 COPY DCL36.
 01  OUTPUT-DATA-ARRAY.                                            COPY
     02  OUTPUT-ELEMENT                  PICTURE X OCCURS 9 TIMES. COPY
*************************************************************
```

(a)

Figure 15.33. *Right justify module in COBOL.*

(continued on next page)

```
/*****************************************************************
 PROCEDURE DIVISION USING INPUT-DATA-ARRAY,
                          OUTPUT-DATA-ARRAY,
                          NUMBER-OF-DECIMAL-PLACES,
                          MESSAGE,
                          NUMBER-OF-INPUT-CHARACTERS,
                          NUMBER-OF-OUTPUT-CHARACTERS.

     IF NUMBER-OF-OUTPUT-CHARACTERS LESS THAN
         NUMBER-OF-INPUT-CHARACTERS
       THEN
         MOVE "OUTPUT ARRAY TOO SMALL" TO MESSAGE
         EXIT PROGRAM
     END-IF.

     MOVE 0 TO LOCATION-OF-FIRST-NON-BLANK.
     MOVE ZERO TO OUTPUT-DATA-ARRAY.
     MOVE 0 TO LOCATION-OF-DECIMAL-POINT.
     MOVE 0 TO LOCATION-OF-LAST-BLANK.
     MOVE NUMBER-OF-INPUT-CHARACTERS TO INPUT-ARRAY-INDEX.
     MOVE NUMBER-OF-OUTPUT-CHARACTERS TO OUTPUT-ARRAY-INDEX.

     PERFORM WITH TEST BEFORE UNTIL INPUT-ARRAY-INDEX LESS THAN 1

       EVALUATE INPUT-ELEMENT(INPUT-ARRAY-INDEX)
         WHEN SPACES

           IF LOCATION-OF-FIRST-NON-BLANK NOT = 0
             THEN
               MOVE INPUT-ARRAY-INDEX TO LOCATION-OF-LAST-BLANK
           END-IF

         WHEN "."

           IF LOCATION-OF-DECIMAL-POINT NOT = 0
             THEN
               MOVE "MULTIPLE DECIMAL POINTS" TO MESSAGE
               EXIT PROGRAM
           END-IF

           MOVE OUTPUT-ARRAY-INDEX TO LOCATION-OF-DECIMAL-POINT

         WHEN OTHER

           IF LOCATION-OF-LAST-BLANK NOT = 0
             THEN
               MOVE "IMBEDDED BLANKS" TO MESSAGE
               MOVE SPACES TO OUTPUT-DATA-ARRAY
               EXIT PROGRAM
           END-IF

           IF LOCATION-OF-FIRST-NON-BLANK = 0
             THEN
               MOVE INPUT-ARRAY-INDEX TO
                   LOCATION-OF-FIRST-NON-BLANK
           END-IF

           MOVE INPUT-ELEMENT(INPUT-ARRAY-INDEX) TO
               OUTPUT-ELEMENT(OUTPUT-ARRAY-INDEX)
           SUBTRACT 1 FROM OUTPUT-ARRAY-INDEX
       END-EVALUATE

       SUBTRACT 1 FROM INPUT-ARRAY-INDEX
     END-PERFORM.

     IF LOCATION-OF-DECIMAL-POINT = 0
       THEN
         MOVE 0 TO NUMBER-OF-DECIMAL-PLACES
       ELSE
         COMPUTE NUMBER-OF-DECIMAL-PLACES =
          NUMBER-OF-OUTPUT-CHARACTERS - LOCATION-OF-DECIMAL-POINT
     END-IF.

     MOVE SPACES TO MESSAGE.

 END PROGRAM CRRTJS.
*****************************************************************
```

(b)

Figure 15.33. *(Continued)*

```
/*****************************************************************
 IDENTIFICATION DIVISION.

 PROGRAM-ID.        CREOJ.

*****************************************************************
*                                                               *
* CREDIT AUTHORIZATION PROGRAM                                  *
* MODULE - END OF JOB                                           *
*                                                               *
*---------------------------------------------------------------*
* CHANGE HISTORY                                                *
*   090785 NEW PROGRAM                                      GRR *
*****************************************************************

 AUTHOR.            G.R. ROGERS.

 ENVIRONMENT DIVISION.

 INPUT-OUTPUT SECTION.

 FILE-CONTROL.

 COPY DCL64.
     SELECT CREDIT-FILE ASSIGN TO DISK-CRFILE                     COPY
                        ACCESS IS RANDOM                          COPY
                        ORGANIZATION IS INDEXED                   COPY
                        RECORD KEY IS CREDIT-KEY.                 COPY
 COPY DCL65.
     SELECT MERCHANT-FILE ASSIGN TO DISK-MRFILE                   COPY
                          ACCESS IS RANDOM                        COPY
                          ORGANIZATION IS INDEXED                 COPY
                          RECORD KEY IS MERCHANT-KEY.             COPY
 COPY DCL66.
     SELECT ACTIVITY-LOG-FILE ASSIGN TO DISK-LOG.                 COPY
 COPY DCL67.
     SELECT AUTHORIZATION-FILE ASSIGN TO DISK-AUTH                COPY
                               ACCESS IS RANDOM                   COPY
                               ORGANIZATION IS INDEXED            COPY
                               RECORD KEY IS AUTHORIZATION-KEY.   COPY

 DATA DIVISION.

 FILE SECTION.

 COPY DCL46.
 FD  CREDIT-FILE EXTERNAL                                         COPY
     BLOCK CONTAINS 10 RECORDS                                    COPY
     LABEL RECORDS ARE STANDARD.                                  COPY

 COPY DCL34.
 01  CREDIT-MASTER-DATA.                                          COPY
     02  CREDIT-KEY.                                              COPY
         03  CARD-NUMBER                 PICTURE X(9).            COPY
     02  HOLDER-NAME                     PICTURE X(30).           COPY
     02  HOLDER-ADDRESS                  PICTURE X(30).           COPY
     02  CREDIT-STATUS                   PICTURE X.               COPY
         88  GOOD                        VALUE "G".               COPY
         88  STOLEN                      VALUE "S".               COPY
         88  OUTDATED                    VALUE "O".               COPY
         88  INELIGIBLE                  VALUE "I".               COPY
     02  FILLER                          PICTURE X.               COPY

 COPY DCL47.
 FD  MERCHANT-FILE EXTERNAL                                       COPY
     BLOCK CONTAINS 10 RECORDS                                    COPY
     LABEL RECORDS ARE STANDARD.                                  COPY

 COPY DCL40.
 01  MERCHANT-MASTER-DATA.                                        COPY
     02  MERCHANT-KEY.                                            COPY
         03  MERCHANT-NUMBER             PICTURE X(9).            COPY
     02  MERCHANT-NAME                   PICTURE X(30).           COPY
     02  MERCHANT-ADDRESS                PICTURE X(30).           COPY
     02  FILLER                          PICTURE X.               COPY

 COPY DCL48.
 FD  ACTIVITY-LOG-FILE EXTERNAL                                   COPY
     BLOCK CONTAINS 10 RECORDS                                    COPY
     LABEL RECORDS ARE STANDARD.                                  COPY
```

(a)

Figure 15.34. *End of job module in COBOL.*

(*continued on next page*)

```
COPY DCL42.
01  ACTIVITY-LOG-DATA.                                                      COPY
    02  AUTHORIZATION-NUMBER            PICTURE X(9).                       COPY
    02  CARD-NUMBER                     PICTURE X(9).                       COPY
    02  HOLDER-NAME                     PICTURE X(30).                      COPY
    02  HOLDER-ADDRESS                  PICTURE X(30).                      COPY
    02  MERCHANT-NUMBER                 PICTURE X(9).                       COPY
    02  MERCHANT-NAME                   PICTURE X(30).                      COPY
    02  AMOUNT                          PICTURE 9(6)V99.                    COPY
    02  CREDIT-STATUS                   PICTURE X.                          COPY
        88  GOOD                        VALUE "G".                          COPY
        88  STOLEN                      VALUE "S".                          COPY
        88  OUTDATED                    VALUE "O".                          COPY
        88  INELIGIBLE                  VALUE "I".                          COPY
    02  FILLER                          PICTURE X.                          COPY

COPY DCL49.
FD  AUTHORIZATION-FILE EXTERNAL                                             COPY
    BLOCK CONTAINS 10 RECORDS                                               COPY
    LABEL RECORDS ARE STANDARD.                                             COPY

COPY DCL41.
01  AUTHORIZATION-DATA.                                                     COPY
    02  AUTHORIZATION-KEY               PICTURE X(3).                       COPY
    02  AUTHORIZATION-NUMBER            PICTURE X(9).                       COPY
    02  NUMERIC-AUTHORIZATION-NUMBER REDEFINES                              COPY
             AUTHORIZATION-NUMBER       PICTURE 9(9).                       COPY
    02  FILLER                          PICTURE X.                          COPY

WORKING-STORAGE SECTION.

77  VERSION-NUMBER                      PICTURE X(27) VALUE
    "VERSION 1     SEPT. 7, 1985".

77  CLOSE-VALUE                         PICTURE X(5) VALUE
    "CLOSE ".

 COPY DCL33.
01  CREDIT-DISPLAY-DATA.                                                    COPY
    02  CURRENT-DISPLAY-KEY.                                                COPY
        03  MERCHANT-NUMBER             PICTURE X(9).                       COPY
        03  CARD-NUMBER                 PICTURE X(9).                       COPY
        03  AMOUNT                      PICTURE X(9).                       COPY
        03  NUMERIC-AMOUNT REDEFINES AMOUNT                                 COPY
                                        PICTURE 9(6).99.                    COPY
        03  FORCE-RECHECK               PICTURE X.                          COPY
    02  ALIGNED-AMOUNT                  PICTURE 9(6)V99.                    COPY
    02  AUTHORIZATION-NUMBER            PICTURE X(9).                       COPY
    02  MESSAGE                         PICTURE X(50).                      COPY
    02  END-INDICATOR                   PICTURE X.                          COPY
    02  FILLER                          PICTURE X.                          COPY
******************************************************************

/*****************************************************************

 PROCEDURE DIVISION.

     CALL "TRANS1" USING CREDIT-DISPLAY-DATA, CLOSE-VALUE.
     CLOSE MERCHANT-FILE
           CREDIT-FILE
           ACTIVITY-LOG-FILE
           AUTHORIZATION-FILE.

 END PROGRAM CREOJ.

******************************************************************
```

(b)

Figure 15.34. *(Continued)*

16 Example Multipanel Interactive Program

PROBLEM DEFINITION

An employee information update program is to be designed for use in a large corporation. The program will be used by the personnel department and all managers to update existing personnel information. More than 1,000 terminals will have access to the program.

The program will utilize the system sign-on facilities to validate user log on IDs and passwords. After log on, the user will be presented with the display shown in Figure 16.1.

Depending on access authority, a terminal user can update name and address information, update salary data, view performance data, or end the program by keying in the correct code.

If the terminal user selects the name and address update (N), he or she then sees the display shown in Figure 16.2.

Employee number is entered and the program responds with the remaining data. The operator updates the data and depresses the enter key. To get data for another employee, the operator simply enters that employee number. If the salary update is selected, the operator will see the display portrayed in Figure 16.3.

Employee number is entered and the program responds with the employee name and current salary. The salary field can be changed and it

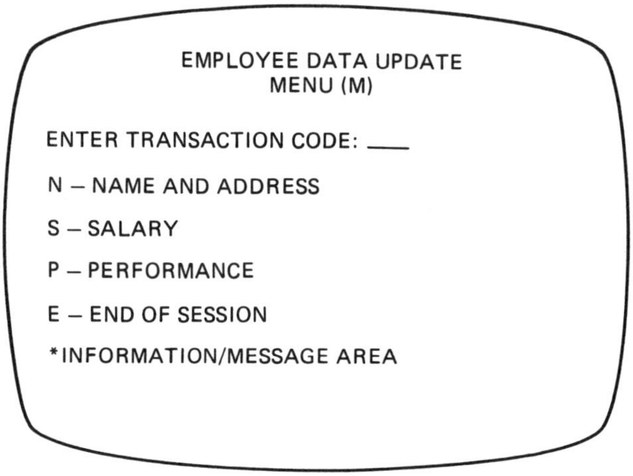

Figure 16.1. *Menu display.*

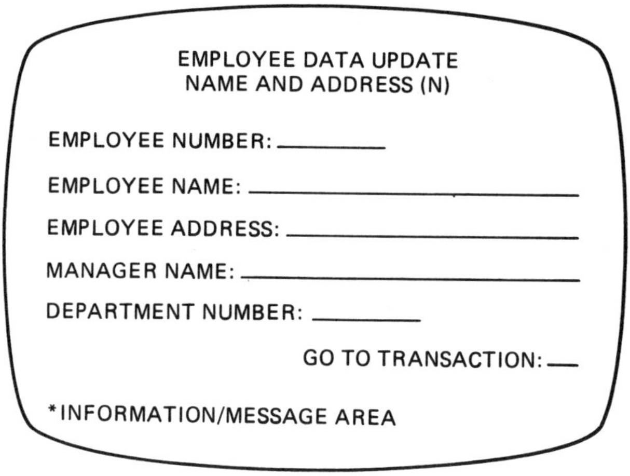

Figure 16.2. *Name and address display.*

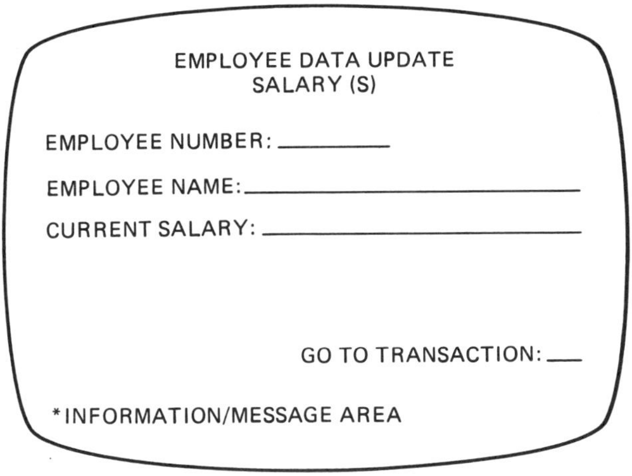

Figure 16.3. *Salary display.*

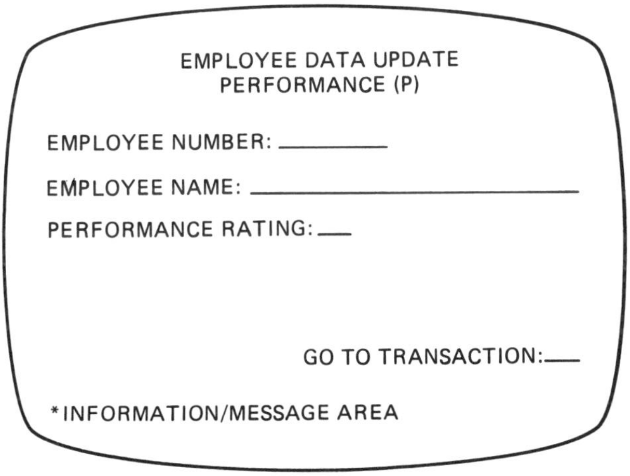

Figure 16.4. *Performance display.*

will be updated when the enter key is depressed. (The name field cannot be changed because it is write protected.) Entering another employee number causes the salary data for that employee to be displayed. For employee performance evaluation updates, the operator views the performance display. (See Figure 16.4.)

The employee number is entered, and the program will show the employee name and the performance evaluation. No data on this display can be updated. Other employees' data can be viewed by entering the employee numbers. The performance evaluation is updated via another program that is not part of this problem.

SYSTEM CONSIDERATIONS

All master data is contained in one segment of an employee data base. The access key data field is employee number. Segments are accessed via calls to the module *DABASE* (which is part of a data base management system) with the appropriate operation code (read, update, insert, open, and close). The data base manager provides automatic backup and recovery capability along with a locking mechanism to control simultaneous update access to the data base segments.

Although a programmer could build an input/output control system to manage the data, the construction task is extremely difficult. If commercial products are available, they should be used as they allow the programmer to concentrate on the real problem: the employee master update.

The displays are controlled by a display manager that is part of the operating system. Formatting rules for the display are handled outside the program. The program passes logical records to and from the formatting tool.

A company user profile security module is available to check access authority. The user ID is passed to it, and it returns a list of the transactions that the user can access.

The program will run under a high performance software manager. This software manager supports a reentrant interactive environment such that each terminal runs a virtual copy of the program, and each copy of the program *sees* a complete terminal session. The software manager does not provide the mainline function.

In high performance terminal environments, there are a number of methods for managing the work areas for the terminals. Some systems automatically assign a copy of the COBOL WORKING STORAGE to each terminal session. Other systems require the program to issue a system command to retrieve an identified terminal work area. Still other systems pass the terminal work as a parameter when control passes from the software control system to the program.

In our environment, the work area for each terminal is passed as a parameter when control enters the program. The terminal user ID is included in this work area and is given a value before control passes to the program. This work area is automatically saved and restored during each input or output operation. Any program data not kept in this work area is lost during input or output operations.

The example program of Chapter 15 has a very simple shutdown capability. The operator simply enters a code to tell the program to finish. In this environment the problem is much more complex. A power outage may occur or the system administrator may decide that it is time to end the day's processing. However, a number of terminals could be temporarily unattended. Many systems pass the shutdown signal through the terminal read mechanism and so does our system. If shutdown occurs, either through a power failure or system administrator intervention, the system has been set up to simulate all operators entering an *E* in the transaction code area. (In your own programming setting, you will, instead, have to test the appropriate value—end of transaction file, special indicator data field, and so on—to set the signal to end the program.)

MODULE HIERARCHY

Because the software control system does not provide the mainline function, we must code it ourselves. As with the previous three problems, we can use the standard mainline function of Figure 7.1. Figure 16.5 shows the first step of the design for the module hierarchy chart.

Since the problem definition identifies the program as an interactive program, there are two choices for the decision logic: single panel interactive or multipanel interactive. Either one would work for our program. If we choose the single panel interactive solution, we could use a

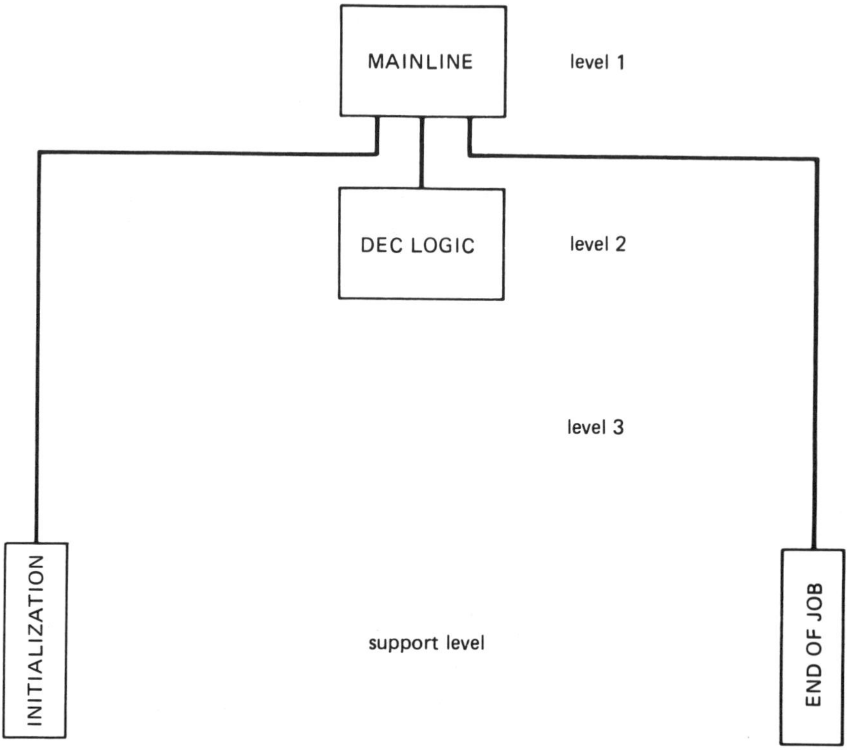

Figure 16.5. *First design step.*

system menu facility to direct the transactions to the correct transaction code. However, it is not clear from the problem definition that such a menu system is available, so, instead, the multipanel interactive logic is the one we will use.

There are many interactive terminals attached to the application. An additional benefit to the multipanel interactive logic is that its performance is probably better because no system overhead is incurred in switching from panel to panel.

Reviewing the classical function of Figure 8.4, we see that there will be one detail processing module for each display panel in the program. The displays are selected via the selection value entered on the displays. One of the selection codes tells the program to end. We could have the processing for each panel check the end code, but it is far easier to sim-

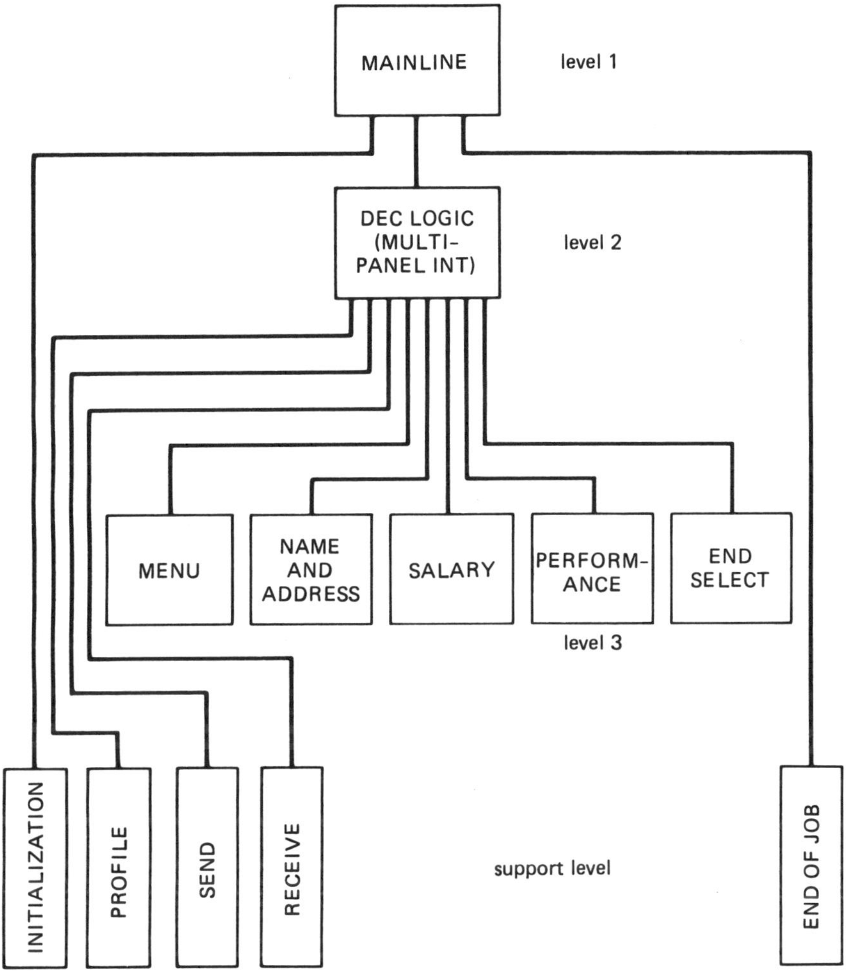

Figure 16.6. *Second design step.*

ply have a separate end module and let the decision logic automatically cause a transfer of control to it.

The classical multipanel interactive decision logic also utilizes three utility modules: a user profile module, a send data to terminal module, and a receive data from terminal module. The addition of these modules completes the second step of the module hierarchy design as portrayed in Figure 16.6.

We next look at the detail processing modules at the third level in the structure hierarchy to define the modules they will invoke.

The menu and end selection modules provide only a switching function. They, therefore, do not call any lower level modules.

Looking at the name and address, salary, and performance modules, we note that all three read employee records. This means that they will call a read function.

Employee number is a key data item for access to the employee records. To give the terminal user flexibility, entering employee number while ensuring consistency of entry, we provide a left justify function called by name and address, salary, and performance modules.

Both the name and address and salary modules are to be able to update the employee records; therefore, they call an update module.

The name and address module can create new employee records and add them to the data base. This requires a call to an insert module.

Finally, when reviewing the specifications, we see that a numeric salary value is processed by the salary function. To make operator data entry easier, we provide a right justify function. It is a utility module called by the salary detail processing module.

This completes the third step in the design of the module hierarchy chart. The result is seen in Figure 16.7.

When the design has reached this state, it is reviewed to see if it can be refined and subdivided into smaller modules. The guidelines of Chapter 2 are applied but no further subdivision can be done. We now proceed to the detail design in the design language.

DETAIL DESIGN

As with the three previous programs of chapters 13, 14, and 15, we begin the detail design with the adaptation of the classical mainline

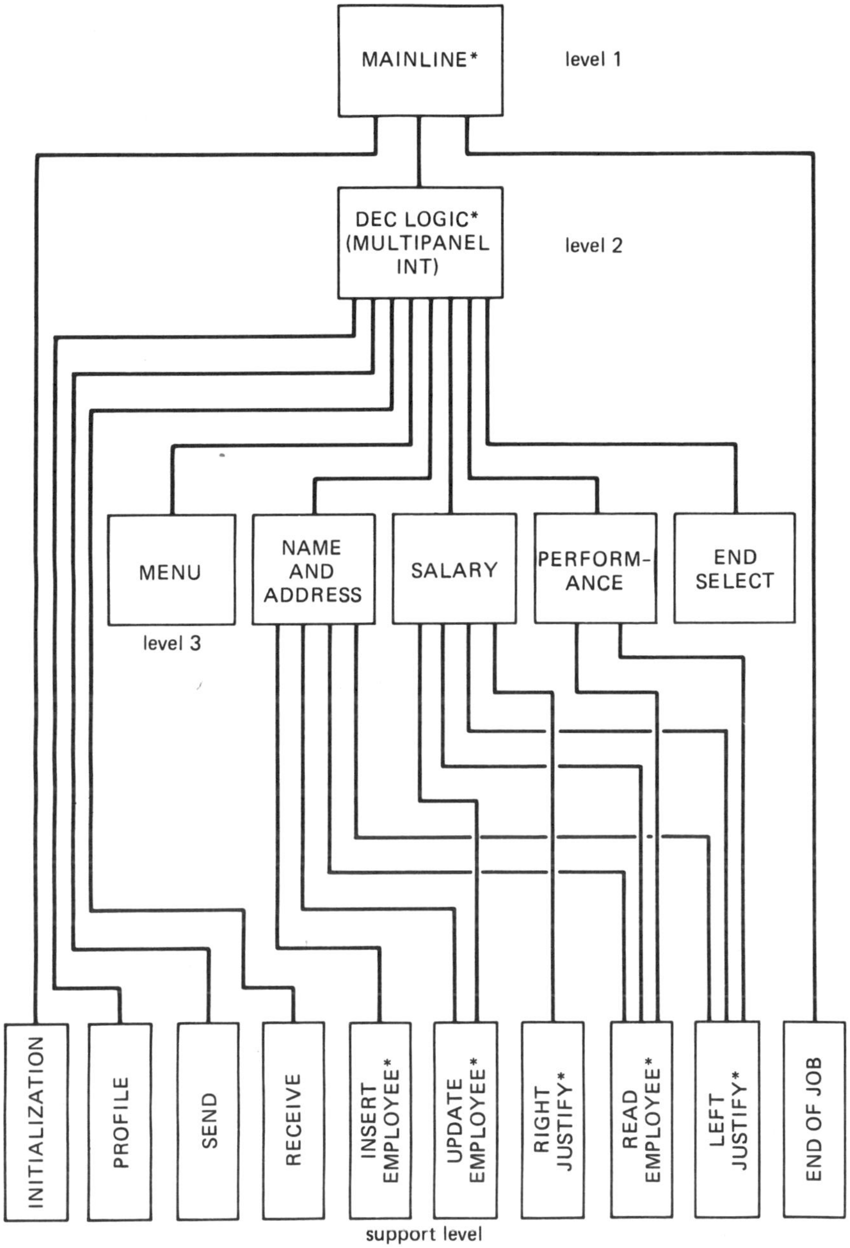

Figure 16.7. *Third design step.*

module at the top of the program hierarchy. The difference between this mainline and the others is the parameter, the terminal work area, that is passed from the software manager to the program when control transfers to the mainline module. In the employee information update program, we name it *terminal user data*. It contains many of the variables that will be used by the program, including the user ID (set by the control system), the variables related to the terminal displays, data base information, and security information. In a reentrant environment, there is one copy of the COBOL code and a copy of terminal user data for each active terminal.

Iteration in the mainline module is based on the end indicator that appears on all displays and is kept in the terminal user data. When a value of *E* appears, processing for that terminal user ends. The design for the mainline module is portrayed in Figure 16.8.

For the next phase of the design, we descend one level lower in the module hierarchy to the decision logic. For this module, the classical multipanel interactive decision logic of Figure 8.4 is used with the data for the employee update problem.

The first time indicator in this module refers to first time for the particular terminal user; thus, it is part of the terminal user data.

The EVALUATE structure has an option for each of the displays, and it calls a module when the end option (*E*) is selected. The WHEN OTHER path sets up the message to be displayed when an invalid transaction is entered. Figure 16.9 shows the employee update decision logic module.

Next the logic for the detail processing modules are designed. Classical functions are not available, so all of them have to be designed by the programmer.

The menu module is not complex. Upon entry, the previous panel code is checked to see if the particular user previously came from this menu module. If not, or if the user accidently entered a blank selection code, control returns and a message is set up to be sent to the terminal, prompting the user to enter a transaction code.

Otherwise, as shown in the design logic of Figure 16.10, the selection code is moved to the panel code field, the selection code is blanked, and the processing control field is given a value of *select* to cause the decision logic to switch control to the proper processing module for the code selected.

```
*              EMPLOYEE INFORMATION—MAINLINE MODULE

 PROGRAM-ID. emmain <MAIN> USING terminal user data.

   CALL "eminit" USING terminal user data.

   PERFORM WITH TEST BEFORE UNTIL panel code
         in terminal user data = "e"
      CALL "emdec" USING terminal user data
   END-PERFORM.

   CALL "emeoj" USING terminal user data.
   stop the program.

 END PROGRAM emmain.
```

Figure 16.8. *Mainline module.*

The name and address module is the most elaborate detail processing module. It is similar to the menu module in that the selection code is also tested upon entry. However, if it does not contain a blank value, control transfers back to the decision logic, which causes a switch to the selected panel processing module. Before control is transferred, the selection code is blanked and a value of *select* is given to the processing control data element. (This data element is used by the decision logic module to select another display processing module or send data to the terminal.)

From here on, in this logic, all results are sent back to the terminal. To accomplish this, the processing control data element is given a value of *send*.

The security data is checked to verify that the user is allowed into the name and address transaction. If not, control leaves this module with an information message set up to be sent to the terminal.

For user convenience, when control passes from one display panel to another and the employee number is not blank, the data is automatically retrieved from the data base. This allows the user to work with one type of data (e.g., salary) and easily switch to access other data (e.g., name and address) for the same employee.

```
*                    EMPLOYEE INFORMATION—DECISION LOGIC

 PROGRAM-ID. emdec USING terminal user data.

    CALL "profil" USING user id, security data.

    IF first time indicator = "yes"
       THEN
          move "no" to first time indicator
          move spaces to previous panel code
       ELSE
          CALL "emrecv" USING terminal user data.
    END-IF.

    PERFORM WITH TEST AFTER UNTIL processing control = "send"

       EVALUATE panel code
          WHEN "m"
             CALL "empnlm" USING terminal user data
             move "m" to previous panel code
          WHEN "n"
             CALL "empnln" USING terminal user data
             move "n" to previous panel code
          WHEN "s"
             CALL "empnls" USING terminal user data.
             move "s" to previous panel code
          WHEN "p"
             CALL "empnlp" USING terminal user data
             move "p" to previous panel code
          WHEN "e"
             CALL "empnle" USING terminal user data
             move "e" to previous panel code
          WHEN OTHER
             move previous panel code to panel code
             move "invalid transaction code-reenter" to message
                  in terminal user data
             move "send" to processing control
       END-EVALUATE

    END-PERFORM.

    CALL "emsend" using terminal user data.

 END PROGRAM emdec.
```

Figure 16.9. *Decision logic module.*

```
*     EMPLOYEE INFORMATION—MENU MODULE

   PROGRAM-ID. empnlm USING terminal user data.

      IF previous panel code not = "m" or
           selection code in display data = spaces
         THEN
            move spaces to selection code in display data
            move "enter transaction code" to message
            move "send" to processing control
            EXIT PROGRAM
      END-IF.

      move selection code to panel code.
      move spaces to selection code.
      move "select" to processing control.

   END PROGRAM empnlm.
```

Figure 16.10. *Menu module.*

If employee number is blank, control leaves the module with a message set up to prompt the terminal user to enter the employee number.

Nonblank employee numbers are left justified to ensure they are properly positioned in the input field. A call to the utility module *emlfjs* handles this function.

If the employee number is not the same as that previously processed, or if a panel switch has occurred, the employee data is read from the data base. Module *emmrrd* conducts the read operation. Since the record can be subsequently updated, the locking indicator should be set to *yes* to ensure other updates cannot occur to this employee segment while the data is being evaluated. If the segment is not found, a message prompting the user to create an employee record is set up, a new employee indicator is set, and control leaves the name and address module. (If the record cannot be found, locks are automatically released by the software system.)

If the previously described logic path is not taken, the employee data is set up from the input area. Then, if the employee is not a new em-

```
*          EMPLOYEE INFORMATION—NAME AND ADDRESS MODULE

 PROGRAM-ID. empnln USING terminal user data.

    IF selection code in display data not = spaces
       THEN
          move selection code to panel code
          move spaces to selection code
          move "select" to processing control
          EXIT PROGRAM
    END-IF.

    move "send" to processing control.

    IF security data shows user not allowed in this transaction
       THEN
          move "transaction access refused" to message
          EXIT PROGRAM
    END-IF.

    IF current employee number = spaces
       THEN
          move "enter employee number" to message in display data
          EXIT PROGRAM
    END-IF.

    CALL "emlfjs" USING current employee number array,
                        justified employee number array, 8, 8.
    set current employee number = justified employee number.

    IF current employee number = previous employee number
       and panel code = previous panel code
       THEN
          continue
       ELSE
          move employee number in terminal user data to
               employee number in employee master data
          CALL "emmrrd" USING employee master data, message, "yes"

          IF message = spaces
             THEN
                set up display fields from data base data
             ELSE
                move "employee data does not exist - enter data to
                     create" to message
                set new employee marker in data
          END-IF
```

Figure 16.11. *Name and address module.*

```
        move current employee number to previous employee number
        EXIT PROGRAM

    END-IF.

    set up employee number and address data in
        employee master data.

    IF not new employee
      THEN
        set up salary and performance data
        CALL "emupdt" USING employee master data, message, "yes"
        EXIT PROGRAM
    END-IF.

    mark as "old" employee.
    move 0 to salary in employee master data.
    move spaces to performance rating in employee master data
    CALL "eminst" USING employee master data, message, "yes".

  END PROGRAM empnln.
```

ployee, the data base segment is updated via module *emupdt*, and control exits from this module.

The final piece of logic in this module creates a new employee record (with a zero salary value and blank performance rating), and inserts it into the data base using module *eminst*. Figure 16.11 provides complete details of the name and address design.

The salary module is similar to the name and address module. However, salary data can be viewed and updated; new segments cannot be added to the data base.

The first check in the logic is for an entered nonblank selection code. This causes the panel code field to take the value of selection code, the selection code field to be blanked, a value of *select* to be put in the processing control field, and control exits from this module.

Next, a value of *send* is put in the processing control data element. This ensures that all subsequent processing in this module results in a confirmation response to the terminal.

The security data is tested to verify that the terminal user is allowed to access this transaction. If not, the message field is given a value showing that access is refused and control leaves the module.

Blank employee numbers cause a prompt message asking for the employee number to be put in the message field. Here, again, control exits from the salary module.

Left justify module *emlfjs* is called to justify the employee number for consistent key access to the master data. The justified value is placed back into the input field area to show the operator that the data value has been processed.

If the user has changed employee numbers or if control has transferred from another display module, The employee data is read and locked. A successful access (blank message) causes the data to be set up for display to the user, while an unsuccessful access causes all display fields to be blanked. The previous employee number is made equal to the current employee number, and control leaves the module.

If neither the employee number nor the panel code has changed, the salary data is right justified. Module *crrtjs* of the credit authorization program (Chapter 15) is available and can perform this service without modification. Since it doesn't make sense to construct a duplicate module for this program we will use the available module.

If any problems are found in right justification, or if the justified salary is not numeric or does not have two decimal places, control leaves the salary module with an appropriate message to be sent to the terminal operator.

Successful completion of all of the tests described means that the entered data is acceptable and the master data can be updated. The justified salary field is placed back into the input salary area and module *emupdt* is called to update the master data.

Finally, salary is added to a total field that is accumulated as an audit value for each terminal. The full design appears in Figure 16.12.

The performance detail processing module has only an inquiry function to perform. It does not update master data.

Upon entry to the module, the selection code is examined in case the user has selected a transfer to another display. If this happens, the value of the selection code field is moved to the panel code, the selection code is blanked, the processing control field is given a value of *select*, and control exits from this module.

As with the name and address and salary modules, the performance module must ascertain that the user is allowed access to the module. If not, an access refused message is set up and control leaves the module.

A blank employee number causes a prompt to be sent to the terminal asking the user to enter an employee number.

Nonblank employee numbers are left justified by module *emlfjs*. Then, the data base is read via a call to module *emmrrd* to retrieve the employee data. Note that the locking indicator is set to *no* for the read. Since we are only looking at the data and not updating it, the segments should not be locked as this only causes a system performance bottleneck. The unlocked segment is accessible to other users while this particular terminal user is examining it.

If the data is found, it is set up for display to the requester. Otherwise, all display fields are blanked to go along with the data not found message produced by read module *emmrrd*. The design for the performance module is laid out in Figure 16.13.

The end selection module is the last of the detail processing modules. It simply sets up a good-bye message to be sent to the user. This can be seen in the design of Figure 16.14.

Having finished with the detail processing modules, we descend in the module hierarchy to design the support level utility modules.

The first module we encounter at this level is the initialization module. Since there is no classical logic for it, we must design this module. The logic must give starting values to indicators and audit accumulators and set a panel code for the first panel that is to be displayed to the requester. The specifications state that the menu (panel code *M*) is to be the first panel displayed.

In this initialization phase, we also identify the data base segment that the program will access. This information will be used by the security test in the profile evaluation module *profil* to verify user identity.

Some data base systems require the files containing the data structure to be opened for processing—others do not. In our example, the files must be specifically opened. Figure 16.15 shows the initialization design.

A user profile evaluation module (named *profil*) does not have to be produced by the programmer. The specifications for the example state that a utility module is available for company-wide use. This is called by the previously designed decision logic module.

```
*                 EMPLOYEE INFORMATION—SALARY MODULE

 PROGRAM-ID. empnls USING terminal user data.

    IF selection code in display data not = spaces
       THEN
          move selection code to panel code
          move spaces to selection code
          move "select" to processing control
          EXIT PROGRAM
    END-IF.

    move "send" to processing control.

    IF security data indicates user not allowed in this
         transaction
       THEN
          move "transaction access refused" to message
          EXIT PROGRAM
    END-IF.

    IF current employee number = spaces
       THEN
          move "enter employee number" to message
          EXIT PROGRAM
    END-IF.

    CALL "emlfjs" USING current employee number array,
                        justified employee number array, 8, 8.
    set current employee number = justified employee number.

    IF current employee number = previous employee number
      and panel code = previous panel code
       THEN
          continue
       ELSE
          move employee number in terminal user data to
               employee number in employee master data
          CALL "emmrrd" USING employee master data, message, "yes"

          IF message = spaces
             THEN
                set up display fields from employee master data
             ELSE
                move spaces to display fields
          END-IF

          move current employee number to previous employee number
          EXIT PROGRAM

    END-IF.
```

Figure 16.12. *Salary module.*

```
    CALL ''crrtjs'' USING salary array,
                          justified salary array,
                          number of decimal places,
                          message in display data, 9, 9.

    IF message not = spaces
       THEN
          EXIT PROGRAM
    END-IF.

    IF number of decimal places not = 2 or
       justified salary array not numeric
       THEN
          move ''invalid salary'' to message
          EXIT PROGRAM
    END-IF.

    set salary in display data = justified salary.
    set up employee master data for update.
    CALL ''emupdt'' USING employee master data, message, ''yes''.
    add  salary in display data to total salary.

END PROGRAM empnls.
```

```
*             EMPLOYEE INFORMATION—PERFORMANCE MODULE

 PROGRAM-ID. empnlp USING terminal user data.

    IF selection code in display data not = spaces
       THEN
          move selection code to panel code
          move spaces to selection code
          move "select" to processing control
          EXIT PROGRAM
    END-IF.

    move "send" to processing control.

    IF security data indicates user not allowed in this
      transaction
       THEN
          move "transaction access refused" to message
          EXIT PROGRAM
    END-IF.

    IF current employee number = spaces
       THEN
          move "enter employee number" to message in display data
          EXIT PROGRAM
    END-IF.

    CALL "emlfjs" USING current employee number array,
                        justified employee number array, 8, 8.
    set current employee number = justified employee number.

    CALL "emmrrd" USING employee master data, message, "no".

    IF message  = spaces
       THEN
          set up display fields from employee master data
       ELSE
          move spaces to display fields
    END-IF.

 END PROGRAM empnlp.
```

Figure 16.13. *Performance module.*

```
*            EMPLOYEE INFORMATION—END SELECTION MODULE

 PROGRAM-ID. empnle USING terminal user data.

     move "good bye" to message in display data.
     move "send" to processing control.

 END PROGRAM empnle.
```

Figure 16.14. *End selection module.*

```
*            EMPLOYEE INFORMATION—INITIALIZATION MODULE

 PROGRAM-ID. eminit USING terminal user data.

     move "yes" to first time indicator.
     move spaces to previous employee number.
     move 0 to total salary.
     move spaces to employee type.
     move spaces to employee display data.
     move "m" to panel code.
     identify data base segments to be accessed.
     open the files.

 END PROGRAM eminit.
```

Figure 16.15. *Initialization module.*

The programmer must also design the receive transaction module of Figure 16.16. Here the data is retrieved from the terminal, and the necessary fields are moved to the terminal user data area. After input is retrieved, the message field in the terminal user data area is blanked to clear out any leftover user messages.

For the send transaction module, which must be designed as shown in Figure 16.17, the display data is formatted for display. It is then sent (or written) to the terminal operator.

For the design of the read employee segment module, we can employ the classical direct read logic of Figure 9.4. We adapt it to the employee update problem by changing the module name to *emmrrd* and incorporating the appropriate data. The result appears in Figure 16.18. Note how the locking logic is employed.

The insert employee segment module is also a classical function. It is the direct insert logic of Figure 9.6, with the employee data for our program. The locking indicator only appears because the data base access module requires a parameter in that position. The content value of a locking indicator field is not utilized. The resulting design for the insert data base function appears in Figure 16.19.

The update employee segment module is adapted from the classical logic of Figure 9.7. The locking options are used with the data for this program. The resulting design is laid out in Figure 16.20.

As can be seen in Figure 16.21, the left justify module of Figure 9.8 is used without change, other than giving it the name *emlfjs* to conform to the naming convention for the program.

```
*         EMPLOYEE INFORMATION—RECEIVE TRANSACTION MODULE

 PROGRAM-ID. emrecv USING terminal user data.

     read display data from terminal.
     set up fields in terminal user data.
     move spaces to message in terminal user data.

 END PROGRAM emrecv.
```

Figure 16.16. *Receive transaction module.*

```
*          EMPLOYEE INFORMATION—SEND TRANSACTION MODULE

 PROGRAM-ID. emsend USING terminal user data.

     format data for the terminal.
     write display data to the terminal.

 END PROGRAM emsend.
```

Figure 16.17. *Send transaction module.*

```
*       EMPLOYEE INFORMATION—READ EMPLOYEE SEGMENT MODULE

 PROGRAM-ID. emmrrd USING employee master data, message,
                          locking indicator.

     set up data base access parameters and key.

     IF locking indicator = "yes"
        THEN
           read record with specified key and lock it
        ELSE
           read record with specified key
     END-IF.

     IF record found
        THEN
           move spaces to message
           set up data fields from record
        ELSE
           set message = "employee data does not exist"
     END-IF.

 END PROGRAM emmrrd.
```

Figure 16.18. *Read employee segment module.*

```
* EMPLOYEE INFORMATION—INSERT EMPLOYEE SEGMENT MODULE

    PROGRAM-ID. eminst USING employee master data, message,
                                locking indicator.

        set up data base access parameters and key.
        set up output record.
        insert record into data base.

        IF record already exists
           THEN
              move "employee data already exists" to message
           ELSE
              move "data inserted into employee master" to message
        END-IF.

    END PROGRAM eminst.
```

Figure 16.19. *Insert employee segment module.*

```
* EMPLOYEE INFORMATION—UPDATE EMPLOYEE SEGMENT MODULE

    PROGRAM-ID. emupdt USING employee master data, message,
                                   locking indicator.

       set data base access parameters and key.

       IF locking indicator not = ''yes''
          THEN
             read record with specified key and lock it

             IF record not found or already locked
                THEN
                   move ''employee data does not exist'' to message
                   EXIT PROGRAM
             END-IF

       END-IF.

       update the data in record.
       replace record and unlock it.

       IF replace is successful
          THEN
             move ''employee data updated'' to message
          ELSE
             move ''update unsuccessful-call administrator''
                  to message
       END-IF.

    END PROGRAM emupdt.
```

Figure 16.20. *Update employee segment module.*

```
*              EMPLOYEE INFORMATION—LEFT JUSTIFY MODULE

 PROGRAM-ID. emlfjs USING input array,
                          output array,
                          number of input characters,
                          number of output characters.

    move spaces to output array.
    move "no" to nonblank character indicator.
    move 1 to input array index.
    move 1 to output array index.

    IF number of input characters greater than
       number of output characters
       THEN
          move number of output characters to justify limit
       ELSE
          move number of input characters to justify limit
    END-IF.

    PERFORM WITH TEST BEFORE UNTIL input array index
         greater than justify limit

       IF input array (input array index) = spaces and
            nonblank character indicator = "no"
          THEN
             continue
          ELSE
             move input array (input array index) to
                  output array (output array index)
             add 1 output array index
             move "yes" to nonblank character indicator
       END-IF

       add 1 to input array index
    END-PERFORM.

 END PROGRAM emlfjs.
```

Figure 16.21. *Left justify module.*

```
* EMPLOYEE INFORMATION—END OF JOB MODULE

    PROGRAM-ID. emeoj USING terminal user data.

      display "total salary for user ", user id,
            " is ", salary total on the system printer.
      close the files.

    END PROGRAM emeoj.
```

Figure 16.22. *End of job module.*

The final support level module and the final module in our program is the end of job module. There is no classical function for it, so it must be designed by the programmer. As can be observed in Figure 16.22, this module prints a salary audit total for the terminal on the system printer and closes the files.

THE COBOL CODE

The COBOL code appears in Figures 16.23 through 16.37. These figures clearly show how the design language is a shorthand method for describing the logic. Because of the large amount of data in the terminal user data area and the data base area, one assignment statement in the design language translates into many COBOL MOVE statements.

```
/************************************************************
 IDENTIFICATION DIVISION.

 PROGRAM-ID.        EMMAIN.

 AUTHOR.            G.R. ROGERS.

************************************************************
*                                                          *
* EMPLOYEE INFORMATION UPDATE PROGRAM                      *
* MODULE - MAINLINE                                        *
*                                                          *
*----------------------------------------------------------*
* CHANGE HISTORY                                           *
*    090785 NEW PROGRAM                                GRR *
************************************************************.

 DATA DIVISION.

 WORKING-STORAGE SECTION.

 77  VERSION-NUMBER                      PICTURE X(27) VALUE
     "VERSION 1     SEPT. 7, 1985".

 LINKAGE SECTION.

 COPY DCL51.
 01  TERMINAL-USER-DATA.                                        COPY
     02  USER-ID                         PICTURE X(8).          COPY
     02  FIRST-TIME-INDICATOR            PICTURE XXX.           COPY
     02  PROCESSING-CONTROL              PICTURE X(6).          COPY
     02  PREVIOUS-PANEL-CODE             PICTURE X.             COPY
     02  PREVIOUS-EMPLOYEE-NUMBER        PICTURE X(8).          COPY
     02  TOTAL-SALARY                    PICTURE S9(7)V99.      COPY
     02  EMPLOYEE-TYPE                   PICTURE XXX.           COPY
     02  EMPLOYEE-DISPLAY-DATA.                                 COPY
         03  PANEL-CODE                  PICTURE X.             COPY
         03  CURRENT-DISPLAY-KEY.                               COPY
             04  EMPLOYEE-NUMBER         PICTURE X(8).          COPY
         03  EMPLOYEE-NAME               PICTURE X(30).         COPY
         03  EMPLOYEE-ADDRESS            PICTURE X(30).         COPY
         03  MANAGER-NAME                PICTURE X(30).         COPY
         03  DEPARTMENT-NUMBER           PICTURE X(3).          COPY
         03  SALARY                      PICTURE X(9).          COPY
         03  NUMERIC-SALARY REDEFINES SALARY                    COPY
                                         PICTURE 9(6).99.       COPY
         03  PERFORMANCE-RATING          PICTURE X.             COPY
         03  MESSAGE                     PICTURE X(50).         COPY
         03  SELECTION-CODE              PICTURE X.             COPY
     02  ALIGNED-SALARY                  PICTURE 9(6)V99.       COPY
     02  SECURITY-DATA.                                         COPY
         03  DATA-BASE-CODE              PICTURE X(8).          COPY
         03  TYPE-OF-ACCESS              PICTURE X.             COPY
             88 NONE                     VALUE "N".             COPY
             88 VIEW                     VALUE "V".             COPY
             88 CHANGE                   VALUE "C".             COPY
         03  ALLOWED-TO-ACCESS.                                 COPY
             04  TYPE-N                  PICTURE X.             COPY
             04  TYPE-S                  PICTURE X.             COPY
             04  TYPE-P                  PICTURE X.             COPY
     02  FILLER                          PICTURE X.             COPY
************************************************************

/************************************************************
 PROCEDURE DIVISION USING TERMINAL-USER-DATA.

     CALL "EMINIT" USING TERMINAL-USER-DATA.

     PERFORM WITH TEST BEFORE UNTIL PANEL-CODE = "E"
       CALL "EMDEC" USING TERMINAL-USER-DATA
     END-PERFORM.

     CALL "EMEOJ" USING TERMINAL-USER-DATA.
     STOP RUN.

 END PROGRAM EMMAIN.

************************************************************
```

Figure 16.23. *Mainline module in COBOL.*

```
/*************************************************************
 IDENTIFICATION DIVISION.

 PROGRAM-ID.          EMDEC.

 AUTHOR.              G.R. ROGERS.

*************************************************************
*                                                           *
* EMPLOYEE INFORMATION UPDATE PROGRAM                       *
* MODULE - DECISION LOGIC                                   *
*                                                           *
*-----------------------------------------------------------*
* CHANGE HISTORY                                            *
*   090785 NEW PROGRAM                                  GRR *
*************************************************************

 DATA DIVISION.

 WORKING-STORAGE SECTION.

 77  VERSION-NUMBER                     PICTURE X(27) VALUE
     "VERSION 1     SEPT. 7, 1985".

 77  INVALID-TRANSACTION-MESSAGE        PICTURE X(34) VALUE
     "INVALID TRANSACTION CODE - REENTER".

 LINKAGE SECTION.

 COPY DCL51.
 01  TERMINAL-USER-DATA.                                        COPY
     02  USER-ID                        PICTURE X(8).           COPY
     02  FIRST-TIME-INDICATOR           PICTURE XXX.            COPY
     02  PROCESSING-CONTROL             PICTURE X(6).           COPY
     02  PREVIOUS-PANEL-CODE            PICTURE X.              COPY
     02  PREVIOUS-EMPLOYEE-NUMBER       PICTURE X(8).           COPY
     02  TOTAL-SALARY                   PICTURE S9(7)V99.       COPY
     02  EMPLOYEE-TYPE                  PICTURE XXX.            COPY
     02  EMPLOYEE-DISPLAY-DATA.                                 COPY
         03  PANEL-CODE                 PICTURE X.              COPY
         03  CURRENT-DISPLAY-KEY.                               COPY
             04  EMPLOYEE-NUMBER        PICTURE X(8).           COPY
         03  EMPLOYEE-NAME              PICTURE X(30).          COPY
         03  EMPLOYEE-ADDRESS           PICTURE X(30).          COPY
         03  MANAGER-NAME               PICTURE X(30).          COPY
         03  DEPARTMENT-NUMBER          PICTURE X(3).           COPY
         03  SALARY                     PICTURE X(9).           COPY
         03  NUMERIC-SALARY REDEFINES SALARY                    COPY
                                        PICTURE 9(6).99.        COPY
         03  PERFORMANCE-RATING         PICTURE X.              COPY
         03  MESSAGE                    PICTURE X(50).          COPY
         03  SELECTION-CODE             PICTURE X.              COPY
     02  ALIGNED-SALARY                 PICTURE 9(6)V99.        COPY
     02  SECURITY-DATA.                                         COPY
         03  DATA-BASE-CODE             PICTURE X(8).           COPY
         03  TYPE-OF-ACCESS             PICTURE X.              COPY
             88 NONE                    VALUE "N".              COPY
             88 VIEW                    VALUE "V".              COPY
             88 CHANGE                  VALUE "C".              COPY
         03  ALLOWED-TO-ACCESS.                                 COPY
             04  TYPE-N                 PICTURE X.              COPY
             04  TYPE-S                 PICTURE X.              COPY
             04  TYPE-P                 PICTURE X.              COPY
     02  FILLER                         PICTURE X.              COPY

*************************************************************
```

(a)

Figure 16.24. Decision logic module in COBOL.

(*continued on next page*)

```
/*****************************************************************
 PROCEDURE DIVISION USING TERMINAL-USER-DATA.

     CALL "PROFIL" USING USER-ID, SECURITY-DATA.

     IF FIRST-TIME-INDICATOR = "YES"
       THEN
         MOVE "NO " TO FIRST-TIME-INDICATOR
         MOVE SPACES TO PREVIOUS-PANEL-CODE
       ELSE
         CALL "EMRECV" USING TERMINAL-USER-DATA
     END-IF.

     PERFORM WITH TEST AFTER UNTIL PROCESSING-CONTROL = "SEND"

       EVALUATE PANEL-CODE
         WHEN "M"
           CALL "EMPNLM" USING TERMINAL-USER-DATA
           MOVE "M" TO PREVIOUS-PANEL-CODE
         WHEN "N"
           CALL "EMPNLN" USING TERMINAL-USER-DATA
           MOVE "N" TO PREVIOUS-PANEL-CODE
         WHEN "S"
           CALL "EMPNLS" USING TERMINAL-USER-DATA
           MOVE "S" TO PREVIOUS-PANEL-CODE
         WHEN "P"
           CALL "EMPNLP" USING TERMINAL-USER-DATA
           MOVE "P" TO PREVIOUS-PANEL-CODE
         WHEN "E"
           CALL "EMPNLE" USING TERMINAL-USER-DATA
           MOVE "E" TO PREVIOUS-PANEL-CODE
         WHEN OTHER
           MOVE PREVIOUS-PANEL-CODE TO PANEL-CODE
           MOVE INVALID-TRANSACTION-MESSAGE TO MESSAGE
           MOVE "SEND" TO PROCESSING-CONTROL
       END-EVALUATE

     END-PERFORM.

     CALL "EMSEND" USING TERMINAL-USER-DATA.

 END PROGRAM EMDEC.

*****************************************************************
```

(b)

Figure 16.24. *(Continued)*

```
/*****************************************************************
 IDENTIFICATION DIVISION.

 PROGRAM-ID.        EMPNLM.

 AUTHOR.            G.R. ROGERS.

*****************************************************************
*                                                               *
* EMPLOYEE INFORMATION UPDATE PROGRAM                           *
* MODULE - MENU PROCESSING                                      *
*                                                               *
*---------------------------------------------------------------*
* CHANGE HISTORY                                                *
*   090785 NEW PROGRAM                                      GRR *
*****************************************************************

 DATA DIVISION.

 WORKING-STORAGE SECTION.

 77  VERSION-NUMBER                    PICTURE X(27) VALUE
     "VERSION 1     SEPT. 7, 1985".

 77  SELECT-CODE-MESSAGE               PICTURE X(22) VALUE
     "ENTER TRANSACTION CODE".

 LINKAGE SECTION.

 COPY DCL51.
 01  TERMINAL-USER-DATA.                                           COPY
     02  USER-ID                       PICTURE X(8).               COPY
     02  FIRST-TIME-INDICATOR          PICTURE XXX.                COPY
     02  PROCESSING-CONTROL            PICTURE X(6).               COPY
     02  PREVIOUS-PANEL-CODE           PICTURE X.                  COPY
     02  PREVIOUS-EMPLOYEE-NUMBER      PICTURE X(8).               COPY
     02  TOTAL-SALARY                  PICTURE S9(7)V99.           COPY
     02  EMPLOYEE-TYPE                 PICTURE XXX.                COPY
     02  EMPLOYEE-DISPLAY-DATA.                                    COPY
         03  PANEL-CODE                PICTURE X.                  COPY
         03  CURRENT-DISPLAY-KEY.                                  COPY
             04  EMPLOYEE-NUMBER       PICTURE X(8).               COPY
         03  EMPLOYEE-NAME             PICTURE X(30).              COPY
         03  EMPLOYEE-ADDRESS          PICTURE X(30).              COPY
         03  MANAGER-NAME              PICTURE X(30).              COPY
         03  DEPARTMENT-NUMBER         PICTURE X(3).               COPY
         03  SALARY                    PICTURE X(9).               COPY
         03  NUMERIC-SALARY REDEFINES  SALARY                      COPY
                                       PICTURE 9(6).99.            COPY
         03  PERFORMANCE-RATING        PICTURE X.                  COPY
         03  MESSAGE                   PICTURE X(50).              COPY
         03  SELECTION-CODE            PICTURE X.                  COPY
     02  ALIGNED-SALARY                PICTURE 9(6)V99.            COPY
     02  SECURITY-DATA.                                            COPY
         03  DATA-BASE-CODE            PICTURE X(8).               COPY
         03  TYPE-OF-ACCESS            PICTURE X.                  COPY
             88 NONE                   VALUE "N".                  COPY
             88 VIEW                   VALUE "V".                  COPY
             88 CHANGE                 VALUE "C".                  COPY
         03  ALLOWED-TO-ACCESS.                                    COPY
             04  TYPE-N                PICTURE X.                  COPY
             04  TYPE-S                PICTURE X.                  COPY
             04  TYPE-P                PICTURE X.                  COPY
     02  FILLER                        PICTURE X.                  COPY
*****************************************************************

/*****************************************************************
 PROCEDURE DIVISION USING TERMINAL-USER-DATA.

     IF PREVIOUS-PANEL-CODE NOT = "M" OR
        SELECTION-CODE = SPACES
       THEN
         MOVE SPACES TO SELECTION-CODE
         MOVE SELECT-CODE-MESSAGE TO MESSAGE
         MOVE "SEND" TO PROCESSING-CONTROL
         EXIT PROGRAM
     END-IF.

     MOVE SELECTION-CODE TO PANEL-CODE.
     MOVE SPACES TO SELECTION-CODE.
     MOVE "SELECT" TO PROCESSING-CONTROL.

 END PROGRAM EMPNLM.

*****************************************************************
```

Figure 16.25. *Menu module in COBOL.*

```
/*****************************************************************
 IDENTIFICATION DIVISION.

 PROGRAM-ID.          EMPNLN.

 AUTHOR.              G.R. ROGERS.

*****************************************************************
*                                                               *
* EMPLOYEE INFORMATION UPDATE PROGRAM                           *
* MODULE - PROCESS NAME AND ADDRESS DATA                        *
*                                                               *
*---------------------------------------------------------------*
* CHANGE HISTORY                                                *
*   090785 NEW PROGRAM                                      GRR *
*****************************************************************

 DATA DIVISION.

 WORKING-STORAGE SECTION.

 77  VERSION-NUMBER                      PICTURE X(27) VALUE
     "VERSION 1      SEPT. 7, 1985".

 77  EMPLOYEE-NUMBER-MESSAGE             PICTURE X(21) VALUE
     "ENTER EMPLOYEE NUMBER".
 77  ACCESS-REFUSED-MESSAGE              PICTURE X(46) VALUE
     "YOU ARE NOT ALLOWED TO ACCESS THIS TRANSACTION".
 77  EMPLOYEE-NOT-EXIST-MESSAGE          PICTURE X(46) VALUE
     "EMPLOYEE DATA DOES NOT EXIST - ENTER TO CREATE".

 77  EIGHT                               PICTURE S99 VALUE 8.

 77  YES-VALUE                           PICTURE XXX VALUE "YES".

 COPY DCL52.
 01  INPUT-CHARACTER-ARRAY.                                          COPY
     02  INPUT-CHARACTER-ELEMENT         PICTURE X OCCURS 30 TIMES.  COPY

 COPY DCL53.
 01  OUTPUT-CHARACTER-ARRAY.                                         COPY
     02  OUTPUT-CHARACTER-ELEMENT        PICTURE X OCCURS 30 TIMES.  COPY

 COPY DCL50.
 01  EMPLOYEE-MASTER-DATA.                                           COPY
     02  EMPLOYEE-NUMBER                 PICTURE X(8).               COPY
     02  EMPLOYEE-NAME                   PICTURE X(30).              COPY
     02  EMPLOYEE-ADDRESS                PICTURE X(30).              COPY
     02  MANAGER-NAME                    PICTURE X(30).              COPY
     02  DEPARTMENT-NUMBER               PICTURE X(3).               COPY
     02  PERFORMANCE-RATING              PICTURE X.                  COPY
     02  SALARY                          PICTURE S9(6)V99.           COPY
     02  FILLER                          PICTURE X.                  COPY

 LINKAGE SECTION.

 COPY DCL51.
 01  TERMINAL-USER-DATA.                                             COPY
     02  USER-ID                         PICTURE X(8).               COPY
     02  FIRST-TIME-INDICATOR            PICTURE XXX.                COPY
     02  PROCESSING-CONTROL              PICTURE X(6).               COPY
     02  PREVIOUS-PANEL-CODE             PICTURE X.                  COPY
     02  PREVIOUS-EMPLOYEE-NUMBER        PICTURE X(8).               COPY
     02  TOTAL-SALARY                    PICTURE S9(7)V99.           COPY
     02  EMPLOYEE-TYPE                   PICTURE XXX.                COPY
     02  EMPLOYEE-DISPLAY-DATA.                                      COPY
         03  PANEL-CODE                  PICTURE X.                  COPY
         03  CURRENT-DISPLAY-KEY.                                    COPY
             04  EMPLOYEE-NUMBER         PICTURE X(8).               COPY
         03  EMPLOYEE-NAME               PICTURE X(30).              COPY
         03  EMPLOYEE-ADDRESS            PICTURE X(30).              COPY
         03  MANAGER-NAME                PICTURE X(30).              COPY
         03  DEPARTMENT-NUMBER           PICTURE X(3).               COPY
         03  SALARY                      PICTURE X(9).               COPY
         03  NUMERIC-SALARY REDEFINES SALARY                         COPY
                                         PICTURE 9(6).99.            COPY
         03  PERFORMANCE-RATING          PICTURE X.                  COPY
         03  MESSAGE                     PICTURE X(50).              COPY
         03  SELECTION-CODE              PICTURE X.                  COPY
     02  ALIGNED-SALARY                  PICTURE 9(6)V99.            COPY
     02  SECURITY-DATA.                                              COPY
         03  DATA-BASE-CODE              PICTURE X(8).               COPY
         03  TYPE-OF-ACCESS              PICTURE X.                  COPY
             88 NONE                     VALUE "N".                  COPY
             88 VIEW                     VALUE "V".                  COPY
             88 CHANGE                   VALUE "C".                  COPY
         03  ALLOWED-TO-ACCESS.                                      COPY
             04  TYPE-N                  PICTURE X.                  COPY
             04  TYPE-S                  PICTURE X.                  COPY
             04  TYPE-P                  PICTURE X.                  COPY
     02  FILLER                          PICTURE X.                  COPY

*****************************************************************
```

(a)

Figure 16.26. Name and address module in COBOL.

```
/***************************************************************
 PROCEDURE DIVISION USING TERMINAL-USER-DATA.

     IF SELECTION-CODE NOT = SPACES
       THEN
         MOVE SELECTION-CODE TO PANEL-CODE
         MOVE SPACES TO SELECTION-CODE
         MOVE "SELECT" TO PROCESSING-CONTROL
         EXIT PROGRAM
     END-IF.

     MOVE "SEND" TO PROCESSING-CONTROL.

     IF TYPE-N NOT = "Y"
       THEN
         MOVE ACCESS-REFUSED-MESSAGE TO MESSAGE
         EXIT PROGRAM
     END-IF.

     IF EMPLOYEE-NUMBER IN TERMINAL-USER-DATA = SPACES
       THEN
         MOVE EMPLOYEE-NUMBER-MESSAGE TO MESSAGE
         EXIT PROGRAM
     END-IF.

     MOVE EMPLOYEE-NUMBER IN TERMINAL-USER-DATA TO
        INPUT-CHARACTER-ARRAY.
     CALL "EMLFJS" USING INPUT-CHARACTER-ARRAY,
                         OUTPUT-CHARACTER-ARRAY,
                         EIGHT, EIGHT.
     MOVE OUTPUT-CHARACTER-ARRAY TO EMPLOYEE-NUMBER
        IN TERMINAL-USER-DATA.

     IF EMPLOYEE-NUMBER IN TERMINAL-USER-DATA =
        PREVIOUS-EMPLOYEE-NUMBER AND
        PANEL-CODE = PREVIOUS-PANEL-CODE
       THEN
         CONTINUE
       ELSE
         MOVE EMPLOYEE-NUMBER IN TERMINAL-USER-DATA TO
            EMPLOYEE-NUMBER IN EMPLOYEE-MASTER-DATA
         CALL "EMMRRD" USING EMPLOYEE-MASTER-DATA,
                             MESSAGE, YES-VALUE

         IF MESSAGE = SPACES
           THEN
             MOVE EMPLOYEE-NAME IN EMPLOYEE-MASTER-DATA TO
                EMPLOYEE-NAME IN TERMINAL-USER-DATA
             MOVE EMPLOYEE-ADDRESS IN EMPLOYEE-MASTER-DATA TO
                EMPLOYEE-ADDRESS IN TERMINAL-USER-DATA
             MOVE MANAGER-NAME IN EMPLOYEE-MASTER-DATA TO
                MANAGER-NAME IN TERMINAL-USER-DATA
             MOVE DEPARTMENT-NUMBER IN EMPLOYEE-MASTER-DATA TO
                DEPARTMENT-NUMBER IN TERMINAL-USER-DATA
             MOVE SALARY IN EMPLOYEE-MASTER-DATA TO
                ALIGNED-SALARY IN TERMINAL-USER-DATA
             MOVE PERFORMANCE-RATING IN EMPLOYEE-MASTER-DATA TO
                PERFORMANCE-RATING IN TERMINAL-USER-DATA
           ELSE
             MOVE EMPLOYEE-NOT-EXIST-MESSAGE TO MESSAGE
             MOVE "NEW" TO EMPLOYEE-TYPE
             MOVE SPACES TO EMPLOYEE-NAME IN TERMINAL-USER-DATA
             MOVE SPACES TO
                EMPLOYEE-ADDRESS IN TERMINAL-USER-DATA
             MOVE SPACES TO MANAGER-NAME IN TERMINAL-USER-DATA
             MOVE SPACES TO
                DEPARTMENT-NUMBER IN TERMINAL-USER-DATA
             MOVE SPACES TO SALARY IN TERMINAL-USER-DATA
             MOVE SPACES TO
                PERFORMANCE-RATING IN TERMINAL-USER-DATA
         END-IF

         MOVE EMPLOYEE-NUMBER IN TERMINAL-USER-DATA TO
            PREVIOUS-EMPLOYEE-NUMBER
         EXIT PROGRAM
     END-IF.

     MOVE EMPLOYEE-NUMBER IN TERMINAL-USER-DATA TO
        EMPLOYEE-NUMBER IN EMPLOYEE-MASTER-DATA.
     MOVE EMPLOYEE-NAME IN TERMINAL-USER-DATA TO
        EMPLOYEE-NAME IN EMPLOYEE-MASTER-DATA.
     MOVE EMPLOYEE-ADDRESS IN TERMINAL-USER-DATA TO
        EMPLOYEE-ADDRESS IN EMPLOYEE-MASTER-DATA.
     MOVE MANAGER-NAME IN TERMINAL-USER-DATA TO
        MANAGER-NAME IN EMPLOYEE-MASTER-DATA.
     MOVE DEPARTMENT-NUMBER IN TERMINAL-USER-DATA TO
        DEPARTMENT-NUMBER IN EMPLOYEE-MASTER-DATA.
```

(b)

(continued on next page)

```
     IF EMPLOYEE-TYPE NOT = "NEW"
       THEN
         MOVE ALIGNED-SALARY IN TERMINAL-USER-DATA TO
            SALARY IN EMPLOYEE-MASTER-DATA
         MOVE PERFORMANCE-RATING IN TERMINAL-USER-DATA TO
            PERFORMANCE-RATING IN EMPLOYEE-MASTER-DATA
         CALL "EMUPDT" USING EMPLOYEE-MASTER-DATA,
                             MESSAGE, YES-VALUE
         EXIT PROGRAM
     END-IF.

     MOVE "OLD" TO EMPLOYEE-TYPE.
     MOVE 0 TO SALARY IN EMPLOYEE-MASTER-DATA.
     MOVE SPACES TO PERFORMANCE-RATING IN EMPLOYEE-MASTER-DATA.
     CALL "EMINST" USING EMPLOYEE-MASTER-DATA, MESSAGE,
                         YES-VALUE.

 END PROGRAM EMPNLN.

*****************************************************************
```

(c)

Figure 16.26. *(Continued)*

```
/*************************************************************
 IDENTIFICATION DIVISION.

 PROGRAM-ID.        EMPNLS.

 AUTHOR.            G.R. ROGERS.

**************************************************************
*                                                            *
* EMPLOYEE INFORMATION UPDATE PROGRAM                        *
* MODULE - PROCESS SALARY DATA                               *
*                                                            *
*------------------------------------------------------------*
* CHANGE HISTORY                                             *
*   090785 NEW PROGRAM                                   GRR *
**************************************************************

 DATA DIVISION.

 WORKING-STORAGE SECTION.

 77  VERSION-NUMBER                  PICTURE X(27) VALUE
     "VERSION 1     SEPT. 7, 1985".

 77  EMPLOYEE-NUMBER-MESSAGE         PICTURE X(21) VALUE
     "ENTER EMPLOYEE NUMBER".
 77  ACCESS-REFUSED-MESSAGE          PICTURE X(46) VALUE
     "YOU ARE NOT ALLOWED TO ACCESS THIS TRANSACTION".
 77  INVALID-SALARY-MESSAGE          PICTURE X(14) VALUE
     "INVALID SALARY".

 77  AMOUNT-1                        PICTURE X(9).
 77  AMOUNT-2 REDEFINES AMOUNT-1     PICTURE 9(7)V99.

 77  EIGHT                           PICTURE S99 VALUE 8.

 77  NINE                            PICTURE S99 VALUE 9.

 77  YES-VALUE                       PICTURE XXX VALUE "YES".

 COPY DCL38.
 77  NUMBER-OF-DECIMAL-PLACES        PICTURE S99.                COPY

 COPY DCL35.
 01  INPUT-DATA-ARRAY.                                           COPY
     02  INPUT-ELEMENT               PICTURE X OCCURS 9 TIMES.   COPY

 COPY DCL36.
 01  OUTPUT-DATA-ARRAY.                                          COPY
     02  OUTPUT-ELEMENT              PICTURE X OCCURS 9 TIMES.   COPY

 COPY DCL52.
 01  INPUT-CHARACTER-ARRAY.                                      COPY
     02  INPUT-CHARACTER-ELEMENT     PICTURE X OCCURS 30 TIMES.  COPY

 COPY DCL53.
 01  OUTPUT-CHARACTER-ARRAY.                                     COPY
     02  OUTPUT-CHARACTER-ELEMENT    PICTURE X OCCURS 30 TIMES.  COPY

 COPY DCL50.
 01  EMPLOYEE-MASTER-DATA.                                       COPY
     02  EMPLOYEE-NUMBER             PICTURE X(8).               COPY
     02  EMPLOYEE-NAME               PICTURE X(30).              COPY
     02  EMPLOYEE-ADDRESS            PICTURE X(30).              COPY
     02  MANAGER-NAME                PICTURE X(30).              COPY
     02  DEPARTMENT-NUMBER           PICTURE X(3).               COPY
     02  PERFORMANCE-RATING          PICTURE X.                  COPY
     02  SALARY                      PICTURE S9(6)V99.           COPY
     02  FILLER                      PICTURE X.                  COPY
```

(a)

Figure 16.27. Salary module in COBOL.

(continued on next page)

```
LINKAGE SECTION.

COPY DCL51.
01  TERMINAL-USER-DATA.                                              COPY
    02  USER-ID                        PICTURE X(8).                 COPY
    02  FIRST-TIME-INDICATOR           PICTURE XXX.                  COPY
    02  PROCESSING-CONTROL             PICTURE X(6).                 COPY
    02  PREVIOUS-PANEL-CODE            PICTURE X.                    COPY
    02  PREVIOUS-EMPLOYEE-NUMBER       PICTURE X(8).                 COPY
    02  TOTAL-SALARY                   PICTURE S9(7)V99.             COPY
    02  EMPLOYEE-TYPE                  PICTURE XXX.                  COPY
    02  EMPLOYEE-DISPLAY-DATA.                                       COPY
        03  PANEL-CODE                 PICTURE X.                    COPY
        03  CURRENT-DISPLAY-KEY.                                     COPY
            04  EMPLOYEE-NUMBER        PICTURE X(8).                 COPY
        03  EMPLOYEE-NAME              PICTURE X(30).                COPY
        03  EMPLOYEE-ADDRESS           PICTURE X(30).                COPY
        03  MANAGER-NAME               PICTURE X(30).                COPY
        03  DEPARTMENT-NUMBER          PICTURE X(3).                 COPY
        03  SALARY                     PICTURE X(9).                 COPY
        03  NUMERIC-SALARY REDEFINES SALARY                          COPY
                                       PICTURE 9(6).99.              COPY
        03  PERFORMANCE-RATING         PICTURE X.                    COPY
        03  MESSAGE                    PICTURE X(50).                COPY
        03  SELECTION-CODE             PICTURE X.                    COPY
    02  ALIGNED-SALARY                 PICTURE 9(6)V99.              COPY

    02  SECURITY-DATA.                                               COPY
        03  DATA-BASE-CODE             PICTURE X(8).                 COPY
        03  TYPE-OF-ACCESS             PICTURE X.                    COPY
            88 NONE                    VALUE "N".                    COPY
            88 VIEW                    VALUE "V".                    COPY
            88 CHANGE                  VALUE "C".                    COPY
        03  ALLOWED-TO-ACCESS.                                       COPY
            04  TYPE-N                 PICTURE X.                    COPY
            04  TYPE-S                 PICTURE X.                    COPY
            04  TYPE-P                 PICTURE X.                    COPY
    02  FILLER                         PICTURE X.                    COPY
*****************************************************************


/****************************************************************
 PROCEDURE DIVISION USING TERMINAL-USER-DATA.

     IF SELECTION-CODE NOT = SPACES
       THEN
         MOVE SELECTION-CODE TO PANEL-CODE
         MOVE SPACES TO SELECTION-CODE
         MOVE "SELECT" TO PROCESSING-CONTROL
         EXIT PROGRAM
     END-IF.

     MOVE "SEND" TO PROCESSING-CONTROL.

     IF TYPE-S NOT = "Y"
       THEN
         MOVE ACCESS-REFUSED-MESSAGE TO MESSAGE
         EXIT PROGRAM
     END-IF.

     IF EMPLOYEE-NUMBER IN TERMINAL-USER-DATA = SPACES
       THEN
         MOVE EMPLOYEE-NUMBER-MESSAGE TO MESSAGE
         EXIT PROGRAM
     END-IF.

     MOVE EMPLOYEE-NUMBER IN TERMINAL-USER-DATA TO
        INPUT-CHARACTER-ARRAY.
     CALL "EMLFJS" USING INPUT-CHARACTER-ARRAY,
                         OUTPUT-CHARACTER-ARRAY,
                         EIGHT, EIGHT.

     MOVE OUTPUT-CHARACTER-ARRAY TO EMPLOYEE-NUMBER
        IN TERMINAL-USER-DATA.

     IF EMPLOYEE-NUMBER IN TERMINAL-USER-DATA =
        PREVIOUS-EMPLOYEE-NUMBER AND
        PANEL-CODE = PREVIOUS-PANEL-CODE
       THEN
         CONTINUE
       ELSE
         MOVE EMPLOYEE-NUMBER IN TERMINAL-USER-DATA TO
            EMPLOYEE-NUMBER IN EMPLOYEE-MASTER-DATA
         CALL "EMMRRD" USING EMPLOYEE-MASTER-DATA,
                             MESSAGE, YES-VALUE
```

(b)

Figure 16.27. *(Continued)*

```
          IF MESSAGE = SPACES
            THEN
              MOVE EMPLOYEE-NAME IN EMPLOYEE-MASTER-DATA TO
                 EMPLOYEE-NAME IN TERMINAL-USER-DATA
              MOVE EMPLOYEE-ADDRESS IN EMPLOYEE-MASTER-DATA TO
                 EMPLOYEE-ADDRESS IN TERMINAL-USER-DATA
              MOVE MANAGER-NAME IN EMPLOYEE-MASTER-DATA TO
                 MANAGER-NAME IN TERMINAL-USER-DATA
              MOVE DEPARTMENT-NUMBER IN EMPLOYEE-MASTER-DATA TO
                 DEPARTMENT-NUMBER IN TERMINAL-USER-DATA
              MOVE SALARY IN EMPLOYEE-MASTER-DATA TO
                 ALIGNED-SALARY IN TERMINAL-USER-DATA
              MOVE SALARY IN EMPLOYEE-MASTER-DATA TO
                 NUMERIC-SALARY IN TERMINAL-USER-DATA
              MOVE PERFORMANCE-RATING IN EMPLOYEE-MASTER-DATA TO
                 PERFORMANCE-RATING IN TERMINAL-USER-DATA
            ELSE
              MOVE SPACES TO EMPLOYEE-NAME IN TERMINAL-USER-DATA
              MOVE SPACES TO
                 EMPLOYEE-ADDRESS IN TERMINAL-USER-DATA
              MOVE SPACES TO MANAGER-NAME IN TERMINAL-USER-DATA
              MOVE SPACES TO
                 DEPARTMENT-NUMBER IN TERMINAL-USER-DATA
              MOVE SPACES TO SALARY IN TERMINAL-USER-DATA
              MOVE SPACES TO
                 PERFORMANCE-RATING IN TERMINAL-USER-DATA
          END-IF

          MOVE EMPLOYEE-NUMBER IN TERMINAL-USER-DATA TO
             PREVIOUS-EMPLOYEE-NUMBER
          EXIT PROGRAM
      END-IF.

      MOVE SALARY IN TERMINAL-USER-DATA TO INPUT-DATA-ARRAY.
      CALL "CRRTJS" USING INPUT-DATA-ARRAY,
                          OUTPUT-DATA-ARRAY,
                          NUMBER-OF-DECIMAL-PLACES, MESSAGE,
                          NINE, NINE

      IF MESSAGE NOT = SPACES
        THEN
          EXIT PROGRAM
      END-IF.

      MOVE OUTPUT-DATA-ARRAY TO AMOUNT-1.

      IF NUMBER-OF-DECIMAL-PLACES NOT = 2 OR
         AMOUNT-1 NOT NUMERIC
        THEN
          MOVE INVALID-SALARY-MESSAGE TO MESSAGE
          EXIT PROGRAM
      END-IF.

      MOVE AMOUNT-2 TO NUMERIC-SALARY ALIGNED-SALARY.

      MOVE EMPLOYEE-NUMBER IN TERMINAL-USER-DATA TO
         EMPLOYEE-NUMBER IN EMPLOYEE-MASTER-DATA.
      MOVE EMPLOYEE-NAME IN TERMINAL-USER-DATA TO
         EMPLOYEE-NAME IN EMPLOYEE-MASTER-DATA.
      MOVE EMPLOYEE-ADDRESS IN TERMINAL-USER-DATA TO
         EMPLOYEE-ADDRESS IN EMPLOYEE-MASTER-DATA.
      MOVE MANAGER-NAME IN TERMINAL-USER-DATA TO
         MANAGER-NAME IN EMPLOYEE-MASTER-DATA.
      MOVE DEPARTMENT-NUMBER IN TERMINAL-USER-DATA TO
         DEPARTMENT-NUMBER IN EMPLOYEE-MASTER-DATA.
      MOVE ALIGNED-SALARY IN TERMINAL-USER-DATA TO
         SALARY IN EMPLOYEE-MASTER-DATA.
      MOVE PERFORMANCE-RATING IN TERMINAL-USER-DATA TO
            PERFORMANCE-RATING IN EMPLOYEE-MASTER-DATA.
      CALL "EMUPDT" USING EMPLOYEE-MASTER-DATA, MESSAGE,
                          MESSAGE, YES-VALUE.
      ADD ALIGNED-SALARY TO TOTAL-SALARY.

  END PROGRAM EMPNLS.
****************************************************************
```

(c)

```
/******************************************************************
 IDENTIFICATION DIVISION.

 PROGRAM-ID.        EMPNLP.

 AUTHOR.            G.R. ROGERS.

****************************************************************
*                                                              *
* EMPLOYEE INFORMATION UPDATE PROGRAM                          *
* MODULE - PROCESS PERFORMANCE DATA                            *
*                                                              *
*--------------------------------------------------------------*
* CHANGE HISTORY                                               *
*   090785 NEW PROGRAM                                     GRR *
****************************************************************

 DATA DIVISION.

 WORKING-STORAGE SECTION.

 77  VERSION-NUMBER                   PICTURE X(27) VALUE
     "VERSION 1     SEPT. 7, 1985".

 77  EMPLOYEE-NUMBER-MESSAGE          PICTURE X(21) VALUE
     "ENTER EMPLOYEE NUMBER".
 77  ACCESS-REFUSED-MESSAGE           PICTURE X(46) VALUE
     "YOU ARE NOT ALLOWED TO ACCESS THIS TRANSACTION".

 77  EIGHT                            PICTURE S99 VALUE 8.

 77  NO-VALUE                         PICTURE XXX VALUE "NO ".

 COPY DCL52.
 01  INPUT-CHARACTER-ARRAY.                                         COPY
     02  INPUT-CHARACTER-ELEMENT      PICTURE X OCCURS 30 TIMES.    COPY

 COPY DCL53.
 01  OUTPUT-CHARACTER-ARRAY.                                        COPY
     02  OUTPUT-CHARACTER-ELEMENT     PICTURE X OCCURS 30 TIMES.    COPY

 COPY DCL50.
 01  EMPLOYEE-MASTER-DATA.                                          COPY
     02  EMPLOYEE-NUMBER              PICTURE X(8).                 COPY
     02  EMPLOYEE-NAME                PICTURE X(30).                COPY
     02  EMPLOYEE-ADDRESS             PICTURE X(30).                COPY
     02  MANAGER-NAME                 PICTURE X(30).                COPY
     02  DEPARTMENT-NUMBER            PICTURE X(3).                 COPY
     02  PERFORMANCE-RATING           PICTURE X.                    COPY
     02  SALARY                       PICTURE S9(6)V99.             COPY
     02  FILLER                       PICTURE X.                    COPY

 LINKAGE SECTION.

 COPY DCL51.
 01  TERMINAL-USER-DATA.                                            COPY
     02  USER-ID                      PICTURE X(8).                 COPY
     02  FIRST-TIME-INDICATOR         PICTURE XXX.                  COPY
     02  PROCESSING-CONTROL           PICTURE X(6).                 COPY
     02  PREVIOUS-PANEL-CODE          PICTURE X.                    COPY
     02  PREVIOUS-EMPLOYEE-NUMBER     PICTURE X(8).                 COPY
     02  TOTAL-SALARY                 PICTURE S9(7)V99.             COPY
     02  EMPLOYEE-TYPE                PICTURE XXX.                  COPY
     02  EMPLOYEE-DISPLAY-DATA.                                     COPY
         03  PANEL-CODE               PICTURE X.                    COPY
         03  CURRENT-DISPLAY-KEY.                                   COPY
             04  EMPLOYEE-NUMBER      PICTURE X(8).                 COPY
         03  EMPLOYEE-NAME            PICTURE X(30).                COPY
         03  EMPLOYEE-ADDRESS         PICTURE X(30).                COPY
         03  MANAGER-NAME             PICTURE X(30).                COPY
         03  DEPARTMENT-NUMBER        PICTURE X(3).                 COPY
         03  SALARY                   PICTURE X(9).                 COPY
         03  NUMERIC-SALARY REDEFINES SALARY                        COPY
                                      PICTURE 9(6).99.              COPY
         03  PERFORMANCE-RATING       PICTURE X.                    COPY
         03  MESSAGE                  PICTURE X(50).                COPY
         03  SELECTION-CODE           PICTURE X.                    COPY
     02  ALIGNED-SALARY               PICTURE 9(6)V99.              COPY
     02  SECURITY-DATA.                                             COPY
         03  DATA-BASE-CODE           PICTURE X(8).                 COPY
         03  TYPE-OF-ACCESS           PICTURE X.                    COPY
             88 NONE                  VALUE "N".                    COPY
             88 VIEW                  VALUE "V".                    COPY
             88 CHANGE                VALUE "C".                    COPY
         03  ALLOWED-TO-ACCESS.                                     COPY
             04  TYPE-N               PICTURE X.                    COPY
             04  TYPE-S               PICTURE X.                    COPY
             04  TYPE-P               PICTURE X.                    COPY
     02  FILLER                       PICTURE X.                    COPY

******************************************************************
```

(a)

Figure 16.28. *Performance Module in COBOL*

```
/*****************************************************************
 PROCEDURE DIVISION USING TERMINAL-USER-DATA.

     IF SELECTION-CODE NOT = SPACES
       THEN
         MOVE SELECTION-CODE TO PANEL-CODE
         MOVE SPACES TO SELECTION-CODE
         MOVE "SELECT" TO PROCESSING-CONTROL
         EXIT PROGRAM
     END-IF.

     MOVE "SEND" TO PROCESSING-CONTROL.

     IF TYPE-P NOT = "Y"
       THEN
         MOVE ACCESS-REFUSED-MESSAGE TO MESSAGE
         EXIT PROGRAM
     END-IF.

     IF EMPLOYEE-NUMBER IN TERMINAL-USER-DATA = SPACES
       THEN
         MOVE EMPLOYEE-NUMBER-MESSAGE TO MESSAGE
         EXIT PROGRAM
     END-IF.

     MOVE EMPLOYEE-NUMBER IN TERMINAL-USER-DATA TO
        INPUT-CHARACTER-ARRAY.
     CALL "EMLFJS" USING INPUT-CHARACTER-ARRAY,
                         OUTPUT-CHARACTER-ARRAY,
                         EIGHT, EIGHT.

     MOVE OUTPUT-CHARACTER-ARRAY TO EMPLOYEE-NUMBER
        IN TERMINAL-USER-DATA.
     MOVE EMPLOYEE-NUMBER IN TERMINAL-USER-DATA TO
        EMPLOYEE-NUMBER IN EMPLOYEE-MASTER-DATA.
     CALL "EMMRRD" USING EMPLOYEE-MASTER-DATA,
                         MESSAGE, NO-VALUE.

     IF MESSAGE = SPACES
       THEN
         MOVE EMPLOYEE-NAME IN EMPLOYEE-MASTER-DATA TO
            EMPLOYEE-NAME IN TERMINAL-USER-DATA
         MOVE PERFORMANCE-RATING IN EMPLOYEE-MASTER-DATA TO
            PERFORMANCE-RATING IN TERMINAL-USER-DATA
       ELSE
         MOVE SPACES TO EMPLOYEE-NAME IN TERMINAL-USER-DATA
         MOVE SPACES TO
            EMPLOYEE-ADDRESS IN TERMINAL-USER-DATA
         MOVE SPACES TO MANAGER-NAME IN TERMINAL-USER-DATA
         MOVE SPACES TO
            DEPARTMENT-NUMBER IN TERMINAL-USER-DATA
         MOVE SPACES TO SALARY IN TERMINAL-USER-DATA
         MOVE SPACES TO
            PERFORMANCE-RATING IN TERMINAL-USER-DATA
     END-IF.

 END PROGRAM EMPNLP.
******************************************************************
```

(b)

```
/*************************************************************
 IDENTIFICATION DIVISION.

 PROGRAM-ID.         EMPNLE.

 AUTHOR.             G.R. ROGERS.

*************************************************************
*                                                           *
* EMPLOYEE INFORMATION UPDATE PROGRAM                       *
* MODULE - PROCESS END OF SESSION REQUEST                   *
*                                                           *
*-----------------------------------------------------------*
* CHANGE HISTORY                                            *
*    090785 NEW PROGRAM                                 GRR *
*************************************************************

 DATA DIVISION.

 WORKING-STORAGE SECTION.

 77  VERSION-NUMBER                    PICTURE X(27) VALUE
     "VERSION 1      SEPT. 7, 1985".

 77  GOOD-BYE-MESSAGE                  PICTURE X(20) VALUE
     "***** GOOD BYE *****".

 LINKAGE SECTION.

 COPY DCL51.
 01  TERMINAL-USER-DATA.                                         COPY
     02  USER-ID                       PICTURE X(8).             COPY
     02  FIRST-TIME-INDICATOR          PICTURE XXX.              COPY
     02  PROCESSING-CONTROL            PICTURE X(6).             COPY
     02  PREVIOUS-PANEL-CODE           PICTURE X.                COPY
     02  PREVIOUS-EMPLOYEE-NUMBER      PICTURE X(8).             COPY
     02  TOTAL-SALARY                  PICTURE S9(7)V99.         COPY
     02  EMPLOYEE-TYPE                 PICTURE XXX.              COPY
     02  EMPLOYEE-DISPLAY-DATA.                                  COPY
         03  PANEL-CODE                PICTURE X.                COPY
         03  CURRENT-DISPLAY-KEY.                                COPY
             04  EMPLOYEE-NUMBER       PICTURE X(8).             COPY
         03  EMPLOYEE-NAME             PICTURE X(30).            COPY
         03  EMPLOYEE-ADDRESS          PICTURE X(30).            COPY
         03  MANAGER-NAME              PICTURE X(30).            COPY
         03  DEPARTMENT-NUMBER         PICTURE X(3).             COPY
         03  SALARY                    PICTURE X(9).             COPY
         03  NUMERIC-SALARY REDEFINES  SALARY                    COPY
                                       PICTURE 9(6).99.          COPY
         03  PERFORMANCE-RATING        PICTURE X.                COPY
         03  MESSAGE                   PICTURE X(50).            COPY
         03  SELECTION-CODE            PICTURE X.                COPY
     02  ALIGNED-SALARY                PICTURE 9(6)V99.          COPY
     02  SECURITY-DATA.                                          COPY
         03  DATA-BASE-CODE            PICTURE X(8).             COPY
         03  TYPE-OF-ACCESS            PICTURE X.                COPY
             88 NONE                   VALUE "N".                COPY
             88 VIEW                   VALUE "V".                COPY
             88 CHANGE                 VALUE "C".                COPY
         03  ALLOWED-TO-ACCESS.                                  COPY
             04  TYPE-N                PICTURE X.                COPY
             04  TYPE-S                PICTURE X.                COPY
             04  TYPE-P                PICTURE X.                COPY
     02  FILLER                        PICTURE X.                COPY
*************************************************************

/*************************************************************
 PROCEDURE DIVISION USING TERMINAL-USER-DATA.

     MOVE GOOD-BYE-MESSAGE TO MESSAGE.
     MOVE "SEND" TO PROCESSING-CONTROL.

 END PROGRAM EMPNLE.

*************************************************************
```

Figure 16.29. *End Selection Module in COBOL*

```
/*****************************************************************

 IDENTIFICATION DIVISION.

 PROGRAM-ID.        EMINIT.

 AUTHOR.            G.R. ROGERS.

*****************************************************************
*                                                               *
* EMPLOYEE INFORMATION UPDATE PROGRAM                           *
* MODULE - INITIALIZATION                                       *
*                                                               *
*---------------------------------------------------------------*
* CHANGE HISTORY                                                *
*    090785 NEW PROGRAM                                     GRR *
*****************************************************************

 DATA DIVISION.

 WORKING-STORAGE SECTION.

 77  VERSION-NUMBER                  PICTURE X(27) VALUE
     "VERSION 1     SEPT. 7, 1985".

 COPY DCL14.
 77  OPERATION                       PICTURE XX.                COPY

 COPY DCL55.
 77  DATA-SEGMENT-NAME               PICTURE X(8).              COPY

 COPY DCL56.
 77  STATUS-CODE                     PICTURE XX.                COPY

 COPY DCL54.
 77  LOCKING-INDICATOR               PICTURE X(3).              COPY

 COPY DCL68.
 01  MENU-RECORD.                                               COPY
     02  SCREEN-ID                   PICTURE X(8).              COPY
     02  INPUT-AREA-1.                                          COPY
         03  SELECTION-CODE          PICTURE X.                 COPY
         03  FILLER                  PICTURE X(49).             COPY
     02  OUTPUT-AREA-1 REDEFINES INPUT-AREA-1.                  COPY
         03  MESSAGE                 PICTURE X(50).             COPY
     02  FILLER                      PICTURE X(102).            COPY
                                                                COPY
 01  NAME-AND-ADDRESS-RECORD REDEFINES MENU-RECORD.             COPY
     02  SCREEN-ID                   PICTURE X(8).              COPY
     02  EMPLOYEE-NUMBER             PICTURE X(8).              COPY
     02  EMPLOYEE-NAME               PICTURE X(30).             COPY
     02  EMPLOYEE-ADDRESS            PICTURE X(30).             COPY
     02  MANAGER-NAME                PICTURE X(30).             COPY
     02  DEPARTMENT-NUMBER           PICTURE X(3).              COPY
     02  SELECTION-CODE              PICTURE X.                 COPY
     02  MESSAGE                     PICTURE X(50).             COPY
                                                                COPY
 01  SALARY-RECORD REDEFINES NAME-AND-ADDRESS-RECORD.           COPY
     02  SCREEN-ID                   PICTURE X(8).              COPY
     02  EMPLOYEE-NUMBER             PICTURE X(8).              COPY
     02  INPUT-AREA-2.                                          COPY
         03  SALARY                  PICTURE X(9).              COPY
         03  SELECTION-CODE          PICTURE X.                 COPY
         03  FILLER                  PICTURE X(79).             COPY
     02  OUTPUT-AREA-2 REDEFINES INPUT-AREA-2.                  COPY
         03  EMPLOYEE-NAME           PICTURE X(30).             COPY
         03  SALARY                  PICTURE X(9).              COPY
         03  MESSAGE                 PICTURE X(50).             COPY
     02  FILLER                      PICTURE X(55).             COPY
                                                                COPY
 01  PERFORMANCE-RECORD REDEFINES SALARY-RECORD.                COPY
     02  SCREEN-ID                   PICTURE X(8).              COPY
     02  EMPLOYEE-NUMBER             PICTURE X(8).              COPY
     02  INPUT-AREA-3.                                          COPY
         03  SELECTION-CODE          PICTURE X.                 COPY
         03  FILLER                  PICTURE X(80).             COPY
     02  OUTPUT-AREA-3 REDEFINES INPUT-AREA-3.                  COPY
         03  EMPLOYEE-NAME           PICTURE X(30).             COPY
         03  PERFORMANCE-RATING      PICTURE X.                 COPY
         03  MESSAGE                 PICTURE X(50).             COPY
     02  FILLER                      PICTURE X(63).             COPY
```

(a)

Figure 16.30. *Initialization Module in COBOL*

(*continued on next page*)

```
COPY DCL50.
01  EMPLOYEE-MASTER-DATA.                                           COPY
    02  EMPLOYEE-NUMBER                  PICTURE X(8).              COPY
    02  EMPLOYEE-NAME                    PICTURE X(30).             COPY
    02  EMPLOYEE-ADDRESS                 PICTURE X(30).             COPY
    02  MANAGER-NAME                     PICTURE X(30).             COPY
    02  DEPARTMENT-NUMBER                PICTURE X(3).              COPY
    02  PERFORMANCE-RATING               PICTURE X.                 COPY
    02  SALARY                           PICTURE S9(6)V99.          COPY
    02  FILLER                           PICTURE X.                 COPY

LINKAGE SECTION.

COPY DCL51.
01  TERMINAL-USER-DATA.                                             COPY
    02  USER-ID                          PICTURE X(8).              COPY
    02  FIRST-TIME-INDICATOR             PICTURE XXX.               COPY
    02  PROCESSING-CONTROL               PICTURE X(6).              COPY
    02  PREVIOUS-PANEL-CODE              PICTURE X.                 COPY
    02  PREVIOUS-EMPLOYEE-NUMBER         PICTURE X(8).              COPY
    02  TOTAL-SALARY                     PICTURE S9(7)V99.          COPY
    02  EMPLOYEE-TYPE                    PICTURE XXX.               COPY
    02  EMPLOYEE-DISPLAY-DATA.                                      COPY
        03  PANEL-CODE                   PICTURE X.                 COPY
        03  CURRENT-DISPLAY-KEY.                                    COPY
            04  EMPLOYEE-NUMBER          PICTURE X(8).              COPY
        03  EMPLOYEE-NAME                PICTURE X(30).             COPY
        03  EMPLOYEE-ADDRESS             PICTURE X(30).             COPY
        03  MANAGER-NAME                 PICTURE X(30).             COPY
        03  DEPARTMENT-NUMBER            PICTURE X(3).              COPY
        03  SALARY                       PICTURE X(9).              COPY
        03  NUMERIC-SALARY REDEFINES SALARY                         COPY
                                         PICTURE 9(6).99.           COPY
        03  PERFORMANCE-RATING           PICTURE X.                 COPY
        03  MESSAGE                      PICTURE X(50).             COPY
        03  SELECTION-CODE               PICTURE X.                 COPY
    02  ALIGNED-SALARY                   PICTURE 9(6)V99.           COPY
    02  SECURITY-DATA.                                              COPY
        03  DATA-BASE-CODE               PICTURE X(8).              COPY
        03  TYPE-OF-ACCESS               PICTURE X.                 COPY
            88 NONE                      VALUE "N".                 COPY
            88 VIEW                      VALUE "V".                 COPY
            88 CHANGE                    VALUE "C".                 COPY
        03  ALLOWED-TO-ACCESS.                                      COPY
            04  TYPE-N                   PICTURE X.                 COPY
            04  TYPE-S                   PICTURE X.                 COPY
            04  TYPE-P                   PICTURE X.                 COPY
    02  FILLER                           PICTURE X.                 COPY
*****************************************************************


/****************************************************************
PROCEDURE DIVISION USING TERMINAL-USER-DATA.

    MOVE "YES" TO FIRST-TIME-INDICATOR.
    MOVE SPACES TO PREVIOUS-EMPLOYEE-NUMBER.
    MOVE 0 TO TOTAL-SALARY.
    MOVE SPACES TO EMPLOYEE-TYPE.
    MOVE SPACES TO EMPLOYEE-DISPLAY-DATA.
    MOVE "M" TO PANEL-CODE.
    MOVE "EMPDB   " TO DATA-BASE-CODE.
    MOVE "EMPDB   " TO DATA-SEGMENT-NAME.
    MOVE "O " TO OPERATION.
    CALL "TRANS2" USING OPERATION, MENU-RECORD.
    CALL "DABASE" USING EMPLOYEE-MASTER-DATA, STATUS-CODE,
                        LOCKING-INDICATOR, OPERATION,
                        DATA-SEGMENT-NAME.

END PROGRAM EMINIT.

*****************************************************************
```

(b)

Figure 16.30. *(Continued)*

```
/************************************************************************
 IDENTIFICATION DIVISION.

 PROGRAM-ID.        EMRECV.

 AUTHOR.            G.R. ROGERS.

***********************************************************************
*                                                                     *
* EMPLOYEE INFORMATION UPDATE PROGRAM                                 *
* MODULE - RECEIVE DATA FROM TERMINAL                                 *
*                                                                     *
*---------------------------------------------------------------------*
* CHANGE HISTORY                                                      *
*    090785 NEW PROGRAM                                           GRR *
***********************************************************************

 DATA DIVISION.

 WORKING-STORAGE SECTION.

 77  VERSION-NUMBER                  PICTURE X(27) VALUE
     "VERSION 1     SEPT. 7, 1985".

 COPY DCL14.
 77  OPERATION                       PICTURE XX.             COPY

 COPY DCL68.
 01  MENU-RECORD.                                            COPY
     02  SCREEN-ID                   PICTURE X(8).           COPY
     02  INPUT-AREA-1.                                       COPY
         03  SELECTION-CODE          PICTURE X.              COPY
         03  FILLER                  PICTURE X(49).          COPY
     02  OUTPUT-AREA-1 REDEFINES INPUT-AREA-1.               COPY
         03  MESSAGE                 PICTURE X(50).          COPY
     02  FILLER                      PICTURE X(102).         COPY
                                                             COPY
 01  NAME-AND-ADDRESS-RECORD REDEFINES MENU-RECORD.          COPY
     02  SCREEN-ID                   PICTURE X(8).           COPY
     02  EMPLOYEE-NUMBER             PICTURE X(8).           COPY
     02  EMPLOYEE-NAME               PICTURE X(30).          COPY
     02  EMPLOYEE-ADDRESS            PICTURE X(30).          COPY
     02  MANAGER-NAME                PICTURE X(30).          COPY
     02  DEPARTMENT-NUMBER           PICTURE X(3).           COPY
     02  SELECTION-CODE              PICTURE X.              COPY
     02  MESSAGE                     PICTURE X(50).          COPY
                                                             COPY
 01  SALARY-RECORD REDEFINES NAME-AND-ADDRESS-RECORD.        COPY
     02  SCREEN-ID                   PICTURE X(8).           COPY
     02  EMPLOYEE-NUMBER             PICTURE X(8).           COPY
     02  INPUT-AREA-2.                                       COPY
         03  SALARY                  PICTURE X(9).           COPY
         03  SELECTION-CODE          PICTURE X.              COPY
         03  FILLER                  PICTURE X(79).          COPY
     02  OUTPUT-AREA-2 REDEFINES INPUT-AREA-2.               COPY
         03  EMPLOYEE-NAME           PICTURE X(30).          COPY
         03  SALARY                  PICTURE X(9).           COPY
         03  MESSAGE                 PICTURE X(50).          COPY
     02  FILLER                      PICTURE X(55).          COPY
                                                             COPY
 01  PERFORMANCE-RECORD REDEFINES SALARY-RECORD.             COPY
     02  SCREEN-ID                   PICTURE X(8).           COPY
     02  EMPLOYEE-NUMBER             PICTURE X(8).           COPY
     02  INPUT-AREA-3.                                       COPY
         03  SELECTION-CODE          PICTURE X.              COPY
         03  FILLER                  PICTURE X(80).          COPY
     02  OUTPUT-AREA-3 REDEFINES INPUT-AREA-3.               COPY
         03  EMPLOYEE-NAME           PICTURE X(30).          COPY
         03  PERFORMANCE-RATING      PICTURE X.              COPY
         03  MESSAGE                 PICTURE X(50).          COPY
     02  FILLER                      PICTURE X(63).          COPY
```

(a)

Figure 16.31. *Receive transaction module in COBOL.*

(continued on next page)

```
LINKAGE SECTION.

COPY DCL51.
01  TERMINAL-USER-DATA.                                              COPY
    02  USER-ID                         PICTURE X(8).                COPY
    02  FIRST-TIME-INDICATOR            PICTURE XXX.                 COPY
    02  PROCESSING-CONTROL              PICTURE X(6).                COPY
    02  PREVIOUS-PANEL-CODE             PICTURE X.                   COPY
    02  PREVIOUS-EMPLOYEE-NUMBER        PICTURE X(8).                COPY
    02  TOTAL-SALARY                    PICTURE S9(7)V99.            COPY
    02  EMPLOYEE-TYPE                   PICTURE XXX.                 COPY
    02  EMPLOYEE-DISPLAY-DATA.                                       COPY
        03  PANEL-CODE                  PICTURE X.                   COPY
        03  CURRENT-DISPLAY-KEY.                                     COPY
            04  EMPLOYEE-NUMBER         PICTURE X(8).                COPY
        03  EMPLOYEE-NAME               PICTURE X(30).               COPY
        03  EMPLOYEE-ADDRESS            PICTURE X(30).               COPY
        03  MANAGER-NAME                PICTURE X(30).               COPY
        03  DEPARTMENT-NUMBER           PICTURE X(3).                COPY
        03  SALARY                      PICTURE X(9).                COPY
        03  NUMERIC-SALARY REDEFINES SALARY                          COPY
                                        PICTURE 9(6).99.             COPY
        03  PERFORMANCE-RATING          PICTURE X.                   COPY
        03  MESSAGE                     PICTURE X(50).               COPY
        03  SELECTION-CODE              PICTURE X.                   COPY
    02  ALIGNED-SALARY                  PICTURE 9(6)V99.             COPY
    02  SECURITY-DATA.                                               COPY
        03  DATA-BASE-CODE              PICTURE X(8).                COPY
        03  TYPE-OF-ACCESS              PICTURE X.                   COPY
            88 NONE                     VALUE "N".                   COPY
            88 VIEW                     VALUE "V".                   COPY
            88 CHANGE                   VALUE "C".                   COPY
        03  ALLOWED-TO-ACCESS.                                       COPY
            04  TYPE-N                  PICTURE X.                   COPY
            04  TYPE-S                  PICTURE X.                   COPY
            04  TYPE-P                  PICTURE X.                   COPY
    02  FILLER                          PICTURE X.                   COPY
*****************************************************************

/*****************************************************************

 PROCEDURE DIVISION USING TERMINAL-USER-DATA.

     MOVE SPACES TO MESSAGE IN TERMINAL-USER-DATA.
     MOVE "R " TO OPERATION.
     CALL "TRANS2" USING OPERATION, MENU-RECORD.

     IF PREVIOUS-PANEL-CODE = "M"
       THEN
         MOVE SELECTION-CODE IN MENU-RECORD TO
           SELECTION-CODE IN TERMINAL-USER-DATA
         EXIT PROGRAM
     END-IF.

     MOVE EMPLOYEE-NUMBER IN NAME-AND-ADDRESS-RECORD TO
        EMPLOYEE-NUMBER IN TERMINAL-USER-DATA.

     IF PREVIOUS-PANEL-CODE = "N"
       THEN
         MOVE EMPLOYEE-NAME IN NAME-AND-ADDRESS-RECORD TO
            EMPLOYEE-NAME IN TERMINAL-USER-DATA
         MOVE EMPLOYEE-ADDRESS IN NAME-AND-ADDRESS-RECORD TO
            EMPLOYEE-ADDRESS IN TERMINAL-USER-DATA
         MOVE MANAGER-NAME IN NAME-AND-ADDRESS-RECORD TO
            MANAGER-NAME IN TERMINAL-USER-DATA
         MOVE DEPARTMENT-NUMBER IN NAME-AND-ADDRESS-RECORD TO
            DEPARTMENT-NUMBER IN TERMINAL-USER-DATA
         MOVE SELECTION-CODE IN NAME-AND-ADDRESS-RECORD TO
           SELECTION-CODE IN TERMINAL-USER-DATA
         EXIT PROGRAM
     END-IF.

     IF PREVIOUS-PANEL-CODE = "S"
       THEN
         MOVE SALARY IN INPUT-AREA-2 TO
            SALARY IN TERMINAL-USER-DATA
         MOVE SELECTION-CODE IN SALARY-RECORD TO
           SELECTION-CODE IN TERMINAL-USER-DATA
         EXIT PROGRAM
     END-IF.

     MOVE SELECTION-CODE IN PERFORMANCE-RECORD TO
       SELECTION-CODE IN TERMINAL-USER-DATA.

 END PROGRAM EMRECV.

*****************************************************************
```

(b)

Figure 16.31. *(Continued)*

```
/*****************************************************************
 IDENTIFICATION DIVISION.

 PROGRAM-ID.        EMSEND.

 AUTHOR.            G.R. ROGERS.

*****************************************************************
*                                                               *
* EMPLOYEE INFORMATION UPDATE PROGRAM                           *
* MODULE - SEND DATA TO TERMINAL                                *
*                                                               *
*---------------------------------------------------------------*
* CHANGE HISTORY                                                *
*   090785 NEW PROGRAM                                      GRR *
*****************************************************************

 DATA DIVISION.

 WORKING-STORAGE SECTION.

 77  VERSION-NUMBER                 PICTURE X(27) VALUE
     "VERSION 1      SEPT. 7, 1985".

 COPY DCL14.
 77  OPERATION                      PICTURE XX.              COPY

 COPY DCL68.
 01  MENU-RECORD.                                            COPY
     02  SCREEN-ID                  PICTURE X(8).            COPY
     02  INPUT-AREA-1.                                       COPY
         03  SELECTION-CODE         PICTURE X.               COPY
         03  FILLER                 PICTURE X(49).           COPY
     02  OUTPUT-AREA-1 REDEFINES INPUT-AREA-1.               COPY
         03  MESSAGE                PICTURE X(50).           COPY
     02  FILLER                     PICTURE X(102).          COPY
                                                             COPY
 01  NAME-AND-ADDRESS-RECORD REDEFINES MENU-RECORD.          COPY
     02  SCREEN-ID                  PICTURE X(8).            COPY
     02  EMPLOYEE-NUMBER            PICTURE X(8).            COPY
     02  EMPLOYEE-NAME              PICTURE X(30).           COPY
     02  EMPLOYEE-ADDRESS           PICTURE X(30).           COPY
     02  MANAGER-NAME               PICTURE X(30).           COPY
     02  DEPARTMENT-NUMBER          PICTURE X(3).            COPY
     02  SELECTION-CODE             PICTURE X.               COPY
     02  MESSAGE                    PICTURE X(50).           COPY
                                                             COPY
 01  SALARY-RECORD REDEFINES NAME-AND-ADDRESS-RECORD.        COPY
     02  SCREEN-ID                  PICTURE X(8).            COPY
     02  EMPLOYEE-NUMBER            PICTURE X(8).            COPY
     02  INPUT-AREA-2.                                       COPY
         03  SALARY                 PICTURE X(9).            COPY
         03  SELECTION-CODE         PICTURE X.               COPY
         03  FILLER                 PICTURE X(79).           COPY
     02  OUTPUT-AREA-2 REDEFINES INPUT-AREA-2.               COPY
         03  EMPLOYEE-NAME          PICTURE X(30).           COPY
         03  SALARY                 PICTURE X(9).            COPY
         03  MESSAGE                PICTURE X(50).           COPY
     02  FILLER                     PICTURE X(55).           COPY
                                                             COPY
 01  PERFORMANCE-RECORD REDEFINES SALARY-RECORD.             COPY
     02  SCREEN-ID                  PICTURE X(8).            COPY
     02  EMPLOYEE-NUMBER            PICTURE X(8).            COPY
     02  INPUT-AREA-3.                                       COPY
         03  SELECTION-CODE         PICTURE X.               COPY
         03  FILLER                 PICTURE X(80).           COPY
     02  OUTPUT-AREA-3 REDEFINES INPUT-AREA-3.               COPY
         03  EMPLOYEE-NAME          PICTURE X(30).           COPY
         03  PERFORMANCE-RATING     PICTURE X.               COPY
         03  MESSAGE                PICTURE X(50).           COPY
     02  FILLER                     PICTURE X(63).           COPY
```

(a)

Figure 16.32. *Send transaction module in COBOL.*

(continued on next page)

```
 LINKAGE SECTION.

 COPY DCL51.
 01  TERMINAL-USER-DATA.                                                   COPY
     02  USER-ID                         PICTURE X(8).                    COPY
     02  FIRST-TIME-INDICATOR            PICTURE XXX.                     COPY
     02  PROCESSING-CONTROL              PICTURE X(6).                    COPY
     02  PREVIOUS-PANEL-CODE             PICTURE X.                       COPY
     02  PREVIOUS-EMPLOYEE-NUMBER        PICTURE X(8).                    COPY
     02  TOTAL-SALARY                    PICTURE S9(7)V99.                COPY
     02  EMPLOYEE-TYPE                   PICTURE XXX.                     COPY
     02  EMPLOYEE-DISPLAY-DATA.                                           COPY
         03  PANEL-CODE                  PICTURE X.                       COPY
         03  CURRENT-DISPLAY-KEY.                                         COPY
             04  EMPLOYEE-NUMBER         PICTURE X(8).                    COPY
         03  EMPLOYEE-NAME               PICTURE X(30).                   COPY
         03  EMPLOYEE-ADDRESS            PICTURE X(30).                   COPY
         03  MANAGER-NAME                PICTURE X(30).                   COPY
         03  DEPARTMENT-NUMBER           PICTURE X(3).                    COPY
         03  SALARY                      PICTURE X(9).                    COPY
         03  NUMERIC-SALARY REDEFINES SALARY                              COPY
                                         PICTURE 9(6).99.                 COPY
         03  PERFORMANCE-RATING          PICTURE X.                       COPY
         03  MESSAGE                     PICTURE X(50).                   COPY
         03  SELECTION-CODE              PICTURE X.                       COPY
     02  ALIGNED-SALARY                  PICTURE 9(6)V99.                 COPY
     02  SECURITY-DATA.                                                   COPY
         03  DATA-BASE-CODE              PICTURE X(8).                    COPY
         03  TYPE-OF-ACCESS              PICTURE X.                       COPY
             88 NONE                     VALUE "N".                       COPY
             88 VIEW                     VALUE "V".                       COPY
             88 CHANGE                   VALUE "C".                       COPY
         03  ALLOWED-TO-ACCESS.                                           COPY
             04  TYPE-N                  PICTURE X.                       COPY
             04  TYPE-S                  PICTURE X.                       COPY
             04  TYPE-P                  PICTURE X.                       COPY
     02  FILLER                          PICTURE X.                       COPY
*****************************************************************
/****************************************************************
 PROCEDURE DIVISION USING TERMINAL-USER-DATA.

     MOVE "W " TO OPERATION.

     IF PREVIOUS-PANEL-CODE = "M" OR "E"
       THEN
         MOVE "EMPM" TO SCREEN-ID IN MENU-RECORD
         MOVE MESSAGE IN TERMINAL-USER-DATA TO
              MESSAGE IN MENU-RECORD
         CALL "TRANS2" USING OPERATION, MENU-RECORD
         EXIT PROGRAM
     END-IF.

     MOVE EMPLOYEE-NUMBER IN TERMINAL-USER-DATA TO
        EMPLOYEE-NUMBER IN NAME-AND-ADDRESS-RECORD.

     IF PREVIOUS-PANEL-CODE = "N"
       THEN
         MOVE "EMPN" TO SCREEN-ID IN NAME-AND-ADDRESS-RECORD
         MOVE EMPLOYEE-NAME IN TERMINAL-USER-DATA TO
              EMPLOYEE-NAME IN NAME-AND-ADDRESS-RECORD
         MOVE EMPLOYEE-ADDRESS IN TERMINAL-USER-DATA TO
              EMPLOYEE-ADDRESS IN NAME-AND-ADDRESS-RECORD
         MOVE MANAGER-NAME IN TERMINAL-USER-DATA TO
              MANAGER-NAME IN NAME-AND-ADDRESS-RECORD
         MOVE DEPARTMENT-NUMBER IN TERMINAL-USER-DATA TO
              DEPARTMENT-NUMBER IN NAME-AND-ADDRESS-RECORD
         MOVE MESSAGE IN TERMINAL-USER-DATA TO
            MESSAGE IN NAME-AND-ADDRESS-RECORD
         CALL "TRANS2" USING OPERATION, NAME-AND-ADDRESS-RECORD
         EXIT PROGRAM
     END-IF.

     IF PREVIOUS-PANEL-CODE = "S"
       THEN
         MOVE "EMPS" TO SCREEN-ID IN SALARY-RECORD
         MOVE EMPLOYEE-NAME IN TERMINAL-USER-DATA TO
              EMPLOYEE-NAME IN SALARY-RECORD
         MOVE SALARY IN TERMINAL-USER-DATA TO
              SALARY IN OUTPUT-AREA-2
         MOVE MESSAGE IN TERMINAL-USER-DATA TO
            MESSAGE IN SALARY-RECORD
         CALL "TRANS2" USING OPERATION, SALARY-RECORD
         EXIT PROGRAM
     END-IF.

     MOVE "EMPP" TO SCREEN-ID IN PERFORMANCE-RECORD.
     MOVE EMPLOYEE-NAME IN TERMINAL-USER-DATA TO
        EMPLOYEE-NAME IN PERFORMANCE-RECORD.
     MOVE PERFORMANCE-RATING IN TERMINAL-USER-DATA TO
             PERFORMANCE-RATING IN PERFORMANCE-RECORD.
     MOVE MESSAGE IN TERMINAL-USER-DATA TO
           MESSAGE IN PERFORMANCE-RECORD.
     CALL "TRANS2" USING OPERATION, PERFORMANCE-RECORD.

 END PROGRAM EMSEND.

*****************************************************************
```

(b)

Figure 16.32. *(Continued)*

```
/*************************************************************
 IDENTIFICATION DIVISION.

 PROGRAM-ID.        EMMRRD.

 AUTHOR.            G.R. ROGERS.

************************************************************
*                                                          *
* EMPLOYEE INFORMATION UPDATE PROGRAM                      *
* MODULE - READ DATA BASE SEGMENT                          *
*                                                          *
*----------------------------------------------------------*
* CHANGE HISTORY                                           *
*   090785 NEW PROGRAM                                 GRR *
************************************************************

 DATA DIVISION.

 WORKING-STORAGE SECTION.

 77  VERSION-NUMBER                    PICTURE X(27) VALUE
     "VERSION 1     SEPT. 7, 1985".

 77  DATA-NOT-FOUND-MESSAGE            PICTURE X(28) VALUE
     "EMPLOYEE DATA DOES NOT EXIST".

 COPY DCL14.
 77  OPERATION                         PICTURE XX.            COPY

 COPY DCL56.
 77  STATUS-CODE                       PICTURE XX.            COPY

 COPY DCL55.
 77  DATA-SEGMENT-NAME                 PICTURE X(8).          COPY

 LINKAGE SECTION.

 COPY DCL50.
 01  EMPLOYEE-MASTER-DATA.                                    COPY
     02  EMPLOYEE-NUMBER               PICTURE X(8).          COPY
     02  EMPLOYEE-NAME                 PICTURE X(30).         COPY
     02  EMPLOYEE-ADDRESS              PICTURE X(30).         COPY
     02  MANAGER-NAME                  PICTURE X(30).         COPY
     02  DEPARTMENT-NUMBER             PICTURE X(3).          COPY
     02  PERFORMANCE-RATING            PICTURE X.             COPY
     02  SALARY                        PICTURE S9(6)V99.      COPY
     02  FILLER                        PICTURE X.             COPY

 COPY DCL39.
 77  MESSAGE                           PICTURE X(50).         COPY

 COPY DCL54.
 77  LOCKING-INDICATOR                 PICTURE X(3).          COPY

*************************************************************

/*************************************************************

 PROCEDURE DIVISION USING EMPLOYEE-MASTER-DATA, MESSAGE,
                          LOCKING-INDICATOR.

     MOVE "EMPDB   " TO DATA-SEGMENT-NAME.

     IF LOCKING-INDICATOR = "YES"
       THEN
         MOVE "RL" TO OPERATION
         CALL "DABASE" USING EMPLOYEE-MASTER-DATA, STATUS-CODE,
                             LOCKING-INDICATOR, OPERATION,
                             DATA-SEGMENT-NAME
       ELSE
         MOVE "R " TO OPERATION
         CALL "DABASE" USING EMPLOYEE-MASTER-DATA, STATUS-CODE,
                             LOCKING-INDICATOR, OPERATION,
                             DATA-SEGMENT-NAME
     END-IF.

     IF STATUS-CODE = SPACES
       THEN
         MOVE SPACES TO MESSAGE
       ELSE
         MOVE DATA-NOT-FOUND-MESSAGE TO MESSAGE
     END-IF.

 END PROGRAM EMMRRD.

*************************************************************
```

Figure 16.33. *Read employee segment module in COBOL.*

```
/****************************************************************
 IDENTIFICATION DIVISION.

 PROGRAM-ID.        EMINST.

 AUTHOR.            G.R. ROGERS.

***************************************************************
*                                                             *
* EMPLOYEE INFORMATION UPDATE PROGRAM                         *
* MODULE - INSERT SEGMENT INTO DATA BASE                      *
*                                                             *
*-------------------------------------------------------------*
* CHANGE HISTORY                                              *
*   090785 NEW PROGRAM                                    GRR *
***************************************************************

 DATA DIVISION.

 WORKING-STORAGE SECTION.

 77  VERSION-NUMBER                   PICTURE X(27) VALUE
     "VERSION 1      SEPT. 7, 1985".

 77  DATA-EXIST-MESSAGE               PICTURE X(28) VALUE
     "EMPLOYEE DATA ALREADY EXISTS".

 77  DATA-INSERTED-MESSAGE            PICTURE X(32) VALUE
     "EMPLOYEE DATA ADDED TO DATA BASE".

 COPY DCL14.
 77  OPERATION                        PICTURE XX.               COPY

 COPY DCL56.
 77  STATUS-CODE                      PICTURE XX.               COPY

 COPY DCL55.
 77  DATA-SEGMENT-NAME                PICTURE X(8).             COPY

 LINKAGE SECTION.

 COPY DCL50.
 01  EMPLOYEE-MASTER-DATA.                                      COPY
     02  EMPLOYEE-NUMBER              PICTURE X(8).             COPY
     02  EMPLOYEE-NAME                PICTURE X(30).            COPY
     02  EMPLOYEE-ADDRESS             PICTURE X(30).            COPY
     02  MANAGER-NAME                 PICTURE X(30).            COPY
     02  DEPARTMENT-NUMBER            PICTURE X(3).             COPY
     02  PERFORMANCE-RATING           PICTURE X.                COPY
     02  SALARY                       PICTURE S9(6)V99.         COPY
     02  FILLER                       PICTURE X.                COPY

 COPY DCL39.
 77  MESSAGE                          PICTURE X(50).            COPY

 COPY DCL54.
 77  LOCKING-INDICATOR                PICTURE X(3).             COPY
****************************************************************

/****************************************************************

 PROCEDURE DIVISION USING EMPLOYEE-MASTER-DATA, MESSAGE,
                          LOCKING-INDICATOR.

     MOVE "EMPDB    " TO DATA-SEGMENT-NAME.
     MOVE "I " TO OPERATION.
     CALL "DABASE" USING EMPLOYEE-MASTER-DATA, STATUS-CODE,
                         LOCKING-INDICATOR, OPERATION,
                         DATA-SEGMENT-NAME.

     IF STATUS-CODE NOT = SPACES
       THEN
         MOVE DATA-EXIST-MESSAGE TO MESSAGE
       ELSE
         MOVE DATA-INSERTED-MESSAGE TO MESSAGE
     END-IF.

 END PROGRAM EMINST.

****************************************************************
```

Figure 16.34. *Insert employee segment in COBOL.*

```
/**********************************************************************
 IDENTIFICATION DIVISION.

 PROGRAM-ID.         EMUPDT.

 AUTHOR.             G.R. ROGERS.

**********************************************************************
*                                                                    *
* EMPLOYEE INFORMATION UPDATE PROGRAM                                *
* MODULE - UPDATE DATA BASE SEGMENT                                  *
*                                                                    *
*--------------------------------------------------------------------*
* CHANGE HISTORY                                                     *
*   090785 NEW PROGRAM                                           GRR *
**********************************************************************

 DATA DIVISION.

 WORKING-STORAGE SECTION.

 77  VERSION-NUMBER                    PICTURE X(27) VALUE
     "VERSION 1     SEPT. 7, 1985".

 77  DATA-UPDATED-MESSAGE              PICTURE X(21) VALUE
     "EMPLOYEE DATA UPDATED".

 77  DATA-NOT-FOUND-MESSAGE            PICTURE X(28) VALUE
     "EMPLOYEE DATA DOES NOT EXIST".

 77  UPDATE-UNSUCCESSFUL-MESSAGE       PICTURE X(49) VALUE
     "EMPLOYEE UPDATE UNSUCCESSFUL - CALL ADMINISTRATOR".

 COPY DCL14.
 77  OPERATION                         PICTURE XX.              COPY

 COPY DCL56.
 77  STATUS-CODE                       PICTURE XX.              COPY

 COPY DCL55.
 77  DATA-SEGMENT-NAME                 PICTURE X(8).            COPY

 LINKAGE SECTION.

 COPY DCL50.
 01  EMPLOYEE-MASTER-DATA.                                      COPY
     02  EMPLOYEE-NUMBER               PICTURE X(8).            COPY
     02  EMPLOYEE-NAME                 PICTURE X(30).           COPY
     02  EMPLOYEE-ADDRESS              PICTURE X(30).           COPY
     02  MANAGER-NAME                  PICTURE X(30).           COPY
     02  DEPARTMENT-NUMBER             PICTURE X(3).            COPY
     02  PERFORMANCE-RATING            PICTURE X.               COPY
     02  SALARY                        PICTURE S9(6)V99.        COPY
     02  FILLER                        PICTURE X.               COPY

 COPY DCL39.
 77  MESSAGE                           PICTURE X(50).           COPY

 COPY DCL54.
 77  LOCKING-INDICATOR                 PICTURE X(3).            COPY

**********************************************************************
```

(a)

Figure 16.35. *Update employee segment module in COBOL.*

```
/*****************************************************************
 PROCEDURE DIVISION USING EMPLOYEE-MASTER-DATA, MESSAGE,
                          LOCKING-INDICATOR.

     MOVE "EMPDB   " TO DATA-SEGMENT-NAME.

     IF LOCKING-INDICATOR NOT = "YES"
       THEN
         MOVE "RL" TO OPERATION
         CALL "DABASE" USING EMPLOYEE-MASTER-DATA, STATUS-CODE,
                             LOCKING-INDICATOR, OPERATION,
                             DATA-SEGMENT-NAME

         IF STATUS-CODE NOT = SPACES
           THEN
             MOVE DATA-NOT-FOUND-MESSAGE TO MESSAGE
             EXIT PROGRAM
         END-IF

     END-IF.

     MOVE "U " TO OPERATION.
     CALL "DABASE" USING EMPLOYEE-MASTER-DATA, STATUS-CODE,
                         LOCKING-INDICATOR, OPERATION,
                         DATA-SEGMENT-NAME.

     IF STATUS-CODE = SPACES
       THEN
         MOVE DATA-UPDATED-MESSAGE TO MESSAGE
       ELSE
         MOVE UPDATE-UNSUCCESSFUL-MESSAGE TO MESSAGE
     END-IF.

 END PROGRAM EMUPDT.
******************************************************************
```

(b)

Figure 16.35. *(Continued)*

```
/*************************************************************
 IDENTIFICATION DIVISION.

 PROGRAM-ID.        EMLFJS.

 AUTHOR.            G.R. ROGERS.

*************************************************************
*                                                           *
* EMPLOYEE INFORMATION UPDATE PROGRAM                       *
* MODULE - LEFT JUSTIFY                                     *
*                                                           *
*-----------------------------------------------------------*
* CHANGE HISTORY                                            *
*   090785 NEW PROGRAM                                  GRR *
*************************************************************

 DATA DIVISION.

 WORKING-STORAGE SECTION.

 77  VERSION-NUMBER                 PICTURE X(27) VALUE
     "VERSION 1     SEPT. 7, 1985".

 77  INPUT-ARRAY-INDEX              PICTURE S99.

 77  OUTPUT-ARRAY-INDEX             PICTURE S99.

 77  NON-BLANK-CHARACTER-INDICATOR  PICTURE XXX.

 77  JUSTIFY-LIMIT                  PICTURE S99.

 LINKAGE SECTION.

 COPY DCL37.
 77  NUMBER-OF-INPUT-CHARACTERS     PICTURE S99.                COPY
                                                                COPY
 77  NUMBER-OF-OUTPUT-CHARACTERS    PICTURE S99.                COPY

 COPY DCL52.
 01  INPUT-CHARACTER-ARRAY.                                     COPY
     02  INPUT-CHARACTER-ELEMENT    PICTURE X OCCURS 30 TIMES.  COPY

 COPY DCL53.
 01  OUTPUT-CHARACTER-ARRAY.                                    COPY
     02  OUTPUT-CHARACTER-ELEMENT   PICTURE X OCCURS 30 TIMES.  COPY
*************************************************************

/*************************************************************

 PROCEDURE DIVISION USING INPUT-CHARACTER-ARRAY,
                          OUTPUT-CHARACTER-ARRAY,
                          NUMBER-OF-INPUT-CHARACTERS,
                          NUMBER-OF-OUTPUT-CHARACTERS.

     MOVE SPACES TO OUTPUT-CHARACTER-ARRAY.
     MOVE "NO" TO NON-BLANK-CHARACTER-INDICATOR.
     MOVE 1 TO INPUT-ARRAY-INDEX.
     MOVE 1 TO OUTPUT-ARRAY-INDEX.

     IF NUMBER-OF-INPUT-CHARACTERS GREATER THAN
         NUMBER-OF-OUTPUT-CHARACTERS
       THEN
         MOVE NUMBER-OF-OUTPUT-CHARACTERS TO JUSTIFY-LIMIT
       ELSE
         MOVE NUMBER-OF-INPUT-CHARACTERS TO JUSTIFY-LIMIT
     END-IF.

     PERFORM WITH TEST BEFORE UNTIL INPUT-ARRAY-INDEX GREATER THAN
        JUSTIFY-LIMIT

       IF INPUT-CHARACTER-ELEMENT (INPUT-ARRAY-INDEX) = SPACES
           AND NON-BLANK-CHARACTER-INDICATOR = "NO"
         THEN
           CONTINUE
         ELSE
           MOVE INPUT-CHARACTER-ELEMENT (INPUT-ARRAY-INDEX) TO
              OUTPUT-CHARACTER-ELEMENT (OUTPUT-ARRAY-INDEX)
           ADD 1 TO OUTPUT-ARRAY-INDEX
           MOVE "YES" TO NON-BLANK-CHARACTER-INDICATOR
       END-IF

       ADD 1 TO INPUT-ARRAY-INDEX
     END-PERFORM.

 END PROGRAM EMLFJS.

*************************************************************
```

Figure 16.36. *Left justify module in COBOL.*

```
/*****************************************************************
 IDENTIFICATION DIVISION.

 PROGRAM-ID.        EMEOJ.

 AUTHOR.            G.R. ROGERS.

****************************************************************
*                                                              *
* EMPLOYEE INFORMATION UPDATE PROGRAM                          *
* MODULE - END OF JOB                                          *
*                                                              *
*--------------------------------------------------------------*
* CHANGE HISTORY                                               *
*   090785 NEW PROGRAM                                     GRR *
****************************************************************

 DATA DIVISION.

 WORKING-STORAGE SECTION.

 77  VERSION-NUMBER                    PICTURE X(27) VALUE
     "VERSION 1      SEPT. 7, 1985".

  COPY DCL14.
 77  OPERATION                         PICTURE XX.              COPY

  COPY DCL56.
 77  STATUS-CODE                       PICTURE XX.              COPY

  COPY DCL54.
 77  LOCKING-INDICATOR                 PICTURE X(3).            COPY

  COPY DCL55.
 77  DATA-SEGMENT-NAME                 PICTURE X(8).            COPY

 COPY DCL68.
 01  MENU-RECORD.                                               COPY
     02  SCREEN-ID                     PICTURE X(8).            COPY
     02  INPUT-AREA-1.                                          COPY
         03  SELECTION-CODE            PICTURE X.               COPY
         03  FILLER                    PICTURE X(49).           COPY
     02  OUTPUT-AREA-1 REDEFINES INPUT-AREA-1.                  COPY
         03  MESSAGE                   PICTURE X(50).           COPY
     02  FILLER                        PICTURE X(102).          COPY
                                                                COPY
 01  NAME-AND-ADDRESS-RECORD REDEFINES MENU-RECORD.             COPY
     02  SCREEN-ID                     PICTURE X(8).            COPY
     02  EMPLOYEE-NUMBER               PICTURE X(8).            COPY
     02  EMPLOYEE-NAME                 PICTURE X(30).           COPY
     02  EMPLOYEE-ADDRESS              PICTURE X(30).           COPY
     02  MANAGER-NAME                  PICTURE X(30).           COPY
     02  DEPARTMENT-NUMBER             PICTURE X(3).            COPY
     02  SELECTION-CODE                PICTURE X.               COPY
     02  MESSAGE                       PICTURE X(50).           COPY
                                                                COPY
 01  SALARY-RECORD REDEFINES NAME-AND-ADDRESS-RECORD.           COPY
     02  SCREEN-ID                     PICTURE X(8).            COPY
     02  EMPLOYEE-NUMBER               PICTURE X(8).            COPY
     02  INPUT-AREA-2.                                          COPY
         03  SALARY                    PICTURE X(9).            COPY
         03  SELECTION-CODE            PICTURE X.               COPY
         03  FILLER                    PICTURE X(79).           COPY
     02  OUTPUT-AREA-2 REDEFINES INPUT-AREA-2.                  COPY
         03  EMPLOYEE-NAME             PICTURE X(30).           COPY
         03  SALARY                    PICTURE X(9).            COPY
         03  MESSAGE                   PICTURE X(50).           COPY
     02  FILLER                        PICTURE X(55).           COPY
                                                                COPY
 01  PERFORMANCE-RECORD REDEFINES SALARY-RECORD.                COPY
     02  SCREEN-ID                     PICTURE X(8).            COPY
     02  EMPLOYEE-NUMBER               PICTURE X(8).            COPY
     02  INPUT-AREA-3.                                          COPY
         03  SELECTION-CODE            PICTURE X.               COPY
         03  FILLER                    PICTURE X(80).           COPY
     02  OUTPUT-AREA-3 REDEFINES INPUT-AREA-3.                  COPY
         03  EMPLOYEE-NAME             PICTURE X(30).           COPY
         03  PERFORMANCE-RATING        PICTURE X.               COPY
         03  MESSAGE                   PICTURE X(50).           COPY
     02  FILLER                        PICTURE X(63).           COPY
```

(a)

Figure 16.37. *End of job module in COBOL.*

```
COPY DCL50.
01  EMPLOYEE-MASTER-DATA.                                         COPY
    02  EMPLOYEE-NUMBER            PICTURE X(8).                  COPY
    02  EMPLOYEE-NAME              PICTURE X(30).                 COPY
    02  EMPLOYEE-ADDRESS           PICTURE X(30).                 COPY
    02  MANAGER-NAME               PICTURE X(30).                 COPY
    02  DEPARTMENT-NUMBER          PICTURE X(3).                  COPY
    02  PERFORMANCE-RATING         PICTURE X.                     COPY
    02  SALARY                     PICTURE S9(6)V99.              COPY
    02  FILLER                     PICTURE X.                     COPY

LINKAGE SECTION.

COPY DCL51.
01  TERMINAL-USER-DATA.                                           COPY
    02  USER-ID                    PICTURE X(8).                  COPY
    02  FIRST-TIME-INDICATOR       PICTURE XXX.                   COPY
    02  PROCESSING-CONTROL         PICTURE X(6).                  COPY
    02  PREVIOUS-PANEL-CODE        PICTURE X.                     COPY
    02  PREVIOUS-EMPLOYEE-NUMBER   PICTURE X(8).                  COPY
    02  TOTAL-SALARY               PICTURE S9(7)V99.              COPY
    02  EMPLOYEE-TYPE              PICTURE XXX.                   COPY
    02  EMPLOYEE-DISPLAY-DATA.                                    COPY
        03  PANEL-CODE             PICTURE X.                     COPY
        03  CURRENT-DISPLAY-KEY.                                  COPY
            04  EMPLOYEE-NUMBER    PICTURE X(8).                  COPY
        03  EMPLOYEE-NAME          PICTURE X(30).                 COPY
        03  EMPLOYEE-ADDRESS       PICTURE X(30).                 COPY
        03  MANAGER-NAME           PICTURE X(30).                 COPY
        03  DEPARTMENT-NUMBER      PICTURE X(3).                  COPY
        03  SALARY                 PICTURE X(9).                  COPY
        03  NUMERIC-SALARY REDEFINES SALARY                       COPY
                                   PICTURE 9(6).99.               COPY
        03  PERFORMANCE-RATING     PICTURE X.                     COPY
        03  MESSAGE                PICTURE X(50).                 COPY
        03  SELECTION-CODE         PICTURE X.                     COPY
    02  ALIGNED-SALARY             PICTURE 9(6)V99.               COPY
    02  SECURITY-DATA.                                            COPY
        03  DATA-BASE-CODE         PICTURE X(8).                  COPY
        03  TYPE-OF-ACCESS         PICTURE X.                     COPY
            88 NONE                VALUE "N".                     COPY
            88 VIEW                VALUE "V".                     COPY
            88 CHANGE              VALUE "C".                     COPY
        03  ALLOWED-TO-ACCESS.                                    COPY
            04  TYPE-N             PICTURE X.                     COPY
            04  TYPE-S             PICTURE X.                     COPY
            04  TYPE-P             PICTURE X.                     COPY
    02  FILLER                     PICTURE X.                     COPY

*****************************************************************

/****************************************************************

 PROCEDURE DIVISION USING TERMINAL-USER-DATA.

     DISPLAY " TOTAL SALARY FOR USER ", USER-ID,
             " IS ", TOTAL-SALARY.
     MOVE "EMPDB    " TO DATA-SEGMENT-NAME.
     MOVE "C " TO OPERATION.
     CALL "TRANS2" USING OPERATION, MENU-RECORD.
     CALL "DABASE" USING EMPLOYEE-MASTER-DATA, STATUS-CODE,
                         LOCKING-INDICATOR, OPERATION,
                         DATA-SEGMENT-NAME.

 END PROGRAM EMEOJ.

*****************************************************************
```

(b)

Appendix A
Design Language Reference

CONSTRUCT	COMMENTS
PROGRAM-ID. module name [⟨MAIN⟩] [USING parameters].	Must be 1st statement in module. Parameters separated by commas. MAIN module is root of program
END PROGRAM module name.	Must be last statement in module
CALL "module name" [USING parameters]	Passes control to named module Parameters separated by commas.

CONSTRUCT	COMMENTS
	Control returns to next statement.
EXIT PROGRAM	Causes control to leave called module.
imperative statement(s)	Sequence structure.

IF condition
  THEN
    [imperative statement(s)]
  [ELSE
    imperative statement(s)]
END-IF
	Imperative statement(s) can be series of structures. If THEN is null, ELSE must be present.

PERFORM WITH TEST BEFORE UNTIL condition imperative statement(s) END-PERFORM	Imperative statement(s) can be series of structures.
PERFORM WITH TEST AFTER UNTIL condition imperative statement(s) END-PERFORM	Imperative statement(s) can be series of structures.

```
EVALUATE [data variable or conditional statement]
   WHEN condition-1
      imperative statement(s)
   WHEN condition-2
      imperative statement(s)structures.
              .
              .
              .
              .
   WHEN condition-N
      imperative statement(s)
              .
              .
[WHEN OTHER             ]
[imperative statement(s)]
END-EVALUATE
              .
              .
≪ comment ≫
              .
              .
```

Imperative statement(s) can be series of

Used to clarify design.

Bibliography

Bergland, G. D. "A Guided Tour of Program Design Methodologies." *Computer* (October 1981): 18–37.

Bohm, C., and G. Jacopini. "Flow Diagrams, Turing Machines and Languages with Only Two Formation Rules." *Comm. ACM* 9, no. 5 (New York, May 1966): 366–371.

Brooks, W. Douglas. "Software Technology Payoff: Some Statistical Evidence." *The Journal of Systems and Software* 2 (1981): 3–9.

Caine, Stephen H., and E. Kent Gordon. "PDL—A Tool for Software Design." Proceedings of the National Computer Conference, Montvale, New Jersey: (AFIPS Press, 1975): 271–276.

Clark, R. Lawrence. "A Linguistic Contribution to Goto-less Programming." *Datamation* (December 1973).

Dahl, O., E. Dijkstra, and C. Hoare. "Structured Programming." *Academic Press* (London, 1972).

Dijkstra, Edsger W. "Go To Considered Harmful." Letter to the editor, *Comm. ACM* 9 (May 1968): 366–361.

Fagan, M. E. "Design and Code Inspections to Reduce Errors in Program Development." *IBM Systems Journal* 15, no. 3 (New York, 1976): 182–211.

Kernighan, Brian W., and P. J. Plauger. *Elements of Programming Style*. Toronto, McGraw-Hill: 1974.

Mills, H. D. "Mathematical Foundations for Structured Programming." *IBM Technical Report FSC 71-6012* (Gaithersburg, MD, 1972).

Myers, Glenford J. *Composite/Structured Design*. Toronto: Van Nostrand Reinhold, 1978.

Parnas, D. L. "On the Criteria To Be Used in Decomposing Systems into Modules." *Comm. ACM* (New York, 1972).

Rogers, G. R. "A Simple Architecture for Consistent Application Program Design." *IBM Systems Journal* 22, no. 3 (New York, 1983): 199–213.

Tantzen, Robert G. "Conversion Between Calendar Date and Julian Day Number." *Comm. ACM* 8 (August 1963): 444.

Uspenski J. V., and M. A. Heaslet. *Elementary Number Theory*. New York: McGraw-Hill, 1939.

Van Leer, P. "Top Down Development Using a Program Design Language." IBM Systems Journal no. 2 (1976): 155–170.

Yourdon, Edward. *Techniques of Program Structure and Design*. Toronto: Prentice-Hall, 1975.

Index